A Modern Pioneer
One Woman's Ministry

∾

Violet Kochendoerfer

Skinner House Books
Boston

Published by Skinner House Books,
an imprint of the Unitarian Universalist Association,
25 Beacon Street, Boston, MA 02108-2800.

Printed in Canada.

ISBN 1-55896-346-4

10 9 8 7 6 5 4 3 2 1
99 98 97 96

Contents

Preface

After three years at Starr King School for the Ministry, I was the first woman to graduate from that school in 1962. Now, more than thirty years later, women students are the majority! My modern pioneering occurred before the days of the women's movement and had its ups and downs along the way. Although I understood the feelings of those who had problems with a woman in the ministry, I didn't make an issue of it and didn't have to. I had my champions and my detractors—both women and men.

In the perspective of history, all four of my ministries take on added significance. Each occurred during a period of modern history punctuated by three assassinations—Jack and Bobby Kennedy and Martin Luther King. Sermons seemed prophetic as each ministry was involved with controversial social and political issues that are still very much with us today—the acceptance of gays, the Vietnam war and anti-war demonstrations, the early civil rights movement, abortion, questioning and rebelling youth with disintegrating families, and even the subject of death in courts today.

If you read the word "negro" instead of "African American," "chairman" instead of "chairperson" in my letters and sermons, remember that I'm using the language of the time thirty years ago.

I have used pseudonyms in a few instances, and I hope that mention of any persons still living will let them feel honored to have taken a part in this pioneering. I deeply appreciate the interest and support of the Unitarian Universalist Women's Heritage Society for their thoughtful efforts to make my story a part of history.

Becoming a Pioneer

In 1959 I reluctantly left Santa Fe for Berkeley in a loaded Studebaker to start a new phase of my life. Had anyone told me I'd end up in the Unitarian ministry, I'd have told them they were dreaming. I didn't even know a woman *could* be a minister in the 1950s. But in a wonderful roundabout way, that's what happened to me.

I was raised in Minnesota as a Missouri Synod Lutheran in a lower middle-class family in the 1920s. I had no thought of going to college. Few friends were headed that way. At high school graduation the goal for most girls was to find a man to marry and raise a family. That wasn't my choice. I had graduated from the commercial course as salutatorian of my high school class, which brought a good position as secretary to the president of Winona State Teachers College.

I enjoyed the college atmosphere and spent a lot of my spare time at the YWCA. Far more important to my later life than playing on a championship basketball team, there was my friendship with a YWCA secretary. Edna was a curious mixture of practicality and warm friendship, who kept insisting I had to go to college and finally convinced me. I had envied students who could "come home for the holidays," so didn't want to go to Winona State Teachers College

In my search I chose Oregon, where I had relatives. After I made that decision, a professor at Winona College insisted it had to be Reed, a small, liberal arts college in Portland, Oregon, with a reputation as a pioneer in progressive education. Rather than teach from textbooks, the basic premise was to teach students how to think for themselves, and personal interaction between faculty and students was encouraged.

Years later, I learned that Reed College had been founded at the turn of the century from the estate of Unitarian Simeon Reed. Thomas Lamb Eliot, Portland's Unitarian minister at the time, had been the first chairman of Reed's board of trustees and had a primary role in its founding and pioneering design.

The Reed administrators told me that with the $1,800 I'd saved, I could get by financially for four years if I worked on campus. I did work, but they were wrong: my money ran out after two years. At the comptroller's generous urging, I became an employee at the college instead of a student. As assistant to the new Dean of Men, I was to find a lifelong friend and mentor.

Easton Rothwell was a slightly graying, quiet but genial man. In appearance and manner he reminded me of General Eisenhower, whom I had met and admired during my service in the Women's Army Auxiliary Corps in World War II. In later years, Rothwell held high positions and knew important people around the world, yet he always made me feel I was a special part of his large family of friends. Many times when I found myself in a quandary, I would ask myself what he would do in the circumstances. When I thought of my life goals (after No. l, the traditional "marriage and family," which I had not eliminated), I would think that if I could be the kind of person Easton Rothwell was and make a difference in other lives, it would be a worthy goal.

After two memorable years, Rothwell took a leave of absence for a stint in the State Department. He was replaced by an ex-government man, who was everything I couldn't abide in the way of values and approach to students. So, before he could fire me, I resigned and did something I thought I would never do. I took a job with the government as the first employee of the new Office of Price Administration in the State of Oregon in 1941.

I accepted a position as junior stenographer at $1,440 a year, with the stipulation that I could have any position I could handle as the office grew. Growth was rapid and, eventually, I was promoted to personnel director. My salary range moved up to $7,500, at which point the Regional Office insisted on a man. When their man arrived and put a typewriter back on my desk, again I resigned.

This resignation pattern reflected my strong conviction that if I wasn't excited about what I was doing, the inevitable discontent was too high a price to pay for the security of staying. So, instead of looking for another conventional job (in a kind of woman's rebellion and almost against my better judgment) I enrolled in the newly formed WAAC (Women's Army Auxiliary Corps), which pioneered bringing women into the military.

After basic training, I was trained as a Morse code radio operator and assigned to Morris Field, an airbase in North Carolina. In this first assignment we learned that Army regulations didn't allow WAACs to operate on an Army Airways Communication Net. As I began training as a Link Trainer Instructor, I became disenchanted. Eight months later, the WAAC became the Women's Army Corps, which required a two-year enlistment. I refused, feeling fortunate this "out" was possible.

World War II had begun. I applied for overseas service with the American Red Cross. Even though the requirements included a college degree that I didn't have, I received an appointment as director of On-Base Military Service Clubs. We sailed on the troop ship Queen Mary on Easter Sunday of 1944 and I spent three and a half years in the European theater, from D-Day in England to being with the 82nd Airborne Divison as we made the historic crossing of the Elbe to meet the Russians and accept surrender of the 21st German Army.

We celebrated with the Russians in the ballroom of the Duke of Meckelnburg's palace in Ludwigslust, raising our glasses high to toast Stalin as they toasted Roosevelt. A visit to the concentration camp we had liberated brought us back to the horrors of war. Later, we provided a formal mass funeral for its victims and a soup kitchen to feed thousands of starving DPs (displaced persons) from six nations. After the end of the war, we moved into Berlin as occupation troops. It was in Berlin that I had dinner with General Eisenhower.

After three and a half years of war, the coming home was difficult. I felt adrift and accepted assignment with the American Red Cross in the Veteran's Hospital in Dearborn, Michigan, until I could decide what I truly wanted to do. After eight months of questioning the validity of the entire program there, once again I resigned and returned home to Minnesota.

Later that summer, I toyed with an invitation from "Elsie," who had been on my staff in the American Red Cross clubs in Bavaria, to come to the Bay Area in California. But I knew I disliked big cities, so it made no sense to go to San Francisco. I decided to pick a smaller community in a part of the country in which I had never lived. Santa Fe (where I had a hometown friend) turned out to be my new home. I came to love New Mexico deeply enough to stay eight wonderful years.

Santa Fe is where I became a Unitarian. After a long time of not belonging, I felt a need to get back to church. I had a friend who had also formerly been a Lutheran. We decided to give the Santa Fe Lutherans a chance; but the same childhood theological rebellion about not being able to question, only to believe, still bubbled to the surface.

One day, while coming home from skiing, a friend, John Hernandez, mentioned that he and his wife were going to a Unitarian fellowship in Las Vegas the next day. He offered to have our friend "Mark" pick me up. I later wrote to John, "Little did I realize when I said 'yes' to you that day, where it would chart my life!"

I attended the Santa Fe Unitarian Fellowship with John, Frances, and Mark. I thoroughly enjoyed the discussions of many issues of that time, but something seemed lacking. I wondered what was religious about the Unitarians. I realize now that what I was questioning way back in the fifties is still a valid criticism of some of our fellowship groups—an over-emphasis of individual freedom can lead to writing off too much of what I feel a good church experience is all about.

Even so, I liked the people, attended regularly, and spent a lot of time that summer with Mark. This handsome man was a fascinating enigma with whom I became emotionally involved. Mark was admirably idealistic, but also somewhat unrealistic in his liberal dreams of how to go about doing something for the underdog. When I found that many Unitarian groups at that time were actively involved in social action, I suggested to Mark that he become a Unitarian minister. He was accepted at Starr King School for the Ministry in Berkeley, California, and left.

Years of experiences in Santa Fe had been shared with scores of friends, but after comfortable jobs as office manager for the Santa Fe Chamber of Commerce and administrative assistant for an architect, I had that nagging feeling of being in a comfortable rut.

I shared these feelings with my mentor, Easton Rothwell. At this time, he was director of the Hoover Institution on War, Revolution, and Peace at Stanford University. He suggested I take off a week or two and come to the Bay Area where he would set up appointments for me. I decided that when I made the break, it had to be a clean one, without the possibility of going back. It took another year to finally leave my beloved Santa Fe. I belatedly accepted Elsie's invitation to stay with her until I found a job and a place to live.

∾

On the long drive from Santa Fe to Berkeley, I had plenty of time to think. Although leaving my secure position and many friends took courage, there was also relief at having finally made the break. I was also filled with a sense of adventure. I thought of Robert Frost—that a poem can be a "momentary stay against confusion" and "end in wisdom." To try to capture that "momentary stay," I wrote,

What is this thing that seems to guide my steps?
That seems to know a plan that I can't see?
That there is one, I cannot help but feel, for I keep
    wandering in its maze,
Not knowing how, or why, or where.
There is no beaten path ahead; but as I take each step,
    another one comes clear.
I turn my head and marvel at the tiny pieces of the way
    I've come,
Fantastic in minute detail and timing.
And after miles and thoughts of what I've left,
I find myself returning to beginnings on another path,
That beckon far beyond my earlier imaginings.

Stops with friends in Phoenix, Los Angeles, and Santa Barbara brought much gratuitous but unhelpful advice. Elsie's generous invitation to stay with her until I found a job and place to live suppressed any real fears.

On March 15, 1959, I drove up to Elsie's interior decorating studio on LeRoy Avenue in Berkeley—just outside the North Gate of the University of California campus. I had envisioned staying with Elsie a couple of weeks. I stayed four months! Shortly after I arrived, Elsie was booked for a two-month decorator tour to Europe, and asked me to apartment-sit for her while she was gone. How could I refuse? This meant I didn't have to hurry to find a job; I could buy groceries and relax in this posh decorator apartment.

I quickly decided I didn't want to live in San Francisco. My job would have to be in the East Bay, preferably in Berkeley. I liked the houses with lawns, located where it would be easier to take courses at the University. Knowing only what I didn't want to do, the possibilities were limited; back then women were bookkeepers, stenographers, secretaries, or maybe nurses or teachers. Two office jobs I was offered were not nearly as attractive as the one I'd left in Santa Fe.

It was a pleasant surprise that Elsie's apartment was two blocks from Starr King School for the Ministry, where my Santa Fe friend Mark was a student. He was eager for me to know more about his new life at the school and took me to several parties. I soon got to know the small student body and faculty. The students, all men, invited me to come to some of the seminars, and since I wasn't working, I spent a lot of time at the school.

As I learned more about the program, I kept thinking that I would like to find a niche in the Unitarian "family." The area director for the whole Pacific Coast had his office in the Starr King building, and I learned that his administrative assistant, Rosemary Mattson, was leaving to accompany her husband to his new position in Boston. My experience as office manager of the Santa Fe Chamber of Commerce meant I was eminently qualified for the job.

I applied, but the area director hired a friend of his from the East Coast. No one in Berkeley was ever interviewed. It was a disappointment, but the irony is that had I gotten the job, I might never have become a minister.

I decided that as long as I wasn't yet working, I would attend the summer session at Starr King, where I could register without an undergraduate degree. Their regular graduate program was a three-year course leading to a BD or Bachelor of Divinity degree. I was the only woman that summer in the philosophy of religion seminar among Unitarian ministers from all across the country. Most seemed to be strict rationalists devoted to logic and "the scientific process." I often found myself saying, "Maybe it's because I'm a woman, but I 'feel' or 'sense' things that I can't rationally explain, but which are a valid part of the religious dimension." I questioned the boundaries they set that allowed no place for these imponderables.

The summer school experience whetted my appetite for more study. In a crazy, wonderful way I felt comfortable with the informal climate, and warmly at home with the interesting people in the Unitarian family. One morning I was having coffee with a student's wife and expressed the desire to find a place for myself in the church. When she encouraged me to speak with Josiah Bartlett, president of Starr King, I decided to do just that. I explained my deep desire to become a regular student at Starr King even though I had no undergraduate degree. Bartlett promised to think it over.

Imagine my excitement to receive the following letter dated July 9, 1959: "You are accepted at Starr King as a special student. Such acceptance carries with it our advice and counsel toward the objectives for which you are enrolled. It does not, however, carry with it any endorsement as a candidate for a degree nor eligibility for scholarship or other aid. We are very glad to be of any help to you we can and are happy to have you with us."

From the letter it was obvious that Bartlett thought I would take a course or two and then perhaps move on. I had no idea a woman could be a minister; but I was intrigued with the program and liked the other students. Nothing interesting had turned up on the job hunt, so I enrolled for a full load that fall and found an apartment on the second floor of a building next to the school.

Once I was a student, I asked about the name "Starr King," which sounded to me like a brand of tuna fish. I learned that Thomas Starr King was a Universalist minister called from Boston to the San Francisco Unitarian Church back in 1860 during the Civil War.

Starr King's leadership and humanitarian efforts were pivotal at that time for keeping California both united and in the Union. At his death, after only four short years in San Francisco, streets, Protestant churches, public schools, and American Legion posts were named for him throughout California. Mountain peaks in both California and New Hampshire honor him as an avid naturalist.

For all of this, Starr King was chosen as one of early California's two leading citizens in the Hall of Statuary in Washington. The other honoree was Father Sera, who founded the Catholic missions along the California coasts. Starr King was also the only human buried within the city of San Francisco. His above-ground crypt is just outside the Unitarian Universalist church there.

After summer school and my admission to Starr King, I had time to look for a regular part-time job for September and found one in the University of California Department of Nuclear Energy. It was an especially interesting time, when Edward Teller was director of the famous Livermore Radiation Lab. Teller and Livermore Lab were often in the news, because they made possible the first successful US hydrogen bomb explosion.

That September of 1959, I wrote a form letter to explain the Starr King program to family and friends. "Picture me here—one of fifteen students, all the rest male, with one a compadre from Minnesota. Van was County Attorney in Pine County. There's also an ex-Cal instructor who has his PhD in biochemistry, and several masters degrees in everything from anthropology to philosophy and psychology.

"We have a small permanent faculty here, with visiting professors from Cal, Stanford, and other seminaries. Instead of grades, after each seminar the prof sends an evaluation to Jo, our president. It's a whole page, where our overall performance is checked as 'superior, average, or inferior,' and then they're asked to comment on a long list of parts of our personal performance.

"Each semester these go to Jo, the president. Later, we each have a conference, when he passes on anything he feels we need to know. It's early to make judgments; but I feel already that our intellectual and emotional growth through personal give-and-take, rather than learning from textbooks, is the best possible training for a minister.

"This semester I have a seminar in 'Old Testament Literature and Culture' from Rabbi White of San Francisco. He's a great chap with a wealth of anecdotes and myths that make the Hebraic Bible come alive. For instance, he says that the word 'virgin,' should really have been translated 'young woman.' Just that makes one wonder about many things.

"Another seminar called 'Inservice Training' is exciting, as we hash over weekly written reports of our individual outside assignments. Some assignments are in large churches as pulpit assistants or work in church schools, some doing surveys in the Mission District in San Francisco, with others as chaplain's assistantships at St. Quentin or mental hospitals—whatever we feel we need to round out our experience. My assignment is working with the minister at the church in San Jose."

It was good to be back to this kind of learning. But all through the first half of that first year, the Mark relationship kept interfering just because of the very fact that he was there. Eric Hoffer's definition of the "true believer" seemed more and more to fit Mark as a man. He seemed to repudiate the parts of his life with which he was unhappy by substituting a lofty cause to live by and champion in order to shape the world in this larger image. The cause would become his very life, to the point where (as a woman in a novel about just such a true believer said) "he had so much love for 'the people,' he had none left for a person."

I had been concerned about this during the Santa Fe days, but Mark's departure for California brought relief. Now I found that Berkeley had been like a homecoming for this true believer. He found active groups like the Trotskyites who gloried in making newspaper headlines with their demonstrations. All this came first—before his involvement as a divinity student.

With the ambivalence of one emotionally involved, I somehow knew that I couldn't change him, and yet I kept on feeling that I had to try. After a hike in the hills behind Berkeley one weekend in November, we had a wild discussion that got nowhere. Later, in trying to sort out my own feelings, I wrote long pages of emotional free verse, part of which I sent to Mark, including these closing two lines: "I cannot offer refuge when you're running from yourself; / For this can never help you face what you must face alone."

I did not realize then that they would accomplish what needed to happen. When I returned after the holidays, I found Mark had not registered for the second semester.

∾

In my second semester, the other students kept after me to "give a chapel." This meant doing a service in front of one's peers—a scary thing even to contemplate. Chapels were not something we were assigned; but when we felt we had something to say, we'd sign up on a posted schedule. As the men kept egging me on, I continued to put them off so I could watch what a few of the others did first.

The very next week, "John" (one of the older students) met me in the hall and said, "You're on with me next Thursday at one, Vi. Don't worry. I'll tell you what I want you to do." I still had my doubts. John was a bit arty for my taste. But I liked the reading he asked me to do and the experience provided the breakthrough I needed. This encouragement and inclusion made me appreciate the other students all the more for their concern and support.

Some weeks later, after reading a Quaker pamphlet entitled "Speak Truth to Power," I felt I did have something to say. My title, "Indictment for Unitarians," suggested that we often verbalize well what others ought to do, in contrast to the Friends with their own ongoing commitment to action in implementing an ongoing program that may take years. I mentioned their stand against capital punishment. The Friends had for years held vigils outside San Quentin each time anyone was executed. We had held our first vigil when Caryl Chessman was up for execution after seven reprieves, and it had been high in the news. We had had sermons and panels and discussions, but Caryl was finally executed; and we seemed to forget and turn to other things. Even though I'd been most critical of our short attention span, I received applause after the presentation.

Toward the end of that first year I did another chapel, "Me and We," in which I tried to sort out feelings about that first year and about the Unitarian movement, repeating some of my earlier indictments. "Maybe it's the restlessness of spring and I need a dose of sulfur and molasses to clear the bloodstream. Maybe it's because my first year at Starr King is coming to a close and I'm trying to pull some things together. . . . But I've spent a lot of time asking myself questions. I'm trying to see me as I really am, and as I relate to Unitarianism. I haven't had any great revelations, but there are a few words and ideas that keep popping up again and again.

"I've decided to go back to Minnesota this summer to my folks' fiftieth wedding anniversary and will also visit my sister and her family in Duluth. As I thought about it, I wondered just what I'd say to my sister about us; for I remembered a letter she'd written me years ago when I started attending the fellowship in Santa Fe. I kept it because it seemed significant at the time. So I dug it out. She mentioned attending Unitarian 'lectures' with a friend; and here's some of what she said. 'They're largely university people, the non-conformist type, many of them so immature as individuals. It's as if, being unable to adapt to the larger community life, they find a haven with some semblance of security in a group professing a philosophy that their inquiring minds can accept because it expects so little of them in return. Coming together, they form a clique of intellectual snobbery.

"'Their liberalism is not genuine, but rather an ego builder to cover up their own individual inadequacies, with ideas and activities which are actually an excuse for never having matured. I'm not for one moment saying all are as I see them here. In fact I ask because I hope elsewhere it may be different.'

"In reading it again, I was stopped for a minute; for this could almost have been me speaking. I read it over again more slowly. 'Lectures!' Well, that depends. 'Special breed'—that's for sure! 'University people,' 'non-conformist.' Of course! 'Security in a philosophy that their inquiring minds can accept because it expects so little of them in return.' That really hit home! 'Clique of intellectual snobbery.' I'm with her on that one too! 'Ideas and activities are actually an excuse for never having matured.' Wow! But, come to think of it, I have sometimes seen us as the religious teenagers, rebelling and using Christianity as our parental whipping dog.

"Now these are large generalizations written by a pretty sharp gal from casual meetings with one group of Unitarians. Yet, because what she says puts a finger on some of the very things I feel after all this time, it makes me wonder just how obvious some of our shortcomings must be to a lot of thinking people. Do we really have something to offer all those we keep saying are Unitarians and don't know it? Or are they still outside because by observation they find more rebellious words than significant action or depth?"

I went on to describe some of my very own questioning,

saying that any intelligent naturalist was bound to go along with humanism, but that I agreed with reconstructionist Rabbi Schulweis, who spoke to us in our Old Testament Literature seminar and said that "Humanism is fine as far as it goes, but it isn't enough."

I said that in our rebellion against Christianity we had embraced Judaism with open arms, perhaps because Jews are non-Christian, and so we can readily substitute their Hanukkah at Christmas time or their Seder at Easter and feel good about it. I had also been taken by Rabbi Schulweis's picture of us, "You pick a little here, and you pick a little there, and you don't have something all your own." I felt that in our great pronouncement of freedom of belief, this very fact puzzles newcomers, who find it hard to put their finger on just who we are or what we stand for. I went on, "Humility—that's another thing I've thought much about, since it's almost a dirty word to many Unitarians. Remember Dr. Leavins quoted Phillips Brooks on humility. 'It is not to stoop till you are lower than yourself, but to stand at your real height against some higher nature, which will show you what the real smallness of your greatest greatness is!' In this light I think of those the world places in the "greatness" category—like top scientists. Invariably they are the ones with the greatest humility, in the realization that of all we know, how little it is of all there is to know."

I also took issue with the chairman of the Starr King board who had made the statement, "Unitarians are snobs; that's why I like them!" and labeled us as "constructive iconoclasts." I was glad he'd used the word "constructive," for I wanted so much for what we are building to define us to others as examples of honesty and integrity.

I closed with, "Well, this is what I've been thinking about these past weeks. You can see there are a lot of questions, and several words underlined by repetition—honesty, integrity, humility, discipline, commitment, love, acceptance, understanding. We can watch our sophisticates write them off as naive or trite, but to me they're part of the religious dimension and the only elements that can put the all-necessary guts and human emotions into the intellectual pursuit.

"Seriously, the Starr King merry-go-round has been one of the most exciting and rewarding rides I've ever had. I must confess now and then I've gotten a bit dizzy with it all, but there was always someone there to hold my hand or my head till I could stand up and walk straight again.

"I know I'll always need time now and then to get off that merry-go-round and stand still—so I can see humankind not as an abstract blur, but as the individual Quakers, the Rabbi Whites, the man on the street, and you wonderful characters here at Starr King. I thank each of you for sharing a life full of experience-tarnished truths, as we join together to find all those shiny new ones somewhere up ahead—on our great search together—ME and WE!"

It was about this time the men had started affirming that I could and would become a minister. I hadn't even thought that was possible, but, as I thought about it, I realized that I had always been interested in religion. After my rebellious bout with conservative Lutheranism, I hadn't gone to church, but at Reed College I had enrolled in a non-credit course in comparative religions. I could remember thinking at one time in my younger years that I would like to be the wife of a minister!

Now, as the possibility was talked about as an actuality for me, I mentioned this to President Bartlett. We talked about my academic qualifications, and he said, "Why don't you go back to Cal and finish your BA, Vi?" He explained to me that after a degree from Starr King, a ministerial candidate had to be passed by the Fellowship Committee, which consists of clergy, psychologists, and laypeople in something like a senior oral. This sounded ominous, but I did send Cal my transcripts and found I would need a year and two summers to complete a bachelor's degree, including some requirements that seemed silly at my age. So I decided it would be a waste of time to go back.

Sometime later, Leon Fay, director of the Department of Ministry in Boston, came to Berkeley, and each student had a personal conference with him. He told me he was pleased to have me at Starr King. When I told him I was interested in the ministry, he said, "I'm sure that the Fellowship Committee will accept you on an equivalency basis if Jo can certify that you've completed the requirements here."

I was deeply impressed. It was warmly gratifying to be associated with a group who didn't have to do things by the book, and for me to be considered for what I was as a unique individual. I wrote about this to myself. "That day I emerged into the clearing. I was unceasingly fascinated in looking back over the path I've come. It's been a good path, with stops at quiet lakes and warming campfires, leaving now and then to explore exciting detours, scale new peaks, returning in new directions to stop at other lakes or set up camp beside a rushing stream where one could fish a while for sustenance.

"I now chart my path into the unfamiliar clearing. Although I have so many understanding companions, I must still walk alone. And, as a woman, there lies great challenge. I have encountered no resistance at all so far, yet know this may not always be true. If I am to help pioneer, I would do it never forgetting I am a woman, yet hoping I'll be accepted along the way for the person that I am."

Later, when I reported Fay's thoughts to Jo, he smiled and said, "Well, let's get it in writing from Boston!" The process asked for references, and one of mine was another Red Cross friend who had been on my staff in Bavaria. She sent me a copy of the letter, the last paragraph of which said, "She knew when to listen sympathetically and when to gently prod. The soldiers were very fond of Vi and considered her their friend. She did it all with a delightful sense of humor and a quick, compassionate sympathy for the underdog. My admiration and love for Vi Kochendoerfer has a very firm foundation."

It had been a year full of many opening doors and in personal associations that helped me find the true meaning of community and even family. My fellow students, all men, were not only welcoming, but supporting and encouraging, to the point where I felt that indeed I had something to say and could minister to others.

Jo and Laile Bartlett built on this family feeling by having each of us to dinner separately, and by hosting great dinner parties for the whole student body. In addition to all that, I had another home away from home with the Vanstrom family, whom I had met while working at the University of California Department of Nuclear Energy. Because County Attorney Van had taken his three sons from a small-town high school where they were "somebody," into the maelstrom of high school in Berkeley, he bought a lovely home for the three years they were to be there. It was a home where I could drop in at any time. Van, the tall, genial but logical-legal mind, and I had many verbal battles around the kitchen table, with motherly Millie as referee. They were to remain family during my first ministry in New England and throughout our lives.

In May I quit my part-time job to go home for my parents' golden wedding anniversary. It was the first time all the Kochendoerfer kids had been home together in years. We decided we would redo the kitchen for the folks' gift. Relatives and friends gathered for the big day. We spent hours taping reminiscences and were delighted to learn things we had never known about each other. How many times I heard, "But you never told us!" We all left with a deeper appreciation of each other and of our parents.

I stayed home four weeks, but wanted to come back for summer school because Henry Nelson Wieman was to be there, and he was someone I wanted to know and learn from. Wieman was a Unitarian theologian, and I'd done a paper on one of his books, *The Source of Human Good*. It was a banner day when I found that theologically he was a "naturalistic mystic!" In my paper at Starr King I said, "For a long time I've felt that being a naturalistic mystic was low on the intellectual scale. Now that I find I can be one and still be in good company, I feel I can make good headway. I do believe there is knowledge that comes without, or in addition to, the rational, logical intellectual search—a kind of innate knowing; and perhaps it is that added element in the difference between knowledge and wisdom."

I found new definition and support for my own theological foundations, and even new language in Wieman's discussion of "Creative Interchange," which echoed Martin Buber's "I and Thou." It gave grounding to my evolving theology of growth through relationships and gave me courage to hold my own in the give and take of our seminars. It was what I once called "this thing at Starr King," that happens at times when there is a sense of deep mutual understanding and acceptance between two persons or within a group. When this happens, intellectual and personal differences dissolve into a new relationship, offering us freedom to say things that are deeply and lastingly significant.

The others too fell in love with Wieman—a tall white-haired gentleman, whose quiet wisdoms we listened to and could accept and experience, rather than have to dissect in discussions. I felt a victory on another front: there was now greater acceptance of what I saw as the feminine ingredient—that element that links nature and "Mother," whose mystical role in reproduction and qualities of appreciation, caring, and nurturing we're now beginning to accept and revere.

Later that summer, I and four of the other students shared Wieman's wisdoms with Unitarian high schoolers at a summer conference of The Starr King Federation of Liberal Religious Youth. I wrote a play encompassing the concepts of creative interchange, which captured the imagination of kids like "Ted," who later wrote me from Oakland, "Thank you SO much for your warm and wonderful letter. I loved the play and still remember sitting there on the grass in the morning sun and marvelling at the thoughtful and entertaining way you gave us 'Freedom, Fear, and Conformity.' I was thrilled and stimulated, and you won't believe it, but I'm now able to get along better with my family and others, and even myself. This changed my attitude toward life. Everything is so much happier now that I'm not fighting life.

"When I came to the conference, Starr King School meant just that to me—a fine school. Today, it means something completely different. It means people. It means the most wonderful people I've ever met. Thank you and all the others for the most wonderful week of my life."

That was it as far as conferences go. It was talked about for years. For me, I'm sure it played a part in the fact that young people were to become highlights in my later ministries. The experience of this conference also reminded me of another LRY experience I often shared with parents, which illustrates my feeling that busy Unitarian parents often allowed their children questionable freedoms when the children would have welcomed boundaries. Parents also frequently spent time and money trying to give their children material things and outside opportunities, when the children might have welcomed instead a little more time and intimate attention.

The experience I have in mind happened at a Liberal Religious Youth Conference at our Palo Alto church. A sixteen year old, whose parents were both psychiatrists, said, "My folks are always tired." I could see him coming home, waiting to talk with them, only to hear, "Don't bug me, I've had a bad day." He told us that they had given him a red Triumph sports car, and went on, "One night—I can't tell you just why I did it—but I went out, jumped in the Triumph, and started for the coast. As I drove I kept stepping on the gas—from sixty to seventy to eighty—and when I'd hit ninety-two miles per hour the State Patrol caught up with me. I was never so glad in all my life that somebody stopped me!"

ॐ

Jo and Laile Bartlett were the beloved parents in what we all felt was our Starr King family. Jo Bartlett's innovations bothered conservative New England Unitarians, who were accustomed to the Harvard Theological School approach, and often put down a Starr King student as "one of Jo Bartlett's boys." The Starr King process didn't produce scholars well versed in biblical and historic textbook theology. We grew as persons, in the knowledge that ministry is more than scholarly presentations from the pulpit. An announcement in the *Midsummer Communique* gives an example of one of Jo's innovations: "The Live Arts. I'm willing to work up a brand new venture—a regular series of evenings, taking us to live performances of ballet, theater, concerts of jazz, folk songs, dance, or exhibits of art. In each case we could shoot for discussion with performers or critics about the creative process."

The Lively Arts (as we called it) was a great seminar. We spent evenings with an architect and with an outstanding Bay Area painter. We sponsored a modern dance group and had sessions on jazz, folk music, and poetry, each time trying to discover with the artists or among ourselves, just what the process of creation involved.

A special requisite of the Live Arts program was an individual project. Jo said, "You're always saying there are things you'd like to do if only you had the time. This will give you 'company time' and I hope you enjoy it."

I had been wanting to mount and do something with a fabulous piece of driftwood I had found on Island Lake in Minnesota. I asked if I could do a chapel on driftwood. Bartlett's response was to tip his head to one side and grin. "This isn't exactly what I had in mind." But he finally said I could. I entitled it "Credo in Driftwood."

Our chapel was a lovely octagonal room with ceiling-to-floor windows all around, lovely drapes, and excellent sound equipment with speakers in the ceiling. I had the mounted driftwood up front on a pedestal as a focal piece, and with soft music playing from Debussy's "La Mer" (the part which seems to have waves welling up and receding) I read from the rear,

DRIFTWOOD . . .
A word?
A piece of wood?
Something to gather and to burn?
A feeling that recalls—or nags without explaining?
What does it conjure in your mind?
Nostalgic fires on a beach?
The solitude of sheltered coves?
The loneliness of not belonging? Or
Spontaneity—freedom—beauty—joy!

From nature's patterned precision in crystals
We have learned the secrets of our universe.
In driftwood, she speaks to us of other things—
She speaks to me of people—
Of myself, and others I have known.

I think of towering giants once firmly rooted in
     the earth,
Attacked by sudden storms of wind and rain . . .
Or some, where anchoring earth
Was melted imperceptibly by streams or waves
     until they fell.
And those which fell in water
And were buffeted and tossed for years,
Gave up one earthly body
To be reborn in myriad forms and shapes.

And in this drifting evolution,
Some were soft and sick and could not
    weather through;
Their bodies, waterlogged and rotting,
Slowly sank and disappeared.
But others, with a strong and sturdy heart
Lived on, and grew in beauty,
The jagged edges of their fractures healed
And softly smoothed
By intimate communion with their world

Not each one is a jewel . . .
If life were good,
And growth within the first carnation easy
    and unbound,
Reincarnation might be often straight and uniform.
But, if twisted, knarled and strong
From bending with the wind,
Or growing round some hurt of life
To seal it in with understanding love,
Then evolution might produce
Unique and fascinating forms
Beyond our own imagination to create.

I like to think that our religion
Is a way of looking—a sensitive awareness
That ever sees in new perspective,
All with overtones of warmth, commitment,
    and concern.
And each in his own way of looking
Will discover different things
That only he can know, or feel, or see
Through his own eyes, his fingertips, his heart.
This is HIS need . . . HIS destiny . . .

So if you do not share my feeling
For this simple gift of nature,
It does not matter;
For you are you, and I am I!
But this I know,
For those who do
Is given life in more abundance—greater depth—
That will sustain through wind and storm and rain
Year after year.

As I finished, Jo smiled and said, "I liked that Vi. I had my doubts. People get so drippy about driftwood!" "Credo in Driftwood" turned out to be a part of my life in many ways over the years; I could build a whole personal philosophy around that gift of nature, a philosophy that I shared at several summer conferences.

∾

On February 17, 1961 I had a call from my mother that Dad was quite ill and not expected to live. Before I could get a plane reservation, Mom called again to say that Dad had died. Airlines were on strike, but I finally got a reservation to Chicago, back to Minneapolis, and then home to Winona.

Because Dad had been a member of the Redman Lodge (which had rituals built around those of the Native American), he could not become a member of the Missouri Synod Lutheran church. This meant that our family Lutheran minister couldn't do the service, even though Mom was a staunch member. She found a minister of another small denomination who was willing to fill in, as I was to do many times in years to come for other families.

There had been a blizzard, so the usual graveside Committal Service was conducted in the funeral home by officials of the Redman Lodge with their own ceremonies. The man in charge explained that the term "Great Spirit" was synonymous with the Lutheran "God." At one point, each of the pall bearers went up to the casket, took a sprig of evergreen from his lapel, and placed it on the casket as he said, "Farewell, Brother." Finally, because the casket could not be buried in the frozen ground, the procession went to the big vault in Woodlawn Cemetery across the lake. As the casket was carried in, the Redmen released a white dove and said their final farewells to their brother.

I remember my last glance at Dad's body and the feeling of regret that there had been so much creative potential in him that had never been realized. He had expressed it partially in his work, because he was a skilled tool and die maker. Mom said of him, "He wouldn't be bossed. He was good enough to be able to do things his own way without being fired." As I heard that, I truly felt I was his daughter.

∾

I returned to Starr King to catch up on other interesting seminars that were to shape my thinking and provide foundations for sermons throughout my ministry. One was in the philosophy of religion with Syd Peterman, a minister in San Jose.

Peterman began by saying something that floored me. "If I had my way I wouldn't let anyone into this seminar who hadn't had math up to calculus!" I'd never dreamed that philosophy had any relation to mathematics! He then brought up something else that intrigued me about our crazy world. He said that we in the western Christian society see "time" in a linear dimension. "God created the world and will destroy it." Seeing things in this logical, linear context influenced our scientific-technological development. The Bible said we were given "dominion over nature" so we could control and exploit it for our human comfort and benefit.

This is in contrast to the east, where the concept of time

is circular, without beginning or end, in reincarnation. Human beings are seen as a part of nature, with an innate need to revere and protect, something we're just beginning to learn the hard way, because our very livelihood is threatened.

I found myself indicting western intellectuals for touting the scientific process and pushing the biblical doctrine of "controlling" rather than being a part of nature, and disregarding ancient wisdoms of the world.

I remember a seminar on the New Testament mostly as a basic lesson in personal conflict and relationships. When Jo brought in outside professors, he didn't tell them that we didn't have regular texts, final exams, letter grades, or other things like that. He left it for us to work out. When he told us about Dr. Good from Stanford, he said, "Now be good to Good. I'm running out of New Testament professors!"

I'll not forget our first session. Dr. Good announced that our basic text would be Rudolph Bultmann and passed out mimeographed outlines for the course requirements, which included two written papers. One was to be an exegesis, where we would take a Bible verse and give our explanation or interpretation. Such structure had never been imposed on us at Starr King.

We kept quiet, but in the silence one could actually feel the arrows of rebellion flying through the air at Dr. Good. Afterwards we went to Jo to unload: "Who wants to waste time doing an exegesis?" and a whole lot more. Jo responded, "Well, this is your problem. Why don't you have it out with him?" At that point one student said, "Let's see if he can come some evening rather than in the afternoon. I'll cook clam chowder and we can go on from there."

Dr. Good agreed. Following the meal, we had a session in the lounge that lasted until midnight. After much give and take, we found we liked and respected him. When someone brought up the feelings about Bultmann and the exegesis, he said, "Well, if you're going to throw the New Testament out of the window, at least you ought to know what it is you're throwing out."

We couldn't fault him there. We accepted Bultmann, graciously took the written exam, and even had a special farewell session with Dr. Good. He admitted that it had been an exhilarating learning experience for him too. "At Stanford, I lecture to a theater of sometimes a hundred or more, and all I can see is the top of their heads as they're busy scribbling notes. When I drive up here from Palo Alto for my time with you, I'll tell you honestly, I say to myself, 'I wonder what's going to happen today?' I'm never disappointed!"

That year I said in a Christmas note to family and friends, "Even though I have finished a year and a half at Starr King, I often look back on the days when I first came to Berkeley, and the many little things that led to my taking the less traveled road—the one that has made all the difference. . . .

"Last year I said, 'I suppose you, like everyone else, wonder what I'm doing here. Well, it's just an experiment, and after a year maybe I'll be able to tell you.' And so I can. I'm doing what I've always wanted to do, but not only couldn't define, but didn't even know was possible. Now I can't imagine doing anything else, for I like people. It's almost as though someone or something has been guiding my steps along this incredible journey to a new home where I'll be able to work with people at the most intimate and significant times of their lives.

"Here at school, every day brings new ideas to struggle with and fit together. We're never told we have to do anything, and if you think this is heaven, just try it sometime! And one big thing I've learned is that in sharing thoughts, ideas, emotions so closely and openly, we come to realize that nothing we do affects only we ourselves.

"I love every minute and feel lucky to be here. And though I came in by the back door, I have been accepted not only by the fellows at school (who were overwhelmingly wonderful from the start) but also by the powers that be at Head-quarters in Boston.

"In this three-year program, I'll be here at least another year after this one. And then what? I think it's exciting not to know, but I do keep wondering."

The next summer, after a trip back to Santa Fe, I was eager to start work and began my second seminar with our new theology professor, Bob Kimball. He was a Harvard man who had been an associate of Paul Tillich there. His seminar in ethics was to be memorable in more ways than I realized then.

A basic premise of our long discussions became a foundation for my approach to religious living—that we are what we are only in relationships—first the self/self, then the self/ other, and third, in how we see ourselves in relation to our universe, where we'd put a God if we had one. On the self/ self issue, we had heated discussions on the question, "Does a person have the right to commit suicide?" On the self/other, Kimball suggested using the sex issue. I can recall wondering what I was letting myself in for as the one woman in the seminar, and with no holds barred at Starr King.

Kimball began the three-hour session by having us list on the board all the possible kinds of sexual relationships—from pre- to extra-marital, masturbation, etc. Then we started talking—all around the edges of the issue for an hour and a half with nothing really happening up to the coffee break. When the same thing continued after the break, I said something like, "Why don't we quit talking about why we can't talk about it and *say* something!" I shared a personal experience I'd had as a single woman, which broke the dam. For the next hour and a half we had at it.

That year Kimball changed his evaluation procedure. Instead of sending his report to the president, he started the procedure of writing it as we sat before him. This was a scary encounter, but when Kimball checked "superior" to begin with, I relaxed. After discussions, and his filling in the list of attributes, he turned over the sheet. Writing on the back he said, "Miss Kochendoerfer, the one woman in the group, was able to get this seminar off the ground when I couldn't do it in three hours." Then he said to me, "I have an admission to make, Vi. Last semester in the Psychotherapy and Religion seminar I wanted to use a sex issue, and said to Jo, 'I don't think I can do this with Vi in the seminar.' Jo said, 'Sure this isn't your problem, Kimball?' I'm willing now to admit that it was!"

Whether this was still a problem for Bob Kimball in the Credo seminar in my final year, I'm not sure. He irritated me when he'd say, "Every now and then, Vi, you roll over on your theistic side." This, because I took issue with his concept of "atheist." He felt that we might say we were agnostic, but that what we did exposed either a theistic or atheistic stance. He felt that being an atheist was "not believing in a God up there who's going to take care of us."

During the first session of the Credo seminar, Kimball said, "This time I can't flunk anyone, because this will be your credo—your 'this I believe.'" He said that the historic credo covered five areas—God, man, church, Christ, and salvation. We started with God as the subject for a three-hour seminar. Later, each of us was scheduled for an hour and a half to present our "working credo" for discussion.

Before starting mine, I explained that I found it difficult to get on to my own beliefs before taking issue with something Kimball had intimated in suggesting that at times I operated more with my heart than with my head. Then I began speaking in free verse, first rebelling at my childhood religion, and then unloading on Kimball at some length, saying in part,

If all this makes your little world go round,
Then that's OK for you;
But making it a party line gets close to orthodoxy
in my book.

> For all this labeling won't get rid of God;
> It just confuses all the issues for the other folks.
> Because that little word means different things to
>   different people;
> And many by your definition would be atheists
> And if they knew, they would resent your saying that.

After I had gotten some of that off my chest, I went on with my perennial criticisms of the utterly rational.

> Man is a mystery and a paradox, but he will not
>   believe this.
> Since he found his reason, he thinks he has all the
>   answers.
> He has found in himself a new God.

I went on taking issue with the scientists, suggesting that to them nature is nothing to marvel at in its beauty and mystery, but just a bundle of blind laws and mathematical forces that man can play around with. And I went on about my God,

> I don't really have to use the word "God"
> For God is not so much an idea as it is an experience.
> Not so much an objective abstraction as it is a subjective
>   knowing.
> And maybe this explains why we have so much trouble
>   with the word.

> Sometimes I think of religion as the poetry of life,
> For it is the poet who would break through all the
>   legalism of label and language,
> And try to capture larger meaning by using words in a way
>   that say more than they do.
> He's the kind of person who sees in people more than they
>   look like,

And feels in himself more than he knows.
He's that way because that's the only way he can be,

God is not a being that loves, and creates and forgives
    and demands worship,
But is being itself, in the acts of creativity through love
    and forgiveness and worship
All of which contribute to the process of creation
And becoming more of our human being.

I went on, finding myself in the Japanese concept of *Shibui*,
encompassing words like "sensitivity" and "softness," without
"sentimentality"—modest, quiet, unassuming serenity, illusion
of simplicity, that all is in relationship to all it comes in contact with—that all cannot be seen or felt at once, but there
are depths to be discovered slowly, subtleties that keep appearing out of what you thought you'd seen before—always something more that's waiting to be discovered, but never regular,
for uniformity reveals itself at once. I spoke of pattern and
texture only nature knows—unevenness of bark, or stone, or
moss, or wood, or soil—unevenness that comes from aging
and weathering, which somehow brings great depth of per-
fection in imperfection. I said in closing,

    You see I find great meaning for myself within the
        realms of nature,
    Where, without knowing, nature seems to give so much
        we need to learn of life and death,
    Of growing under constant strife and tension,
    Yet always toward some balance, which is never
        permanent.

As I finished, there was absolute silence—something that never
happened at Starr King! After what seemed an hour, Kimball
said, "I think you'd better put that on tape and listen to it,

Vi." That sounded ominous. I knew my credo shouldn't have included so much of my rebellion, but somehow it didn't bother me. I'd gone on for pages, but it had been therapeutic and meaningful for me. It was difficult for me to follow the final assignment to boil the many pages down to one or two for our last session.

We talked the Kimballs into having a luncheon on their patio for that session. Each of us read our condensed version. All I felt I could do was to distill what I'd said into my definition of God: "God is the experience of feeling a part of the ongoing creative process of the universe, out of which we have evolved with human potential as the knowing part, and therefore the power of choice, to further create or to destroy."

I enlarged on this, suggesting that each human being has an innate need to create; and that if there's no creative outlet, our energy may assert itself in destructive ways. This concept has held meaning for me as I read of the bloodshed, violence, and wanton destruction by some youth, who seem to be crying out, "I'm here! I'm somebody! Pay some attention!" At any rate, because I didn't make this energy a "he" or a "she," it came out as an "it," which I didn't like. Because of this, Kimball's classifying it as "the most impersonal" didn't bother me. So what was to happen some weeks later was a shattering experience.

This time, for the Credo seminar, we had to write our own evaluations. Because I had spent much time in putting myself on paper, and had gotten a lot from the experience, I checked "superior." After answering the specifics, I turned the sheet over and set out once again the controversial issues on which I had clashed with Professor Kimball.

My conference came half an hour before the start of the next seminar. I sat down at the side of Kimball's desk and handed him my evaluation. He read down the front page, checking certain areas in a jerky way. My intuition told me something was wrong. He turned the page over, and when hc finished reading, there was silence. Then he took a deep breath and started. "I think I should tell you, Vi, that I've seriously considered flunking you in this seminar. I'm serious. I went to Jo and asked whether you needed this credit to graduate. It seems that you don't, but. . . ." All this was delivered in a manner most uncharacteristic for the person I thought I had come to know.

As we began our conversation, I reminded him that from the beginning his criteria for this seminar had been highly unusual for Starr King. He brought up the hostility he felt should not have been part of my working credo, and I tried to explain that he was partly to blame. The encounter became so irrational that at one point I said, "Well, Bob, I don't think I need psychiatric help." He insisted that that was not what he meant, "but. . . ." I was floored. I'd never failed anything in my life.

At the close of my next seminar, I climbed the stairs to my apartment, dropped my stuff, and sprawled in my big chair, wondering about it all when the buzzer rang. It was Bob Kimball. As I opened the door, he stretched out his hand and stumbled, "I forgot, Vi, to give you this ticket to the Karl Barth lecture. . . ." It was his way of saying he knew he'd shaken me and was sorry; but he didn't come in.

In three occasions months later, I felt vindicated. The first was at Forest Farms, a rustic camp beside a stream where our whole student body and families had special weekends. We were all spread out across a large deck. Bob was talking with others, but within my hearing—I've always felt calculatedly so. He mentioned his lecture series around the Bay Area and said, "I'm changing the 'atheist' part. I find it gets misunderstood." I was so pleased I could hardly contain myself.

The next was after I graduated. I didn't get to the General Assembly in Washington, DC, that year, but in driving across the country that fall to the New Minister's Meeting in Boston, I spent an overnight with my Starr King friends in Erie,

Pennsylvania. When I told "Lew" of my devastating experience, he said, "Now that you tell me all that Vi, something Kimball said to me at General Assembly makes a lot more sense. He told me that this year's Credo seminar was the most unsatisfactory experience he had ever had. The way he put it, he found he couldn't be objective enough."

I treasure a handwritten letter from Kimball during my first ministry at Provincetown on Cape Cod. He said he envied my being there—that they'd often camped at Truro nearby and he could still hear the waves pounding the shore. He went on, "You always scold me. . . ." I loved him for this admission.

Although the Credo seminar was a devastating experience at the time, in retrospect I'd not have missed it for the world. Like Dr. Good's confession, this was another perfect example of what we called The Starr King Process. It happened not only for students, but also for faculty, a growth process in personal relationships so all-important in a ministry. It can't be taught. It can only be acquired through experience, and is sometimes more meaningful if it evolves through a painful encounter.

∾

Finishing my studies at Starr King took on a new meaning when in the September 15, 1961, issue of *Time* magazine I read an article about corporations and the great success of Litton Industries under its new president, forty-two-year-old Roy Ash.

Because his family had been too poor to send him to college, Ash had no BA—a fact that, he grinned, "I hate to admit because someone's liable to take my master's away." Nevertheless, Ash went off to get an MBA at Harvard Business School.

I clipped a note to this and left it on Jo's desk with a note, "If Harvard [which is our historic training school for Unitarian ministers] can do this for Ash, do you suppose Starr King might skip the BA and let me get a BD? Can I come talk about this?" His response: "Why not take your case to the Student Affairs Committee?"

I did just that with an extensive presentation containing fourteen documents that set forth my background and experience. I was invited to make a personal appearance before the committee, the chair of which was a psychiatrist who later consulted on the Patty Hearst case. We talked for half an hour. Their decision: "On the basis of your presentation, we'd like to say 'yes,' but feel that it would prove a precedent that might be difficult for Jo to handle." I had to accept their decision.

Easter came early that last year. I was asked to be guest speaker for the Unitarian group in Monterey. My spirits soared as hills along the way were ablaze with California poppies. Another pulpit invitation came from the Unitarian church in Marin County. The congregation was in the process of finding a replacement for its minister, Sam Wright, who had joined the Starr King faculty. In their newsletter, in addition to my background and education, it said, "Miss Kochendoerfer is a third-year student and will be the first woman to graduate from Starr King School. She plans to serve in the regular Unitarian Universalist ministry, and says she was delighted to note in our questionnaire that we were willing to acknowledge the presence of women in the ministry and to demonstrate this fact by inviting her to our pulpit."

I learned that in their congregational questionnaire, in response to "Would you be willing to accept a Black?" ninety some percent of these good Unitarians waved their liberal banner with a "yes." The next question was "Would you be willing to accept a woman?" Here the vote was something like 108 "yes," and 67 "no." The Search Committee felt this should be checked out. So in my opening words I said, "I didn't realize until I got here this morning that I am Exhibit A for you to try on for sex!"

The president of the congregation and his wife took me to lunch after the service. I was pleased when Mrs. Nicoll admitted that she was one who voted no, but that she was at least fifty percent convinced by my service that morning. I thanked her for being honest, and shared my feeling that I could fully understand how and why many (especially women) might feel that way. I was encouraged that she could admit it, because that meant it was something we could work on.

A later letter from her husband addressed the issue: "I'm glad you noticed the degree to which you were accepted by the church people—both for what you had to say and for yourself personally. It is rather unusual that anyone asks for copies of a guest speaker's talk. In your case this was done, and for your 'Driftwood' as well. Since then I have asked a number of people what they thought, in view of our conversation at lunch. I tried to contact those who I thought would give serious opinions. All those with whom I spoke thought that 'your Sunday' was excellently done and that their view of it was widespread."

That year was to be the last spring trip—something the students at Starr King had done each year during spring vacation. We'd divide up into groups of six and take off to visit Unitarian Universalist groups on the West Coast. One year we would do the Northwest, and another year go to Southern California. On one trip north there was an episode of discrimination—the only one at Starr King that I remember. It came from a student who years later became a nationally acclaimed author, famed and loved for his homely philosophy. That year, when he found I had signed up for his group, he reportedly said that having a woman along would put a crimp on their style. I could fully understand how some men might feel that way, and realized he was just being honest. But when the student body president learned of it, he was furious, and urged me to sign up for his own group.

On the long bus trip home from Portland to Berkeley, I

shared a motel room with one of the men to save money. Another commented on the last lap, "It was great having Vi along. Somehow it made the trip more family." On the trip South the preceding Easter, we had participated in a service at the large Unitarian Universalist church in Los Angeles. Steve Fritchman, the minister there, was so taken with my being in the group that he made a special statement from the pulpit touting women in the ministry.

We knew we would be appearing before the Ministerial Fellowship Committee shortly after our return. This was the group whose approval we needed to be accepted into the Unitarian Universalist ministry. I had heard that the Fellowship Committee could make it difficult for women and unfairly declined a woman whose primary interest was not in religious education. Although I had taken all the religious education seminars offered, I had "religiously" steered away from getting slotted in religious education. Before leaving Starr King for this last spring trip, and at the suggestion of some of the men who knew her, I wrote to Greta Crosby to ask her opinion of women in the ministry. Greta had a law degree before she studied for the ministry at Meadville/Lombard. She was minister at Utica, New York, one of three or four women in the Unitarian Universalist ministry at that time.

Greta responded: "Dear Vi, I have thought of the ministry as 'my calling' in the deepest sense. It is right for me. But I just have no calling at all 'to prove something about women in general.' I am profoundly grateful to the women who had to be feminists, because they liberated me from many artificial barriers to fulfillment, including that of feminism. Am I right in imputing a like attitude to you? If so, your course will be easier because there is nothing so heavy to carry around as a chip on the shoulder about being 'a woman,' a 'woman minister,' or a 'woman' anything.

"Another preliminary thing, I suppose, is that I developed a rigorous unbelief in the sacramental efficacy of questionnaires. Faced with the question, 'Do you want a woman minister?' I too might well say, 'no.' The point is that in real life no one is ever faced with the question, 'Do you want a woman minister?' The question is, 'Do you want X (or Greta or Vi) as your minister?'"

Greta said that when she first decided to go into the ministry, she was told by a past president of the American Unitarian Association, who was then head of the Department of Ministry, "It is as hard for a woman to find a pulpit as for a Negro." Others told her later her only chance would be to get experience first as an associate minister. She first held out for her own church. She finally weakened and was ready to accept an associateship in a Boston church, when she was turned down at the last minute by a vote too close for a proper vote of confidence. Prejudice had been expressed in an unmistakable way.

She went on, "What hurts, of course, is the sting of injustice—the inward effort of resistance against being condemned on a ground that is irrelevant, impersonal, and beyond your control—or wish to control. It must be like the feeling of a Negro when he's denied access to the normal pursuits solely because he is a Negro.

"The other half of my reaction, of course, was relief. I felt spared and free to continue in the way I had begun. And shortly afterward, the Utica opportunity came about. I thanked my lucky stars that I had been 'banned in Boston!'

"It is so hard to convince anyone that you are called to the whole ministry and not solely to the ministry of children if you are a woman. Perhaps I exaggerate the danger of the labeling, but I had in my own case a strong feeling that if I once got into RE I might never get out again. But a year or two as an associate, barring personality conflicts or jurisdictional disputes with the senior minister, is probably a valuable experience with no pigeonhole."

As to her actual experience, Greta thought a few men

might have felt threatened, and not as free to speak to a woman as to a man, and others felt some unreasoned hostility to any woman in authority. However, she felt it easy to speak and act with most men in a very straightforward relationship such as she had as a lawyer. She felt that some men might even have an easier relationship with a woman than with another man because of a lowered sense of competition, and perhaps because of close relationships with their mothers or wives.

Writing about relationships between men and women, she continued, "Let's not forget the spice of life, the sexual attraction that works in many subtle and legitimate ways to make relationships pleasant far beyond the range of physical touching or flirtation. Obviously, I'm not speaking of any potentially improper or scandalous relationship, the deathknell of many a ministry, because it is the deathknell of trust. I'm speaking of what you must know well in your association with your classmates, the legitimate joy of living enhanced by the added attraction of different sexes.

"Being a woman was particularly valuable in relationship to the women in the church. Now, if you asked them, 'Do you want a woman minister?' many will answer with a categorical 'No!' as I said before. And why not! Obviously a man minister is more attractive to a woman in a church, all things being equal, which they are not. But when it comes right down to it, many women work and talk better with a woman than they do with a man.

"There is still another thing that works in here. It may do something for many women to see a woman minister as a living example of a symbol or public witness to the fact that woman is not necessarily inferior in these areas."

Greta suggested that I wait until the kind of position I wanted became available, and perhaps get a temporary job in a strategic location, and sent all good wishes. I wrote Greta, thanking her for her good letter and told her I'd shown it to some of the men, who agreed it was a classic that should be widely shared.

Appointments were scheduled with the Fellowship Committee shortly after we returned from the spring trip. This committee bestows Preliminary Fellowship (a three-year probational period) on post-graduate ministerial candidates, after which the next step is receiving Full Fellowship and tenure.

We had to write an essay entitled, "Why I Want to be a Unitarian Universalist Minister." I gave some of my early history and then said in part, "To be entering the role of prophet and priest at the frontiers of knowledge, and with the freedom of no authority but that of self, is both the most exciting and most frightening possibility. These emotions are sobered by the great responsibility and trust involved. But it is also a glorious adventure; and I can do no more than offer myself, for I believe it is more in what I am as a person than in anything I may say from the vantage point as prophet that will provide possibilities of genuine encounter with individuals in their integrity, which is at the heart of true religion.

"[His] is the sacred privilege of helping others find meaning in the mysteries of birth; the struggles, conflicts and limitations of life; in the inevitability of death and all the implications this may have for life. His is the precious experience of sharing relationships on every possible human level. His is the sharing of individual Gethsemanes, and hopefully the resurrections and salvations to come. His is the role of protector and catalyst for the greater expressions of human creativity. 'A humanly impossible task,' some may say. But I say, 'No, the most vital, the most dynamic, because it is the most human job of all!'

"Even among Unitarians and Universalists, I expect to encounter an intellectual boundary situation. As enlightened as we like to think we are, I am sure there is a non-rational feeling with many that women are intellectually and perhaps otherwise inferior to men. So I expect to have to earn my status, and upon my worth as a significant person I will base my ministry."

Up to that time students had to go to Boston to appear before the Fellowship Committee. For us they used what was known as the West Coast Retread Committee—the one used to interview ministers from other denominations wishing to be fellowshiped with us.

This committee had two hours to question us on the basis of our record at school, our personal feelings about lots of things, and a battery of psychiatric tests we had taken. They taped the whole procedure and then sent the tape, together with their recommendation, to the Boston committee. Evidently I said the right things, because I was one of three out of five who received their blessing. The other two had to appear before the Boston committee.

A whole file of letters went back and forth to straighten out my status, first as a woman who wanted to be a pulpit minister, as well as one who would graduate without any degrees, since they had decided they could not give me a BD without my having earned a BA. Since then, I have used my own example many times in counseling people who see impediments blocking their way, suggesting that, in fact, we set our own barriers. I could have said "No church will have me. First of all, I'm a woman in my forties, without any degree in a very degree-conscious association." But I knew I'd find a church, and I did.

Had I not stuck to my principles of not getting slotted in religious education, I might have had a ministry right there in Berkeley. During an in-service assignment at a Berkeley church, the minister tried to set up a quiet candidating situation, meeting with committees, the board, etc. He had been trying to get an assistant minister in religious education, and I felt he thought it would be easy to sell a woman to the congregation. He even promised me a Sunday in the pulpit, which he had not offered men students before me. I told him that I was there to learn about all aspects of churchmanship, and that if at the end of the semester he was still interested in presenting me to the congregation for an assistantship and I was too, we could talk more about it.

He resented my independence, and at one point blew his cool and said, "Well, you'll never get a church of your own unless it's some little one dying on the vine in New England." Then he reneged on my Sunday in the pulpit. The whole experience was a valuable example for me of facades and images. His was a most calculated ministry, with measured steps in the chancel at services emphasizing this image. It built a protective armor, but I had seen the real inner man when the facade had cracked. And I vowed never to build an image to hide behind.

Toward the end of my three years at Starr King, schedules were wild. There was so much to do, knowing we were leaving and wouldn't be coming back. Even more difficult was facing the thought of leaving our Starr King family, and I was touched when one of the other students felt a need to share this emotion.

"Hunter," a handsome, soft-spoken man, signed for a chapel. As we entered, the Swedish modern chairs were set in a circle, each with a tiny paper cup on the tapestry seats. It began with music, after which Hunter recited a long poem about being a small child dwarfed as he stood beside a tall aunt in a long skirt. At the end of each of three parts of the poem describing her deep effect upon him as a child, Hunter paused. A fellow student placed a blindfold on Hunter's eyes after each part until he had three.

Then it was his turn. His passionate words said first how much the school and its administration had meant to him, after which his compadre removed a blindfold. Then from his childlike position, he told how much Jo and the faculty had meant. Another blindfold came off. Finally, in touching words he told us what we students had meant to him as our Starr King family. Now he could see! He reached behind a curtain for a half gallon bottle of wine. Slowly he went around the circle, pouring to each of us as he said, "For what you have meant to me!" There were few dry eyes.

Commencement was at First Church in Berkeley, with an academic procession, of course, and a trumpet voluntary. Following words of greeting and a hymn, President Bartlett began, "Men and women of liberal religion, with your own help we have tried to serve your need for ministers. We recommend these five persons. They have come from all across our land, learning along their way from countless jobs, schools, and people. They have dwelt with our Starr King family for many months and will now leave us, feeling gladness and regret. We have chastised and encouraged them and rejoiced in their achievements. And now, we celebrate. We will miss you. But we wish you well."

Professor Capron welcomed us on behalf of Unitarian Universalist churches, and Dr. Lathrop from the Ministers Association. Then we graduates said in unison, "We affirm and treasure our experience at Starr King. (President Bartlett be seated.) We affirm and pledge our service to our people and our churches. (Laymen be seated.) We affirm and accept the challenge of the ministry. (Dr. Lathrop be seated.)"

Then one of the graduates spoke for us, "We will face the pain and joy, giving and sharing what we can. The course behind us has been both rough and smooth, and we are now prepared to live and work and laugh and cry with those around us. We expect no easy life. Together with others we move into the liberal religious life, assured that our lives are worthy. Now we celebrate!"

After the address by John Brigham from the UUA Department of Ministry, degrees were conferred. My name was listed separately on the program under "Certificate of Completion," because I was not to receive the hood designating the graduate degree of Bachelor of Divinity. This meant that some in the audience felt I had been discriminated against because I was a woman. Nevertheless, dozens flocked around me during the reception expressing their excitement at having a woman in the group. Years later, I was to be granted the MDiv degree retroactively.

There were letters from family and friends. Mom wrote a lovely, simple note saying how proud she was. My sister wrote too: "Congratulations, Sis. We're so proud! I'd like to fill your room with flowers—lavish gifts galore—for that is how we do things nowadays. Because of obvious limitations, but even more so because 'the grand gesture' would be incomplete somehow—I sit here instead, thinking of you, taking pride in you, Sis.

"I don't know which gives me greater joy—having a daughter graduate this year, or having you do so. What Barby has accomplished is expected, even demanded; but for you to have done what you have, is something more in dedication, in denial of the comfortable, and greater still, a wonderful decision in faith. I'm proud—so very proud."

A letter from Francie and Johnny Hernandez, who had introduced me to Unitarianism in Santa Fe, proudly took credit for my being in the ministry, and said, "We're proud not only because it is a momentous personal achievement for you, but also because it is important to the whole denomination and our Santa Fe fellowship especially. We feel very smug and proud."

Plans to drive back to Minnesota via Santa Fe were changed, and on June 4, 1962, I was off to Alaska. I had received a letter from "Audrey and Al," my first Santa Fe family, who were now in Juneau. My friends at Starr King felt I should stay around to look for a church, but I had worked hard for three years and felt I deserved a rest. I had a great time in Juneau and a few good weeks at home in Minnesota before heading to Boston for a meeting of all new ministers. I looked forward to becoming acquainted with the UUA's historic building right next to the Statehouse on Beacon Street in Boston, and to putting faces behind names I had been hearing for years. I didn't feel any different with "The Rev." before my name, but perhaps that was to come after I was called to my first church.

As I left Berkeley, I knew I would always be thankful for the kind of education I had received. I felt fortunate to have been a student at Reed College, whose basic premise had been to not parrot other writers, but to think for ourselves. Starr King went even further in helping each of us become significant human beings. We left the Starr King family as students with sufficient "book learning" to provide congregations with challenging religious thoughts and ideas, but even more important, to be the kind of men and women who could minister to others as real people. I was also thankful to Jo Bartlett for his taking a chance on me, as well as to the other Starr King students who not only accepted me as an equal, but supported and encouraged me along the way.

My First Church

At graduation, the other students at Starr King felt I should hurry about finding a church. But I felt due the vacation that beckoned. This proved a good example of not pushing too hard; upon crossing the country I found a church waiting for me even before I wanted to get involved!

The new ministers' meeting in Boston was a command performance for which I embarked in my little Karmann Ghia with much the same feeling I had had when I left Santa Fe over three years before, wondering what lay ahead. I would be one of many new ministers looking for a church and the only woman. During the long drive to Boston that September, I had long conversations with myself about my religious future. "I want a church of my own! Is this too much to ask? Is it in the cards for this coming church year? Will it have to be, as they say, in New England? Will I have to mark time until it can happen? If so, what will I do, and where?"

I knew I wouldn't be out in the cold until something came through. Just as in Berkeley where I knew I had a home with Elsie, there was a haven with the Vanstroms, who were in Providence, Rhode Island. They offered not only shelter and food for my body, but also caring, encouraging support in whatever I was to face in my future. Van had graduated from Starr King the preceding January and had been called as associate minister at the historic First Unitarian Church of Providence.

Before I could sit down and relax, Millie Vanstrom told me that George Spencer, director of the UUA Department of Ministry, wanted to get in touch with me. He had been trying to track me all across the country. He had a date for me to speak in two days—as a candidate for the ministry of a church.

After all the questions I had since becoming the first woman graduate at Starr King, here was another. I had been led to expect that the complicated candidating process would take at least months of personally working with search committees. Here were the powers-that-be in Boston by-passing all the preliminaries and wanting an immediate answer. My whirling mind rebelled. After a moment, I sat down and said to Millie, "If George should call back, just tell him I've not yet arrived."

Monday, Van and I left early for the fifty-mile drive to Boston for the three-day meeting of all new ministers. In Boston I learned from George Spencer that he was indebted to Provincetown for having promised me as a candidate speaker the previous Sunday. "I'm sorry," I told him. "And I can't go next Sunday, because I've promised to be in Van's ordination service. If they're still interested a week from next Sunday, I'll go."

The Provincetown committee said they would wait. I was excited, I had heard so much about Cape Cod and was intrigued with the thought of seeing Provincetown, the well-known art colony way out on the tip of the Cape.

On the drive to Provincetown, it rained all the way. I was to go to the home of Dorotea Murchison at the far end of Commercial Street, where a big bronze plaque documented the landing of the Pilgrims. I had learned in school that the Pilgrims had landed at Plymouth Rock in 1620. No one had told us back then that they first landed on Cape Cod, where Provincetown is now, and later crossed the bay to Plymouth.

The Murchison home, high on a hill, was a showplace—a Gropius-designed home with a strong Japanese accent. A short, gray-haired woman immediately welcomed me at the gracious entrance with a warm smile, took me by the arm, and brought me in out of the rain. Dorotea Murchison was to become one of my special parishioners whom I could count on for anything from monetary support to scrubbing floors.

As a member of the Search Committee, Dorotea had invited special dinner guests to meet me. We left for the church and a meeting with the full committee. After a short discussion without any pertinent, searching questions, they asked me to be their minister. I couldn't believe it, and thinking of the usual process, I said, "But don't you think you ought to wait until you hear me speak tomorrow morning?" They agreed and we returned to the Murchison home in the rain.

Sunday morning it was still raining—a real nor'easter. Even though the streets were awash, a fair crowd came out to hear me. The church was right downtown—a huge two-story, white colonial building set back from the street with a lawn in front. Famed for its copy of a Christopher Wren tower, the church is said to be one of the most photographed in the area.

The upstairs sanctuary seated 408 on cushioned pews of Cape pine with mahogany railings and arm rests, inset with ivory medallions of carved whales' teeth. There was no traditional pulpit. The minister stood at an impressive broad mahogany rostrum on a raised platform. The huge circular chandelier of Sandwich glass dated from 1847, the year the church was built.

The most striking thing about the sanctuary was the remarkable trompe l'oeil interior sepia wall and ceiling decoration, which gave a three-dimensional effect of Greek columns on the sides, and a marble dome above, copied from the Temple of Jupiter in Athens. This was all explained in the printed orders of service, together with the story of how back in 1820 two little girls playing on the beach had found a book floating in the surf. It was *The Life of the Reverend John Murray, Preacher of Universal Salvation.* The book was dried and passed around. Many read and believed, and thus began Universalism in Provincetown, and in 1829, the Church of the Redeemer, Universalist.

In early days the congregation filled the large church to overflowing. Its members had been largely ship captains during old whaling days, back when the church was not only the community's religious center, but also the social center and its welfare department. On the church books was the provision that if men were lost at sea, the church would be responsible for the welfare of widows and orphans, as the Bible decreed.

My sermon that morning was entitled "The Third Relationship," and I suggested that after the first self/self issue and the next self/other, the third relationship was involved with how we see ourselves in relation to the universe, where some find their God to answer all the unanswerable questions of beginnings and worldly judgment. At a meeting following the service, again the Search Committee asked me to become their minister. Again, I didn't accept.

I couldn't explain why I had reservations about accepting the call. Somehow it seemed unreal, happening so easily and so soon; and I needed some time to think it over. So I said I would have to see if I could find a suitable place to live, having heard that year-round rentals were difficult to find.

After visiting friends in Cambridge and Marblehead, and talking with George Spencer at the UUA, I finally decided that at least I could start with my own church. With a good record there, I would have valid experience to offer other search committees. I also felt that Provincetown, being an art colony, couldn't be too provincial—something that (from many rumors I'd heard at Starr King) I associated with historic New England churches.

To cushion the suddenness of it all, I called Herb Mayo, the committee chairman, on October 8 and told him that I would accept if I could start on November 1, after visiting friends in Connecticut and Marblehead. His answer was dated October 19, 1962: "We are very happy that you are interested in becoming minister of the Church of the Redeemer (Universalist). At a meeting of the Universalist Parish of Provincetown, Inc., held today at the church, you were unanimously elected to serve as our minister. We look forward to your return for the service on the first Sunday in November, and hope that you are having an enjoyable trip around New England."

In my letter of acceptance I agreed to an overall annual remuneration of $5,000. With income tax, ministerial deductions for parsonage, travel, and miscellaneous expenses, this would leave a taxable salary of $2,600. I was to have a one-month vacation, taken at some time other than the busy summer season, and one day a week off from regular duties. They had found a spacious upstairs apartment for me with the Rices on Bradford Street.

Once I had made the decision, I realized that there had been another selfish motive behind my decision to accept. I had fallen in love with the picturesque settings of the town and was eager to begin exploring its dunes and beaches. It was a place others yearn to be able to visit once in a summer or a lifetime, and I could call it home for a couple of years!

As my thoughts returned to the church, it occurred to me that because Provincetown was a Universalist church, I had something else to feel good about. Just the year before, in 1961, the Unitarians and Universalists had joined to form the Unitarian Universalist Association. In my predominantly large-city Unitarian experience, I recalled the many "come-outers" who defined themselves by what they did not believe and who needed time to work through their rebellion. Now I could experience the more positive orientation of the rural and small-town-oriented Universalists. Instead of the Calvanistic doctrine of predestination that only the elect would be saved, their God of love stood for universal salvation in simple and positive religious beliefs.

I was ordained and installed on December 9, 1962. In the Unitarian Universalist denomination, which lacks a religious hierarchy, a minister's first church has the privilege of ordination. Once a minister is ordained, he or she is accepted by a subsequent congregation in an Installation Service. The Vanstroms came from Providence for my ordination, and Ken Warren came from Barnstable on the Cape.

I was pleased when George Spencer accepted my invitation to deliver the ordination sermon. It was entitled, "But Where is the Glory?" He said in part, "This is an historic occasion in our denomination. It is not often that we have the privilege of ordaining a woman to our parish ministry. Though we have long said that there is no prejudice among us to having women in our ministry, there has been no overwhelming number of women admitted over the years. Out of nearly one thousand ministers, I think, Violet, that you are number three or four in the women's group.

"I need not remind you that the way is twice as difficult for a woman. Her ministry has to be superior in every way to make it possible for her to have a career in this profession. She will have to continually hammer at the doors of prejudice to make sure her ministry is taken seriously. But it can be done, and I know you have accepted the challenge that confronts you."

Van, in his Charge to the Congregation, complimented them on choosing a woman, suggesting how easy it would have been to say, "But it's never been done before." Ken Warren, who'd been a Unitarian minister on the Cape for ten years, charged me, counseling me to try to understand my Cape Cod members and their heritage. He also indicated that I would have a wide-open mix during tourist season, where he felt I would be special because I was a woman, and they would all be watching. Nell Silvey, a blunt-spoken Cape Cod member, welcomed me to the church, and Episcopal Vicar Vanderburgh brought welcome from the town. It was hard to believe it was all happening! I was touched to tears—tears of joy and fulfillment.

Sessions with photographers and a church reception followed. Late in the afternoon, after the guests had gone, I sat down to have a good cry. My cup of joy had truly overflowed. My thoughts went back to that day four years ago when I had accepted John's invitation to the Santa Fe Unitarian Fellowship. How could I ever have envisioned my easy evolution to this new status of professional pioneer!

The wonder of it all was overwhelming. Twice I was interrupted by the phone with wires from Starr King compadres in Washington and California, and I reread Mom's letter. "I'm very proud of you, Violet, and I know God is too. I love you and I'll be thinking of you all day and hope the weather will cooperate. . . . Yesterday I had a surprise. A man was at the door with a newspaper. I thought he was wanting me to take a subscription. But it was Clarence St. Peter. His mother lives in Hyannis and sends him the *Cape Cod Standard Times*. He works in the post office here and has been changing your address, and when he saw your picture in the paper he just had to show it to me. He said he'd pass along any more news he finds."

I'd also had a letter from my sister. It was on holiday stationery with "Greetings from Around the World": "The greetings above seem much too 'distant' for a warm person like you. Yet, as an adjective it does partially describe your attitude to life somehow—your interest in people—all people—your love for them and all God's creation. Beyond your reverence, however, is that wonderfully contagious zest for all things with your childlike faith in the good of things and the curiosity that keeps you ever seeking. Keep that quality, Sis. If you gave nothing else to the world it would bring happiness beyond imagination."

I was touched deeply that her feelings so paralleled mine—that the interesting, significant people along the way are those who keep the childlike qualities of wonder, curiosity, and adventure and reverence for life. To have my own sister say it made it even more meaningful.

I had congratulatory letters from Jo Bartlett; "Bob" and "Sam," two professors at Starr King; and Steve Fritchman, the minister I had met in Los Angeles during an Easter service on one of my spring trips.

There was even a letter from the Berkeley minister I'd done In-Service Education with, who had prophesied that I would never get a church of my own unless it was one dying on the vine in New England. "You have been in my thoughts many times since you went East, and your invitation to attend the Installation comes as a most welcome announcement. Those of us who had known you had the deep conviction about your ability to make good once you found an assignment. I wish for you the most wonderful experiences. I am sure I speak for all of us and especially for your friends in our church in sending congratulations to both you and the members of your new parish."

Bob Kimball, who had given me such a hard time with my credo, wrote some weeks later. He said in part, "Well, welcome to the fold. In many ways the church situation there sounds quite ideal as a place for you to begin (continue?) your ministry. The Order of Worship reflects conservative New England piety, but I think you will be able to work comfortably in such a situation without succumbing. New England reflects honesty. That quality, plus the sea around them, could make the Provincetown church an interesting place to minister."

I wondered about his closing words, "Scholefield [a San Francisco minister] agrees with me that all ministers necessarily fulfill father-figure roles in a congregation. It will be interesting to see, with time, how a woman becomes defined in such a situation!"

With all of this, I was one happy, fulfilled woman, ready to begin that "definition" Bob Kimball mentioned, wondering, however, about the responsibilities, and perhaps the difficulties of living my new status of pioneer.

∾

The Thursday after my ordination I was at my typewriter working on my sermon when the phone rang. "Miss Kochendoerfer, this is Mrs. Joseph. My son wonders whether you would marry him tomorrow. The first time wasn't legal. . . ."

Mrs. Joseph was a member of our church, married to a Portuguese fisherman. She worked for another of our members who ran a rest home on Commercial Street and had a small daughter in our church school. All sorts of things went through my mind—but the "wasn't legal" part put me on the alert. As I think of it now, this early experience presaged one strange aspect of my paradoxical stay in Provincetown.

I had not yet performed a wedding. My little black book was somewhere in the unpacked boxes I had stashed away. So I said, "I'm sure we can work something out, but I'll have to check and call you back."

I had talked with the town clerk about Massachusetts laws on marriage. He was a former Catholic priest, and I had an experience with him I would forever associate with New Englanders. I would ask question after question about who could apply for a license, waiting periods and such, and never get a simple, straightforward answer.

I finally learned that Mrs. Joseph's son had been married and divorced, with the decree against him, which meant a two-year waiting period before he could legally remarry. During that period, he had been brought up on a charge of bigamy for impregnating a girl while he was technically still married. However, Dr. Hiebert, a colorful Provincetown physician, felt the girl involved was far enough along in her pregnancy that something should be done. So with his particular influence, he had arranged a waiver with state authorities. This made the present license legal.

I did find some material on weddings I could adapt, and called Mrs. Joseph back. This time I found myself talking with the prospective groom. He said, "We'd like to be married in our living room." I got directions and agreed to be at the address for a four o'clock wedding the following day.

The next day I drove down Bradford Street in the December dusk and found the clapboard house. I knocked and was admitted to a large linoleum-floored kitchen with a stove, sink, and refrigerator lined up at the far end. The setting and room full of Portuguese people brought that uncomfortable feeling one has as a minority in a crowd. Someone finally took my coat.

Mrs. Joseph introduced me to her son, her very pregnant daughter-in-law-to-be, and to her towering husband who had long, curly hair. This was in 1962, before men had started letting their hair grow.

At one point, after much milling around, I said, "Shall we have the ceremony in the living room?" In that barely furnished room, the light on the wall behind cast me in a shadow as I stood before the young man and the very pregnant bride. With a baby crying on the bed in the next room, I conducted the traditional ceremony.

On the way home I said to myself, "Vi, you've always wondered what your first wedding would be like. You never could have dreamed this one up!" I also had that strange feeling I still have after a ceremony—that my words and my signature had somehow made the marriage legal.

Some weeks later the phone rang. It was the young groom wondering whether I would baptize his baby. I tried to explain that what Unitarian Universalists did might not be considered legal by the Catholic church, but he knew something should be done for his son, and it seemed he was willing to take his chances. He told me he'd find sponsors.

Instead of baptisms, it's the usual custom for Unitarian Universalists to perform a child dedication and naming at a regular church service. Since most Unitarians don't accept the concept of original sin, which other denominations feel must be washed away, we name the child and then dedicate the parents and the congregation to the responsibility for producing a healthy climate within which this child may grow. Because young Mr. Joseph mentioned sponsors, which would suggest a more traditional service, I felt it would be best for me to do the ceremony at the home. We made a date for that Friday night.

I was warmly welcomed. They took my coat and explained that they had named the baby Daniel, after Dr. Hiebert, who was to be one of the sponsors. It turned out that Dr. Hiebert had gone "down Cape" on an emergency call, but he planned to be back. We waited half an hour, but knowing I had an eight o'clock appointment, Mrs. Joseph sent a son to find someone else to be a sponsor. He returned and said, "Bill and Ann will come."

There was a knock at the door. It opened a crack. There stood a young man in a GI Army overcoat down to his ankles. He said, "Annie doesn't want to!," and closed the door. Again, the son went out, this time returning with a middle-aged couple who agreed to be sponsors. Once again, we lined up in the living room. With a bud from the chrysanthemum plant I'd received, instead of the rose bud we sometimes used as a symbol of childhood purity, I proceeded.

We had just completed the ceremony when there was a rap at the door. It was Dr. Hiebert, hatless, but with the fur collar of his coat up around his ears, his white hair showing above. He apologized for being late. When he heard that a woman had performed the service, he was fascinated and wondered whether we would reenact the scene so he could take a picture. I agreed to the reenactment. He took two exposures with his County Coroner's stereopticon camera.

Weeks later, when I met Dr. Heibert at a dinner party, he asked whether he had sent me the pictures. When I told him he hadn't, he said, "I should explain. You'll remember I took two exposures. One turned out beautifully, but I'm sorry to say that the other was a double exposure with the next official photograph I took of a body we exhumed down at Truro on an arsenic poisoning case." When he noticed that I was a bit repulsed at the picture of me holding out a chrysanthemum bud above a dead body in a cemetery, this distinguished gentleman went on telling coroner stories for my benefit.

An unforgettable wedding came about later that year as the result of a cocktail party at the home of a wealthy Jewish divorcee. She mentioned that a good friend's daughter was to marry a non-Jewish boy. "They've reconciled themselves to this," she said, "but it means they'll have to be married by a Justice of the Peace." A member of my church who overheard the conversation said, "Oh no! Just call Miss Kochendoerfer."

The bride was attending Duke University and the prospective groom the University of Indiana, both majoring in music. The whole wedding was planned by long distance telephone. But one day the mother of the bride-to-be called to ask whether she might come to talk. She had never heard of the Universalist Church and wanted to know something about it.

Edith London, a tiny, soft-spoken, almost birdlike creature, is one of the most memorable persons I've ever met. We had a long, intimate conversation. Many of Edith's family were lost in the Holocaust. Her husband had taught at the University in Berlin, but then fled Germany for France, where he was a professor at the Sorbonne for a time. Later they came to North Carolina, where he accepted a position at Duke University. At the time of her husband's premature death, he had been a candidate for the Nobel Prize in low-temperature physics. I found out later that Edith herself was a well-known artist, having had one-woman shows in North Carolina galleries.

Rosie London's wedding day was sunny and bright. The ceremony was performed in a lovely private home, with music performed by soloists of the Provincetown Summer Symphony, which attracted talent from across the country. My words touched the bride's heart and Rosie wept.

A few days later I received a note from Edith London, "I am deeply grateful to you for having impressed great beauty and dignity on Rose's wedding ceremony. And I am certain that everyone who witnessed this great event in the lives of our two young people wants to be included in this deepfelt expression of thanks for an experience which went far beyond the expression of passively witnessing. I am so very happy that it was you who joined Rose and Bill into marriage."

Edith asked for a copy of the ceremony so that she would be able to reread it over the years. Since then I have always given couples a copy of their wedding ceremony.

I spent that first Christmas with the Vanstroms and returned for the social event of the Provincetown year—the Murchison Christmas party. With guests in elegant formal dress in the refined, tasteful setting, it seemed to be of another world. Among the fascinating locals, including famous artists, was a sixty-some-year-old woman I was glad to meet. "Mame" was a woman I was to learn more about later. Since many were eager to see my apartment, I invited the congregation for an open house the coming Sunday. The punch and sherry put them in a good mood for the big parish meeting the following week.

In a newsletter, I'd outlined several changes I hoped we could make. I pointed out that we still had the historic dual church/parish membership on the books that we needed to change. This went back to early days when all taxpayers had to support the church and thus were parish [county] members, whether they ever darkened its door or not. They did, however, have a vote in calling a minister, which caused the great controversy when Dr. Ware had been chosen for the Hollis Chair of Theology at Harvard and was considered too liberal. That led to the legal Dedham decision as to whom property belonged when many churches split over the issue.

I also wanted us to vote on joining the Cape Cod Council of Churches. I had learned that Unitarian Universalist churches could be members of the Massachusetts Council. Because of this, some Lutheran churches refused to join.

The most controversial item at our meeting would be a request to change the name of the church. I explained that when summer visitors read the sign as they came into town, CHURCH OF THE REDEEMER (with "Universalist" in small letters underneath) most wouldn't realize there was a liberal church in town.

I needn't have worried about the meeting. Right down the line the congregation backed me up. On the name it was a tie between Universalist and Universalist Unitarian Church of Provincetown, until one woman realized she was still clutching her ballot. That made it The Universalist Church of Provincetown (Universalist-Unitarian). I had not even dared hope they would include "Unitarian!"

After the business meeting, we gathered to see other old papers we had found in the safe. In addition to those of the dual membership we had voted to discontinue was an old treasurer's book. Along with items for pew rent and prisms for the Sandwich glass chandelier, there was an entry for $7.00 to Jack Rosenthal for pumping the organ. Jack was our moderator and swore, "I never got that much in one lump sum!"

Later many retired to his home to celebrate with Rosenthal "tea," our name for a hard liquor drink.

I was proud of my group that night, especially because I had just learned that I was minister to many Methodists who had become Universalists when their historic building had been sold to Walter Chrysler for an art museum some years back. It seems the transfer had been made without consulting the congregation, many of whom hated Chrysler. When it was announced at an annual meeting, many of the good Methodists felt betrayed and left the church.

Those who left couldn't go to the Catholic church, or, for many, even the Episcopal; so they chose ours. With the many ex-Methodists added to our congregation, it had increased to a size where they felt they could call a full-time minister. This was a revelation to me, though it did explain some of dichotomies I'd wondered about.

Many of these erstwhile Methodists were of advanced ages. Who was I to try to ignore religious beliefs that they had chosen and that had shaped their lives? I found that "religion" to many of them meant "going to church on Sunday." They hadn't complained about my sermons, but I did feel I had to be honest with them. I began by defining my own theological terms so that they knew what I meant when I said or didn't say things about religion or God or the Trinity. In light of all this, to minister to my older Methodists, and also to present a weekly program that would attract new and younger members, wasn't going to be easy.

In addition to incorporating the needs of my Methodist/ Universalists, I had to learn to understand old Cape Codders. Their bluntness seemed a protective shield. When I began an after-service coffee hour, two long-time influential members stayed away, saying loudly, "It has never been done before!" It wasn't long before they joined the flock.

Another prestigious member hadn't been to church since I had come. Although she wasn't a native of the Cape, she too was outspoken. When the Mayos had called her one Sunday to ask whether they could pick her up, "Laura" retorted, "I haven't been feeling well for the past month and no one's called. You don't have to bother now. By the way, how do you like the new minister?" I imagine the Mayos said they thought I was okay, to which Laura retorted, "I don't approve of women in the ministry!"

This intrigued me. I decided to call on her one rainy Sunday after church. I had noticed her impressive Cape Cod house with a huge bay window, set back only a yard or so behind a high black wrought-iron fence. As I opened the gate, I stopped to look at shelves in the bay window filled with fascinating objects, together with a sign for tourists, THIS IS NOT A SHOP.

I lifted the heavy knocker and waited. A tall, imposing woman, white hair piled high on her head, opened the door. At her side stood a svelte Afghan dog—a blonde beauty with curlers holding up ears and a topknot. She invited me into a living room with fascinating decor from her many travels. Right off, Laura liked me and told me so. "If I like somebody, I like them. If I don't, they don't have to bother to come around any more."

She asked whether I'd like to see her kitchen. It was a dream, with floor-length windows across the back looking out on one of the loveliest gardens in Provincetown. There Laura introduced me to Reuben, her parrot, who said "Hello" from his large cage in the corner. She insisted I stay for tea. I was told later that after I left, Laura was on the phone calling her friends. "The new minister came to call. She was here two hours and we ate out in the kitchen!"

Laura became one of my best friends and supporters. She told me that "Joe" and "Jeff" (two of our gay members) told her she had to keep me happy so I would stay. She also said they told her they were glad I was a woman, or else, at the salary they were paying, they wouldn't have gotten such a good minister. That reminded me of what Dorotea Murchison had said. "We might have gotten a second-rate man; but we feel we got a first-rate woman!"

Because Laura was such an interesting character, I took all my visiting friends to meet her. In a discussion one time she talked about "niggers." I said, "I wish you wouldn't use that word, Laura." She retorted, "Well, they are!" Then she thought a bit and said, "Now that you mention it, last summer I had some roomers. One of them was black, and now that I think about it, I must admit that she was a cut above the rest." She never used the word again to me.

Another special member of the congregation was a tall, slender woman, beautiful to look at in her stately demeanor, who always reminded me of the heroine pictured in old-time novels. "Grace" was a published author, and had just received great acclaim for her book *The Two Lives of Edith Wharton*. She had started writing back in her suffragist days and had many stories to tell.

One Sunday Grace was home with her leg in a cast. I received a phone call at the church from her daughter in Ohio, who wanted me to tell Grace that her son had died of cancer in New Jersey. As I broke the news to Grace, I saw this stately, elegant woman dissolve in uncontrollable grief.

That afternoon I promised to drive Grace to New Jersey. After looking at a map and seeing the maze of freeways through the New York City area, I was relieved to no end when Grace's physician recommended against her traveling. I had called the minister of her son's Unitarian church, who counseled against Grace seeing her son's emaciated body. Although I had been relieved at not having to drive Grace to New Jersey, with more experience I might have made a different decision. I now feel it important in resolving final separation for many to see the dead body of a close relative.

I remembered a conversation with Bob Kimball after I returned from my father's funeral. He had said, "I envy you Vi.

When I came here from Harvard, my Dad died just ten days later. I felt that because I had seen him so recently, I didn't need to return for the funeral. I'll regret that the rest of my life." Another friend said, "My Dad died when I was overseas with the Peace Corps, so I didn't come back. Now it's hard to think of him as dead. It always seems that he'll be returning from a trip or somewhere."

All this reminds me of my first funeral. The Unitarian Universalist ministers in the area had monthly meetings at Sea Pines Institute in Brewster on the Cape. It was a good experience to get to know them all on an informal basis and to have them to answer the many questions I had as a new minister. I was one woman among twenty men, but they seemed to feel that my being there added something good. One said, "How would you like us to treat you, Vi—as a lady or as a minister?" For a moment I was stopped, and then smiled and said, "As a woman!" What I meant, I guess, was "just as a real person," which is what I hope I am. Somehow, I much dislike being called a "lady" minister, or "lady" anything. To me, it connotes an artificial and polite facade I felt was foreign to me and my ministry.

It was at this meeting while relaxing on the beach that I received a phone call from the funeral director at Wellfleet, a town down Cape from Provincetown, saying that Pa Snow had died. Pa Snow was the father of my finance chairman. I asked one of the older ministers if I had to rush back. He smiled and said, "If you get there so you can talk with the family the day before the funeral, that should be okay. I'd call them and set this up."

I did meet with two sons and daughters-in-law. I had known Pa Snow's death was imminent, so I had already given it thought. They told me stories about Pa as a veteran sailor all Provincetown had known and loved, and that his best sailing buddy, a Catholic, had also died and was to be buried the same day.

Because our santuary was on the second floor, with two

flights of stairs that turned back on themselves, we couldn't have open-casket services there. The funeral home was jammed, with standing room only to honor Pa Snow, and also, I suspect, with a bit of curiosity at what kind of service the new woman minister would do.

It was great to be able to use sailing images, especially with the two buddies sailing off on the same day. The family felt I had captured Pa's lovable personality and tearfully thanked me. The Mayos reported that one of our blunt Cape Codders had said on the way out, "Well, I'm sure glad she didn't just read a bunch of old Bible verses." Several persons I'd not actually met, but knew who I was, stopped me on the street later to say something to the effect of, "It was the best funeral I've ever attended." That was good to hear.

∾

Several members of our congregation were gay. I'd known gays who were accepted in the art atmosphere of Santa Fe and also in the Bay Area of California, so I expected to find gays in this famous art colony.

Joe and Jeff were two gay members who owned a lovely home on the harbor, but spent most of their time in New York City, where they ran a floral shop. They were solid Provincetown citizens, well known in town, and were to be two of my most valued members—always ready with financial support, manual labor, or advice. Joe was a tall, imposing presence with graying wavy hair. One had the sense he was always in charge, though in a warm and gentle way. One was also attracted to genial Jeff—shorter and slimmer—a caring person who accepted his more retiring role in their chosen relationship with perennial cheerfulness.

Shortly after I came, they were in Provincetown for services. They stayed until after everyone else had left. As we were talking in the foyer, Jeff said, "It's really cold here. Why don't we have Miss Kochendoerfer come to dinner this evening and we can continue our conversation." This was the beginning of a standing dinner invitation to their home nearly every time they came to Provincetown.

Their large, three-story home was right on the harbor. As I entered I saw Jeff in an overstuffed chair, some knitting on the arm. Each had a French poodle, one named Touche and the other Bijou. After Joe provided us with drinks, Jeff retired to the kitchen. A handsome, youthful-looking white haired man who ran an antique shop had arrived, bringing a woman guest. After excellent food and drink, we had a good conversation, and I left with an optimistic feeling about the possibility of attracting some of the art crowd.

Joe and Jeff also played a part in beautifying our church on Sunday. Many times members would bring small bouquets of flowers for the sanctuary that were pathetically dwarfed by the large scale of the wide mahogany rostrum. I asked J & J if they would bring some large vases from their New York floral shop, hoping members would get the idea that we needed larger flower arrangements in keeping with the scale of the impressive rostrum.

When Joe brought the vases, he called to ask me to have dinner with him at The Moors. We had a delightful evening. "Ted," the owner of The Moors had drinks sent over and came to talk. When he left, Joe related Ted's story. "Do you know, Vi, he was married to a lesbian and was faithful to her until her death. Now he's married to a woman doctor who lost her license performing abortions and moved to the Cape to open a restaurant in Truro." Our unguarded conversations supported my belief that no matter what kind of difference one has, if one accepts one's self without apology, others will feel comfortable in their acceptance as well.

Another Sunday I was to have dinner with Joe and Jeff. About five Joe called, "Vi, we have a cocktail engagement we wouldn't want to miss. Could you make it seven thirty instead of seven?" A short time later the phone rang again. This time it was Mrs. Adams who lived across from me on Bradford Street. "Miss Kochendoerfer, I'm having some folks in for drinks about five thirty. Would you like to join us?" It seemed made to order, so I said "I'd love to." I liked Mrs. Adams: she had been injured in an auto accident and she couldn't walk, but she nevertheless was an active business-woman. Her lovely colonial home was made for entertain-ing, and she did it like a queen from her wheelchair.

This turned out to be Joe and Jeff's party. The handsome antique shop owner brought Mame, the older woman I'd met at the Murchison Christmas party. Mame was in her late six-ties, a large-bosomed, genial, much-loved person in Provincetown. Her fame, or infamous reputation, lay in the well-known fact that she'd been a high-class call woman for years and still was. We had a merry time.

Two Episcopalians became a vital part of my Provincetown life, and I still count them as treasured friends. One afternoon shortly after I'd come to Provincetown, I had a caller at about four o'clock. A short, slight man wearing a jaunty beret and a worn tweed jacket turned out to be Vicar Ernest Vanderburgh of St. Mary's of the Harbor. I invited him in, and we had a long talk. Ernie had been in Provincetown for years and made me feel welcome. He shared stories about his Episcopalian group and homey things about the community he thought I should know. As he left, he invited me and members of our church to join their weekly adult discussion group. This sounded like a great idea.

One day as I returned from a minister's meeting down Cape, my landlady told me that the vicar's wife had called that afternoon and would call back the next day. I pictured a formal, well-dressed woman. When I opened the door the following day, there stood an attractive young woman with a short, blown bob and a quiet smile. I'm not sure just what expression was on my face because Jane wore a big bulky sweater with torn, paint-stained jeans stuck into a pair of boots.

She stayed to talk a whole hour, for we seemed to sense we had much in common. I found she loved to explore and do outdoor things and seemed eager to find someone outside her congregation to do them with. The next evening, I was their guest for drinks and oyster stew in front of a fire. I got home after one in the morning. That was the beginning of many comfortable sessions when we would share our personal hopes and dreams, as well as the worries and problems of our ministries. Ernie and Jane were to be my closest friends and supporters.

The next Friday morning, Jane called, "We're taking the sailboat out for the last time before putting it up for the winter. Why don't you join us?" I thought a minute and then remembered that in my newsletter I'd announced office hours to begin that very day. I mentioned this to Jane. She laughed and put Ernie on the phone. He said, "Oh Vi, no one's going to come the first day." So I wrestled with my new-minister's conscience and decided to go along.

It was one of those Provincetown days when the atmosphere is so clear you swear you have a new set of eyes—the reason why so many artists were there. It has to do with the extraordinary quality of light on the outer Cape. By the time we returned from an exciting sail across the bay to Race Point, the tide was in. Ernie had to hurry to change into his ministerial garb for a two-o'clock funeral.

Jane talked me into clamming that afternoon. Again my conscience questioned, but I'd never dug clams in my life and was intrigued with the idea. We took my car, parking it along the highway at the edge of town. After a couple of hours of digging clams, Ernie joined us, back in sailing clothes. We took off in their beachbuggy to find oysters and scallops, leaving my Karmann Ghia parked near the Breakwater Motel.

I knew that day why I'd decided to stay in Provincetown, as I became an honored guest, eating steamed clams at the Vanderburgh's outer cape beach house at Wellfleet. We had to hurry to get back in time to pick up my Ghia before the Friday night meeting of our mutual discussion group, which we had decided to call The Inquirers. As we came down the harbor road, we found cars lined up all around the motel and flood lights out over the harbor. As I got into my Ghia the police came up.

They explained they had been called when someone had seen the little car with the California license sitting there for hours. They had found from the registration that it belonged to the new minister in town. The police had been told that someone had headed out on the bar with a clam rake. They probably thought, "This landlubber from California went out and didn't know the tides."

I was so embarrassed! But the police were wonderful. As we hurried home to change clothes and get to our discussion group, Ernie said, "Well, that's one way of getting known in a hurry. It's bound to be a local color story in *The Cape Cod Standard Times* next Tuesday!"

The Inquirers became a well-known local program with our topics announced each week in *The Cape Cod Standard Times*. We discussed issues such as art and religion, euthanasia, birth control, Zen, the race problem, and the cost of death.

At one meeting someone suggested that the next week we discuss "What does it mean to be a Christian?" I called Ernie, who had not been at the meeting. "You know how outspoken my people are. This could be hard on you!" He said he didn't mind.

That evening I led off. "For the purposes of this discussion I would maintain that we, who have long been labeled the heretics, are the Jesus Christians, and therefore the true Christians—and that you, who call yourselves the real Christians, have, over the centuries, been the real heretics!" That brought applause from my group.

I maintained that there was no Trinity for early Christians, but when Constantine became a Christian he Christianized the Holy Roman Empire. At that time people argued about whether Jesus was God or not. Athanasians said he was, and the Arians said he was not. So Constantine called what was perhaps the first ecumenical conference at Nicea in 325 CE to settle the matter. No consensus arose, and the question had to be decided by vote. When the Athanasians won the vote, Jesus became the Son of God, and at the Council of Constantinople in 381, the concept of the Holy Spirit was added to make the Christian Trinity. So I maintained that the Trinity was a man-made concept. Ernie had no rebuttal to my story.

This discussion happened just before the Provincetown Town Meeting, at which I had been invited to do the Invocation. At the meeting, as I was out in the lobby during a break, a little old lady came up to me and said, "That was beautiful, my dear. I can't help think how they all bowed their heads as you reminded them of the responsibilities involved in the freedom of a town meeting—with their responsibilities to themselves, to their neighbors, to their God, and all. But to look at them now, you can see it was nothing but words to them."

I agreed with her and have often questioned the need for the usual perfunctory invoking of the deity before and after certain meetings. Even so, mine made *The Provincetown Advocate* next day, and my parishioners were proud because I was the first Unitarian Universalist minister to have been asked.

ౚ

I was getting a reputation for my weekly newsletter. I called it *The Weathervane*. A church member cut a lovely linoleum block of our Christopher Wren tower for the masthead. I wrote the newsletter, cut the mimeo stencil, and ran it on the first hand-cranked model AB Dick ever put out. I painted the thick, black ink in the big open cylinder with a paint brush. If anything went wrong, the nearest stationery store was in Hyannis, fifty-one miles away. We made the headlines in our district newsletter: "We've just finished reading our first issue of *The Weathervane*, and send a special salute this month to our church at Provincetown. Its minister, the Rev. Violet A. Kochendoerfer, has joined our ministers' group and we watch with eagerness the new spirit and growth of this church. We all know the value of a good 'anchor man' and welcome the new vitality and send greetings to this church at the end of the Cape."

I was pleased I'd been called an "anchor-man," and didn't spoil the compliment by taking issue. I felt I made more inroads with my male compadres by not making them "watch their language."

In the February 12, 1963, issue of *The Weathervane*, I wrote about "The Ecumenical Movement in Provincetown," saying how pleased I was with our co-sponsored discussion group with the Episcopalians. I had run into Mr. Lane, minister of the Methodist church, and Father Duarte the previous week and invited Father Duarte to join our next Inquirer's group. We were planning to discuss the Vatican Council and would have welcomed a Catholic point of view. He accepted! It was the first time we had hosted the Catholic clergy!

When Father Duarte came, he admitted that it was Pope John who made possible his joining us. He was a most gracious guest and openly shared his feelings about the Vatican Council, answering many questions about Roman Catholicism.

In *The Weathervane* of August 25, I addressed international friendship: "RUSSIANS ARE PEOPLE TOO. Russian trawlers are anchored in the harbor again. There are those here who think the Russian fisherman are great because they have met and had communication with them. Stephen, the young son of one of our members, had that privilege. With a grown-up neighbor on Monday they cruised over to the Russian boats anchored in the Pamet area for repairs.

"They went on about the jolly Russians who'd given candy to one of our children. The child was so excited he told all his friends and they made up a package of penny candies for the Russians to give to their children. The child's mother (a member of our congregation) overheard the children discussing this, saying, 'Grown-ups think Russians are bad, but this is silly. They're real people—friendly, happy people—and we like them.'

"Let us learn from our children. Instead of indoctrinating them with our own fears, doubts, and distrusts, let's look at our own racial situation and ask ourselves, 'Would there be any problem of integrating elementary schools if it weren't for parents and teachers and politicians?'"

That spring *The Cape Cod Standard Times* did quite an article entitled "Woman Talk, Do You Know—The Rev. Violet Kochendoerfer of Provincetown?" It surrounded a large picture of me looking at a book and said, in part, "The Rev. Violet Annette Kochendoerfer, minister of the Universalist Church of Provincetown, has come through the last nine months with undimmed enthusiasm for her first post as a clergy woman and her new hometown.

"The fact has something to do with the merits of the job, and wonders of the place, but even more to do with Miss Kochendoerfer's nature and her total intent to seek and find the best in life. In short order, her new friends and parishioners dropped their reserve to address her by her shortened first name, 'Vi.' Startling to many has been the ease and good humor with which major changes in the church have come about.

"Once under pressure of problem-solving and fatigue, this woman minister was embarrassed to find herself in tears. Her comment that as a minister perhaps she had to forget she was a woman, impressed this reporter as an academic daydream. A woman who cares for people, a home, beautiful things, good food, and has irrepressible 'joie de vivre' is going to have a hard time to discount her womanhood. We assume she gave up this idea as a bad one after eight hours of sleep."

After giving a physical description of me and of my parsonage, describing in detail many of my past experiences, and providing a long history of sorts, the article closed with my words in the days before the his/her controversy. "Of the role of the liberal minister she says 'The Unitarian Universalist minister is offered the wealth and expanse of the world of man from which to distill meaning for today. He is the antidote for the specialist in the scientific world. He must be the generalist. He must be on understanding and speaking terms with every part of our culture, yet he must see man as a totality within this culture. His is the impossible task of generalization and integration, and of working in the boundary areas where man can only question, and where he must project meaning within ambiguity and without final answers.'

"Down this traveled but still rugged road, Miss Kochendoerfer has glimpsed her destiny. She is agile of body, mind, and spirit, and gives every indication of being equal to it. Cape Codders who know and like her already wish her Godspeed."

I saw little of the regular members come May. They were off getting ready for their summer jobs running motels and gift shops, or renovating rental quarters to bring them income on which to live for the rest of the year. Beginning in June, many summer residents and visitors came, making an entirely different congregation with whom I could try more creative services.

Because the church was right downtown on Commercial Street, it was open each day as an historic tourist attraction. The downstairs parish hall was converted into the well-known Thrift Shop, which brought saleable ware from friends who came from as far as New York City. Then it had to give up space for the board-approved Moffet Gallery. Ross Moffet, our quiet, genial treasurer, was a well-known artist who had done the murals for the Eisenhower Museum. His wife, Dorothy Moffet, was an acclaimed watercolor artist. Together they were a much-loved pair, and their gallery attracted many visitors.

One of the Moffet's helpers was a young man from a wealthy Congregational church in Connecticut. He said, "I was here last summer just once, because I thought the church was on its last legs. Then when I walked in this year, it was exciting. I felt as though I'd stepped into an alive church!"

We had some long talks and it was he who gave me the idea that perhaps it isn't necessary to stay on in one's first parish too long—not if that first parish is Provincetown. He said, "As much as I'd hate to see you go, I feel it would be wrong to waste all your enthusiasm knocking yourself out here—not when there are so many groups that need and could use you. If not in your denomination, there are plenty of Congregational churches looking for someone like you."

I was told of a conversation going around town about a woman who had come to church and was impressed. She told a friend she ought to come hear me. The friend responded that she was not very religious. And the first woman said, enthusiastically, and as a compliment, "Oh, that's all right. She isn't either!" She meant, of course, that I didn't get too involved in orthodox theology.

Late that spring, problems with my music department had come to a head. Several times, without warning, my music director (who was also our organist) just didn't appear. I found out that she was an alcoholic. Although I could have worked with that, I did have to have reliable talent on Sundays. Often she had real or imagined physical maladies, and much of the time had the choir upset one way or another.

I had talked with fellow ministers about my problem. They all regarded musicians as fellow professionals and trying to tell them what to do was tricky business. I listened, but had to disregard their good advice. Toward the end of spring, after a three-week absence, the director's husband mentioned that she was thinking of taking a leave of absence for the busy summer. I took the opportunity to locate a fine musician from the Andover faculty who was on the Cape for the summer.

When fall came, I talked Jane Vanderburgh into taking over as organist. She was a top-flight musician who could handle our precious tracker organ like the pro she was, picking up pedals on one end when she ran out on the other end of the limited pedalboard. Jane's moving classical preludes and offertories added immeasurably to our services.

Ernie and Jane were both musicians and were teaching me the bass recorder so I could join them in a trio. Through them I was to learn that Provincetown was a treasurehouse of musical talent, in addition to artistic talent. A young couple who lived up the hill behind my house had joined the church. "Sal" ran a well-known Portuguese restaurant. One day he stopped by to ask whether I thought we might invite some recorder players to be soloists at one of our services.

The players were Joel Newman, assistant professor of music at Columbia University, and Elloyd Hanson, who was then editor of *The American Recorder*. I said I would ask them, and got directions to their sail loft apartment. I climbed to the deck, which hung out over the harbor, and heard music through a closed screen door. Joel and Elloyd invited me in. They had just been out picking blueberries and had made some blueberry flunnery (sort of like strawberry shortcake made with blueberries). They sat me down in a comfortable chair with a plate of flunnery and a perculator of coffee, and I was the audience! They agreed to play at the church if their instruments were in tune with our organ. Luckily, they were!

Joel and Elloyd played four movements of a Telemann sonata at our Sunday service, and were entranced with the acoustics. I received a letter from Joel, "The acoustics of your beautiful building are so perfect we could hardly believe it. I'd compare them with the time we played in the Spoleto Festival in Italy. We found a little old church way up in the hills which we wanted to use. We were told we had to get the permission of the Bishop. We played for him. He listened, paused, and then brought his two palms together. And we knew we were in!

"And, Vi, your building is like that! Our playing there made two recorders sound like several! And to come to this spot on the tip of the Cape and find an organ like yours and an organist like Mr. Flint who can play really great music—is just something one doesn't expect to find. If we don't go to Europe next summer, we'd love to come back and play for you again!"

Ernie and Jane were both at that service, and together we later arranged for recorder concerts at our church. Experiences like this, together with sharing their sailboat expeditions and dunebuggy picnics on the sand dunes, as well as my regular escapades with Jane on beachcombing trips after storms when we'd come home laden with treasures, made me feel fortunate indeed. Yet, there were reservations, because some of my deepest satisfactions came not from my ministry with those who had called me, but with the exciting people, experiences, and possibilities the summers and summer congregations provided.

Later that first summer, Dr. Heibert died at the age of eighty-three after serving the town as a general practitioner for fifty-three years. Dr. Heibert *was* Provincetown. Henry Morgan's local column said, "It's common knowledge that half of the population of Provincetown was delivered by Doctor

Hiebert." *The Provincetown Advocate* said "He carried the tradition of the country doctor into the space age, and it will probably be impossible to find anyone to take his place." The article told of his friendship with Eugene O'Neill, with whom Dr. Heibert had shared a room during college days. Years later, O'Neill showed up in Provincetown and came to Dr. Heibert for help as an alcoholic. The good doctor offered his help if O'Neill would promise to write one good play. "Beyond the Horizon" was the result. Later came "Anna Christie," "The Hairy Ape," and "All God's Children." Dr. Heibert later said, "I feel that if I had done nothing else in my life, this accomplishment was worth living for."

I mention this because Eugene O'Neill reminds me of how fortunate I felt to have a close association with the famous Provincetown Playhouse. The group started back in 1915 when an unusually talented group of artists and writers built a playhouse in an old shed at the end of a wharf and formed the Provincetown Players. The following summer, the young, unknown playwright came to Provincetown, and with the Players' production of his "Bound East for Cardiff," O'Neill's career began. Since that time The Playhouse has been associated with him.

Ours was the church of The Playhouse. One of its members had been married there; and I received as many tickets as I wanted for any performance. Tiny, aging Catharine Huntington had been both actress and producer since 1940. I wrote a thank you note at the end of the season, to which she replied, "Thank you so very much for what you say. It is one of the rewards we treasure—messages which give heart, for there are discouraging things so often! You have given us opportunities and real inspiration. Thank you for being with us, and please come back, or stay on and on for as many summers as we can look forward to."

During that first year, I had many notes and letters from friends. I kept a letter from the wife of a San Francisco psychologist who had led our seminar on marriage at Starr King. She said, "Last Friday, Saturday, and Sunday there was a symposium at the University of California on 'The Potential of Woman.' It was quite marvelous. Sheldon and I watched it practically the three full days, as it was televised on KQED. During the discussions, someone raised the question as to why women have been excluded from the clergy, whereupon Sheldon commented with great glee, 'Vi made it!'"

But letters weren't all sweetness and light, like this one from my hometown Missouri Synod Lutheran Sunday school teacher. "Your letter to your mother with accounts of your varied experiences and trips made interesting reading, but left me disappointed and a little sad. I cannot, like your many friends, congratulate you on your ordination as pastor of your first church because I believe the church you've chosen is a false one. I'm disappointed that you, who once possessed the 'pearl of great price' have discarded it for a religion that appeals to man's intellect, and pride in his own conceit.

"I say this because Unitarians by their own admission do not believe in the great doctrines of the Bible. They do not accept the Bible as the infallible Word of God. They do not believe in the Triune God. What then do they teach or preach? Mere morality? Pleasant man-pleasing phrases?"

She went on for a whole page on our lack of theology and closed, "Dear girl, you would have such a wonderful opportunity to bring Christ's saving Word to your people, but I fear you are going to rob yourself and them of the salvation that Christ paid such a great price to gain for us. May the Holy Spirit guide you into paths of truth, so you won't let Him down Who once died for you."

I had to answer, and did it with a long letter in which I said, "I left the Lutheran church a long, long time ago, because it did not seem very religious to me. When I questioned, I rebelled at Rev. Sauer, saying I must 'only believe.' If I'm going to believe something, I have to know why! But when

I tried to explain how I felt, I was told to keep quiet.

"Then I learned that Dad belonged to the Redmen's Lodge and so wasn't allowed to be a member or 'partake of Holy Communion,' which I was taught was necessary if one were to get to Heaven. Well, as a child, I hated a God that would do that to me, and I didn't want to go to Heaven if Dad couldn't be there.

"Lutheranism always seemed so negative to me. I was a 'poor sinful being, begging for forgiveness'; and I didn't like this at all. Jesus said, 'I come that ye may have life, and that ye may have it more abundantly.' His religion was more one of joy it seemed to me. So, as a result, I didn't belong to any church for many years, even though I still think I'm a more 'religious' person than most.

"I never could see how just 'believing' something (and I've wondered just what this 'believing' means to lots of people) could make you better than if you didn't believe and yet lived a life of love and truth and service."

I went on at length on the subject of love, thanking her for her concern and ending with "For love includes understanding (which I don't feel you've tried to give me) and forgiveness (which you have not afforded me either). And Jesus said too, 'Judge not, lest ye be judged.'"

I sometimes took issue in Provincetown on topics I felt important. I sent an open letter to Governor Peabody of Massachusetts in *The Cape Cod Standard Times*. "At the bottom of the many Proclamations you send out is the statement, 'God Save the Commonwealth of Massachusetts.' The invocation of divine intervention to do something which is our own responsibility seems to reflect an unwillingness to face the obligations of our own God-given freedom. Our ideals and goals may be divine, but the striving must be human. The Kingdom of God, if and when it comes, will be the work of human minds and hearts and hands.

"As a Universalist-Unitarian, I believe there is no rigid

separation between the religious and the secular—that the truly religious is a certain dimension with which we approach anything we do—a certain commitment to what is of highest worth in each part of our existence—a call for action in accepting the responsibility of freedom arising out of our integrity as a whole human being."

I closed in saying I was heartened with his enlightened stand on capital punishment and asked that he join the Massachusetts Council of Churches in their crusade against corruption in our Commonwealth. In response I got an article with a half-inch headline across a whole page in *The Cape Cod Standard Times*—"Woman Minister Lauds Peabody's Stand on Capital Punishment." In the Sunday edition of *The Times* my picture was on the front page with an article, "Minister Forecasts End to Death Penality."

In addition to our imaginative, paid weekly announcement of services, *The Cape Cod Standard Times* and *The New Beacon* (our local weekly) gave us regular coverage on our art gallery and any special programming, even now and then highlighting one of my sermon topics.

∾

We all looked forward to the September exit of tourists as families left to get their children ready for school. In the newsletter I commented on the summer at church when it seemed the line coming out of the service would never end! To our visitors I said, "The church will seem empty without you, just as the house does after guests leave." I was ready for the October vacation I felt I had truly earned; and I had begun to wonder about staying on in Provincetown another year.

At the close of that long summer, my wondering shifted into a real quandary, and on September 8, 1963, I wrote eight single-spaced pages for the record and marked it "confidential." I'm not sure why. It was just for myself. It seemed to help to put thoughts and feelings on paper, weighing the pros and cons of Provincetown and my ministry there. "When I came to Provincetown last November 1, I was told that one has to be here a year before he can understand the whole picture. How true! With a summer season just closing, I'm beginning to wonder, and have many ambivalent feelings about this beautiful place.

"Last night at seven, I performed a lovely wedding ceremony at the church for two summer residents—a young professional pianist and a beautiful, serious young girl. I hardly recognized their art-colony friends dressed for the wedding, because I'd met them at our winter foreign movie series in a drafty warehouse building where we huddled together on long planks. Sitting there among beards, sandals, bulky sweaters, and get-ups, I'd almost felt as though I were in a foreign country.

"At the wedding reception we got into a serious talk about Provincetown, and Eric said, 'When we came three years ago, we found people leaving, and asked them how they could leave this idyllic spot with all its beauty and atmosphere.' They said, 'Just wait a couple of years, and you'll have your answer!' When I mentioned that several of the young families I knew were leaving, he said, 'Well, we are too! I'm slightly psychotic myself [that's the word he used] but I can't take this!'

"I walked out of the reception into Saturday night in Ptown. My car was parked across from our church, where I could hear the live music from the show in the Hep Gazebo of the Crown and Anchor, one of our best nightclubs.

"The conversation I'd just had didn't seem real somehow. Yet, words coming from someone I respected (and one of the art crowd at that), pointed up what I've been thinking about for sometime, but especially during this past month of August. I do know one must discount things because of the 'summer something' here, with the thousands and thousands of visitors and summer residents. Everyone is under such tension just being a slave, often ruining health to make enough in eight weeks to exist on the rest of the year. Nevertheless, one comes to see that PROVINCETOWN IS A TOWN OF PARADOX.

"It has one of the loveliest settings, with a physically elemental, clean, clear natural vitality that can be one of the greatest, most inspiring, life-giving experiences. It does attract healthy, vital people, especially in the summer. But come September, when thousands become hundreds, the sorting out seems to leave too many whom I feel are running away from life. They come here—the farthest out place on the East coast—to escape, and some never get back. They come with the most complicated messed-up lives I've ever run into—hardly any whole families; and children who seem unwanted, without identity, and almost out of place.

"Life here can at times be exciting and fascinating. I have many fine people in our church. Yet, at public gatherings, I find myself looking hopefully for a few stable, my-kind-of people! Now and then I have a strong feeling I'd like to go to a church where even though there would be many of the same problems, there would at least be some normal families of mama and papa and children. I told Dotty Spoerl in Boston they'd have to rewrite the Beacon curriculum for places like this. We can't use the Martin and Judy series in our church school. Such a normal family would be too confusing for our children!

"On one end of the spectrum we have a great many old people—and they do grow old here! The Cape Codders who never left home are to me often sick in the sense that they live in a small, cramped existence behind their rigid exterior, which opens up only to another of their clan—those who have also lived here for generations back in a sort of inbred fashion.

"In between we have the Portuguese Catholics (whom I've heard make up from 75 to 90% of our people) who are kept under the thumb of Rome much like the Spanish around Santa Fe. It's like what one hears about in Mexico and other places where, because the Church can get away with it, they play on superstitions in a shocking fashion.

"The artists who discovered this place, and now bring the tourists, have never really been accepted by the native Cape Codders; yet they must be tolerated, for they help the economy. And since I'm told there actually was a Communist cell operating here sometime ago, this could explain the atmosphere where almost anything that's slightly liberal, old timers readily label 'pink' if not 'red.' It's a town afraid—afraid to take a firm stand, yet resenting much of what's happening. We came to this decision at one of our weekly discussion groups.

"All this doesn't give a true picture, but it gets a lot off my mind. In each of our groups there are truly significant people, even among the old Cape Codders I've been so hard on, but especially those who did get away and came back—and among the Portuguese, and also among the gays and the artists. Even so, younger persons who see the need for a more normal community situation for their kids are leaving one by one.

"Another paradox. Provincetown has been designated as one of the most severely depressed areas in the country, with the highest unemployment rate; yet one can't find anyone here who's willing to do any of the jobs that need doing. They'll work six months during the summer to qualify for unemployment and then use the money to exist on, or for fare to Florida, Acapulco, and such."

As I think of this now, many of these feelings, especially those relating to children and the breakdown of the family, seem to be forerunners to many of the familiar societal and family problems our society is facing thirty years later. I went on to say, "ALL THIS IS GENERAL. NOW FOR A RUN-DOWN ON THE CHURCH I TOOK OVER LAST NO-VEMBER."

I went on for pages with some of the problems, and then turned over the coin to think of the pluses, which had mostly to do with the summer programs where I felt I could truly be myself, but then went on, "After all the acclaim, many of my own group do not approve—and I feel a bit guilty—like a child who makes good but can't please his parents, whose approval is important. Still I've just gotten a glimpse of all that could be done during the summers here, if our Association wished to sponsor programming that made use of the fabulous talents that abound.

"I keep meeting so many unusual and colorful people I know any other place will be a big let-down. Truro, the next town down Cape, is packed with famous writers and artists, who have discovered that perfect hideaway. Selfishly, the ones I've met are the kind I'd like to see in our congregation, but who are not attracted to us in our present winter program. And though some of our good and warmly accepted members are part of the gay community, the atmosphere as a whole with the predominance of older members, is not too attractive to the busy younger members of the gay or art crowd.

"On the other hand, I came to serve the people who called me. I can look at our group and feel quite proud of them. They've gone along with many more changes than the average New England groups might listen to, largely, perhaps because it's easier that way. And, to be honest, how could one expect them to make big changes at their ages—and who's to say they should? It's their church and we can't take it from them. Even so, I do feel they'd be happier by far with an older person who came to preach a sermon on Sunday, perhaps get out a newsletter (for they do like the one we have) and be here to bury them when they die. At the age of many of them this won't be too far off.

"If they'd be willing to let our building be a community center for outreach programs (which I'd hoped for), we might have reason for existence beyond ourselves; but actually I feel they'd like to put up a sign, FOR MEMBERS ONLY! Seen from their point of view, outsiders (even our summer groups) seem to take their church away from them, and they no longer feel at home. This too I can understand, but I don't want to be part of a dying church, or a too exclusive one.

"I can see now that if I stay I'd just be either settling down into the kind of church these largely older members want and are comfortable with, or I'll be knocking myself out on a program for my own satisfaction and to the interest of those watching from the outside community. I've met several who are curious and interested in what I'm doing, but don't want to be a paying part of the show.

"Perhaps for the next decade or so, some retired minister who likes the Cape and wants nothing more than to preach on Sunday and be here to bury them when they die, supplementing his Social Security in a comfortable spot, would fit best here. And yet I say this, knowing there could one day be a renaissance."

After this long talk with myself, I put it in the files.

My vacation came in October. On September 18 I put several second sheets and carbon in the typewriter, and started out, TO POTENTIAL UNITARIAN UNIVERSALIST FRIENDS. I gave them my travel dates and itinerary, asking whether someone in their group would be interested in trading bed and breakfast for an evening of talking shop about Unitarian Universalism. I sent a copy to the groups I had found in the UUA Directory in towns I'd pass through on my way to Duluth around the north shore of Lake Superior.

It brought an exciting evening at an interracial summer camp at Trumbull Hill, a speaking engagement to the women at Montpelier in Vermont, and a long-distance call from Port Arthur, Ontario, asking whether I'd do a Sunday service. Each stop brought new Unitarian friends. I drove back from Minnesota through the States.

Returning from a rejuvenating vacation in November, I found a letter from Dr. Killam, chairman of the UU Ministerial Fellowship Committee, waiting for me in Provincetown. As a requirement for renewing my three-year Preliminary Fellowship, I was to write about my reactions to my first year in the ministry. I started my two-and-a-half page letter, "Dear Dr. Killam: I realize you would like a brief statement for the records; but when one could write a book about her first year in the ministry in Provincetown that few would believe, it is difficult to set down briefly how I feel about it. So, may I have a few minutes of your time to give you some background on the basis of which my conclusions may make some sense. I hope it's interesting enough to make up for the extra time it takes you to read it."

The second paragraph began, "Provincetown is a series of paradoxes." Then I pulled out all the stops about my ex-Methodist parishioners, my alcoholic-schizophrenic organist, my gay parishioners, the antique mimeograph, and the winter climate (not weatherwise but humanity wise). I did share much of what I liked, suggesting that if the church belonged to the Association and they wished to make of it a showplace in the summer, there was endless potential for working with the arts, music, drama, dance, etc., which we had barely tapped this past year.

"Now for the conclusions. I am thankful for the experience and believe that it has been a good one for me and for our group here. For me it has been a great unusual education. Any place else I go from here is bound to be dull in comparison.

"But I want to make religion more relevant for living today—to work with younger people—with whole families—with a liberally oriented group. I know I will have some of the same basic problems in any group I ever serve, but I can't keep up my enthusiasm (which I feel is an important part of the religious dimension) all by myself. A one-man show is not a church."

Sometime later George Spencer, director of the UUA Department of Ministry, said to me, "Vi, I wish you might have been at that Fellowship Committee meeting. Bob was so taken with your Provincetown report, he read your whole letter out loud. The committee joined him with laughter at points, one even pounding the table!" The official response from Boston said it was voted to renew my Preliminary Certificate of Fellowship for the second year. Dr. Bob Killam sent a personal letter from his First Unitarian Church of Cleveland in Shaker Heights: "Dear Violet: I have read and re-read with great interest your letter dated November 11th to me as chairman of the UUA Ministerial Fellowship Committee.

"It is in every way quite the most interesting letter I have received from candidates for fellowship renewal. I feel that I have a very clear picture of the Provincetown church, and I am most certain that I would not want to attempt to be its minister! You are to be congratulated on being able to provide so effective a ministry in such a difficult situation.

"I would like very much to have your newsletter. Would you please be kind enough to put my name on your mailing list? We shall send you *The Cleveland Unitarian* in exchange, and hope that it may be of interest to you. With kind personal regards and all good wishes."

I received a letter from a Starr King friend who was minister in Newburgh, New York. He had submitted his resignation and told their Search Committee they needed me! Again, this was bypassing the Boston office when Newburgh asked me to come by to talk with them.

Just before I was to leave, I had a phone call from Dr. Killam, who told me his assistant minister was leaving. He asked if I would meet him and his board chairman in Boston. Once again it was all so sudden. My response was a long silence as all sorts of thoughts went through my mind. I finally asked whether I could think it over and call him back.

I had heard that the Shaker Heights church had an 800-

child church school with three sessions on Sunday morning. I didn't like large churches—they were too impersonal. I surely didn't want to get pigeon-holed in religious education for children, which is where many saw women. So I called him back, "Dr. Killam, I've decided I don't like big cities, and I don't want to get slotted in religious education." He countered my negative feelings to the point where I agreed to meet him in Boston.

I liked the people on the committee at Newburg, and they said they'd get back to me after having interviewed other prospective candidates. Three days after returning from Newburgh, I drove into Boston to have dinner with Dr. Killam and his board chairman, Dr. Wilson. After dinner we went up to their hotel room.

Because I felt sure I wasn't greatly interested in their position, I was relaxed and quite outspoken. At one point Dr. Wilson said something that didn't quite fit in our conversation. I said, "Oh, I thought you were chairman of the board at Cleveland, sir." He smiled and said, "I'm sorry. I should have explained. I wear two hats. I'm also a psychologist on the Fellowship Committee." I caught my breath. That's why he was here; and he'd be one who would have to one day pass on my continuing fellowship!

Finally I said that I was quite sure I wouldn't want to be considered for their opening. At this, Dr. Wilson said, "Oh, please don't say 'no' Miss Kochendoerfer, until you come look us over." I thought of their big church where they had Robert Shaw as minister of music and Angus MacLean (one of our all-time greats) as minister of education, with whom I'd have loved to be associated, and replied, "Well, I've heard of your show church for years. I'd love to see it if you want to pay the expenses "

The date was set. I was to go for a whole week with two Sundays just as in a real candidating situation. I arranged for Van to substitute in Provincetown. Ken Warren, the Brewster minister, would be on call for emergencies. Of course I couldn't tell anyone, except our moderator, and I wondered whether I'd have the kind of clothes for a week in Shaker Heights. I decided they'd have to take me as I was!

Dr. Killam called one day to ask whether I wanted to stay in a hotel, motel, or with people. I didn't hesitate. "Oh, I enjoy people!" So when I arrived, I was given a packet with an itinerary. Each day I was to have dinner with one family and spend the night with another.

I had a lot of time with the assistant minister who was leaving. He told me that much of his time was spent in recruiting church school teachers and drawing traffic plans to get the cars in and out of the parking lot between the three sessions. He also told me about a recent conflict with the church board.

It seems the LRY (the high school Liberal Religious Youth) had hosted a conference at the church when an incident occurred that the board felt should not happen at First Church Cleveland, given their standing in the Shaker Heights community. The assistant minister said, "They didn't even give me or the kids a decent hearing when we might have explained some things."

In meeting with committees and groups and reading over records, I learned a great deal about their renowned top-flight music program. They had ordained Robert Shaw as minister of music. At his request they'd purchased a new baroque organ and imported union musicians from New York City. Nothing but the best!

Genial Angus Maclean and I hit it off beautifully. He was a beloved old man, considered an authority in religious education. His acclaim had been earned the best way—by being, rather than saying—being a warm, caring, kind old man children loved. We had warm conversations when I learned he regretted the fact he seldom had the privilege of speaking on Sundays. I realized this meant I could forget that part of my ministry, which I enjoyed, if I were to join them.

On Saturday noon there was a luncheon at a gourmet restaurant with the executive of the board and the planning committee. They wanted my impressions. Because I was sure I didn't want to be their new assistant minister, I was bluntly honest. "I was looking over some of your budgets and was amazed to see that you spend more money on your adult music program than you do on your 800-child church school." One of them admitted that they felt this was something they needed to look at. "And when I heard that the board had just wiped your LRY off the program, without giving their representatives a valid hearing, I'm not sure I'd feel comfortable working with such a board." At that point Dr. Killam rudely interrupted. He stood up abruptly with, "I'm sorry you feel that way, but if you knew what really happened, you wouldn't say that. I have an appointment at the church," and left.

I shared my thoughts with the rest. "I feel that what might have been a great learning experience for the young people, as well as for the board, in working this through together, you precluded from happening by your arbitrary decision." They agreed and liked some of my other recommendations.

That evening after dinner at the MacLeans, Angus's wife brought up the LRY situation again. I kept out of the discussion, but Dr. Killam brought it up again as he was taking me home, admitting I'd put my finger on his conscience. Before I left for home the next day, we had a meeting in his office. I told him. "I can see that what you really need and want is someone to take your impressive church school off your hands. This is a wonderful opportunity for someone, but it's not for me."

Shortly after returning to Provincetown, I sent a written critique of my week's visit to the Cleveland board. Dr. Killam liked the advice I had sent and said, "In keeping with it, the board decided at its meeting Monday night that we should engage a director of religious education. Your visit here helped us greatly in clarifying our problem, and we hope that you will feel the trip was worthwhile." Dr. Wilson also wrote, saying he felt I'd served as a good consultant and they felt they'd gotten more than their money's worth. All in all it was a great experience—unique in that it was a reverse candidating situation.

❧

On Saturday morning, November 23, 1963, a friend took a picture of me outside the church changing the announcement for Sunday's sermon. Late the preceding afternoon the phone had rung. It was Ernie. "Should we cancel the Inquirers meeting tonight?" When I wondered why, he almost yelled over the wires, "Turn on your radio, Kennedy's been shot!" After giving myself a few seconds to take in what I'd heard, I said, "No, Ernie, I feel it might be a good catharsis for us to be together in a group to talk about it." That next morning I changed the sermon topic from "Thanksgiving, An Examination of the Art of Receiving," to "Memorial for JFK" and went home to work on a special sermon.

In *The Weathervane* of December 1, a long article started, "DURING THESE UNFORGETTABLE PAST DAYS, did you wonder, as I did, how much can happen in one split second? As I stood in the church yard changing the sermon topic last Saturday, I thought of all the churches across the country who were doing the same. I thought of the whole world, stopped in its tracks—everyone from heads of state to school children—forgetting everyday schedules, turning steps in new directions, and minds and hearts to greater, higher, deeper thoughts of life and death. Did you ask too, as I did time after time, 'What is the meaning of it all?' I thought about it, and I said in part on Sunday,

Death is our common end. It comes to great and small. When man is called when he has lived out all his years,

it is beyond our comprehension.
But when a man is taken in his prime—a man who car-
    ried on his shoulders and within his mind and heart
Perhaps the greatest burdens and responsibilities one man
    has ever borne, and bore them gallantly—
When he is taken from our midst in but the twinkling
    of an eye
We must cry out—must ask the question—'Why? Why?
    Why?'

And at this time of year, when thanks and prayers are
    given,
What is there we can say we're thankful for?
Perhaps that in our time of sorrow, the greatness of one
    man, and what he meant to other men,
Could raise us in our grief and wonderment until we
    find no hatred or revenge within our hearts,
But only find the strong resolve that he who died shall
    not have died in vain . . .
That what he stands for in the hearts of men will be a
    beacon up ahead to light our way;
And from our common, world-wide sense of loss, will
    find one day within our midst,
That brotherhood that Jesus also willed we find."

The next week I suggested more self-examination in a service at Falmouth. In my sermon, "The Experience of Fact
and Feeling," I shared the thought that we may verbally express love and democracy and freedom and human dignity,
but until we're actually involved—emotionally involved—it
will have little meaning.

I said in part, "In our world today, where we have come
to adjust to our malnutritious diet of violence, revolution,
bloodshed, and even potential total destruction, until nothing any more seems really real—I can't help but feel that the

President's assassination has proved a shock treatment of the kind used with mental patients who have lost touch with reality. I understand that after such treatment, the patient is often confused, and not able to recall past experiences, before hopefully reorganizing the present into something more in touch with life as it really is.

"I think peoples around the world are confused and amazed at themselves. Pettiness and party politics are forgotten in such comments as, 'I did not vote for John F. Kennedy; but that murderer killed *my* president!' or 'I always used to think of President Kennedy as a Madison Avenue Charlatan and agreed with few of his ideas; but now I find myself asking, What can I do for my country?'

"Is it because the shock did reach beyond the realms of the rational and often stubborn minds to the depths of people's hearts? Is it because it reminded us of the unanswerable questions—the religious questions of life and death? How many times did we hear the expressions, 'unbelievable,' 'beyond belief,' 'it can't be true!' But the fact of the matter is that it was true, and we must look beyond the fact and ask, 'Why do we feel as we do? What is the truth behind what has happened to us?'

"None can deny that as the shadow of the news spread around the world, people of every nation—every race, every creed, every political party—the whole world—were caught up in a shared emotional climate, which, in itself has greater significance and power than we, in our analytic, scientific generation, are willing to admit."

Because of this service, and the Robert Frost one I'd done with them, the Falmouth fellowship felt they needed to examine their programming. The group included several from Woods Hole Marine Biological Institute, who, even though they were scientists, felt their field did involve dimensions beyond logic and reasoning. In discussions, the group came to realize that a depth of feeling in their services was missing and important. I was pleased to have brought them to this realization.

After the assassination and Thanksgiving, I got out my Christmas "card," to friends in England, Bavaria, Japan, Canada, and many states of the Union. I began by saying I'd met more famous, odd, and wonderful people and had more unreal and unbelievable experiences in one year than many pack into a whole lifetime. I went on, "And I must say, too, that in the ministry—with its disillusionments, its disappointments and heartaches, but also with its joys, its triumphs and glories—I have at last found myself. If I have had any success, I believe it is because I have tried to be honest, open, and real. This openness has been threatening to some clannish Cape Codders I realize; but most have grown in the process.

"I've tried to be courageous too, for I feel the church is on trial for its very life these days. With our older congregation here, which doesn't attract young people, I'm cheated, for I so desperately feel we're not speaking to the youth of our country—to those rebelling souls we hand the problems we can't solve. I can sense their disappointment at what is going on in the churches under the name of religion which hasn't offered them very much. I often mention this in sermons, and find validation in acclaim I've received from visitors in our large summer congregation. I think of a woman who firmly shook my hand and said, 'My dear, you have courage!'"

After the Christmas Eve service, I drove to Providence for my second Christmas with the Vanstroms. It was snowing and I loved it. We drove out to the farmhouse of Van's senior minister—way out in Cumberland Hills near Woonsocket. I returned to Provincetown the next day.

In January, our New England ministers had their Winter Institute at Rolling Ridge, a Methodist retreat center up in New Hampshire near North Andover, Massachusetts. I drove up with Carl, who I knew had brought his fifth along. The men were all billeted in a kind of dormitory arrangement. As the one woman, I drew the bishop's apartment with private bath! A lot of the fellows had brought bottles, one a whole gallon of his own homemade wine. Then we found a Methodist regulation that there was to be no liquor! So I told the men, "No one is going to invade my boudoir. Bring your bottles up." So my room was the drinking headquarters of the Institute.

In February I had another first! New England Unitarian Universalist ministers had a historic body called the Greenfield Group. To become a member your name had to be submitted and voted on. A friend of Greta Crosby's had submitted her name more than once, but the men decided they didn't want to break the masculine mold. Then, one by one they got to meet Greta and liked her. They were just about to vote her in when she left that part of the country, so I feel Greta ran the gauntlet for me. When Van submitted my name, they voted "yes!"

Meetings were at a lovely old lodge in Vermont. I was asked to do one of the worship services, and will not forget the evening meeting we were considering protest literature. Someone read from Ginsberg's *Howl,* which of course had a lot of four-letter words. When they finished, a professor from Harvard, and a gentleman of the old school, got up to question the propriety of reading something like that "in mixed company!" I smiled because I'd enjoyed supplying the "mix!"

❧

One of the highlights that winter occurred at one of the Inquirer meetings. A new couple joined. "Deneal" was black, about medium height with brown, short-cropped hair and a pointy little beard. His white wife, "Daleen," was about his height with naturally curly hair and big brown eyes. Their casual dress fit into the Provincetown scene.

I learned later that Deneal was a graduate of the University of California at Berkeley in economic marketing. He had been around colleges for eight years and in all that time had worked through many of life's problems, including that of race. He was not a shouting anarchist, but, as he put it, a kind of traveling pilgrim. The couple was experimenting with life and living, and at one time had lived off the land in the Sierras for several months just to see if they could do it.

They had come to New England via Canada because Deneal felt it would be easier to travel together there. This was long before intermarriage became more common. They both had jobs at Atlantic Coast Fisheries, Daleen as secretary and Deneal as statistical analyst. They weren't loaded down with possessions and could move on at any time—the most truly free couple I had ever met. In many ways we were opposites, but nevertheless there was an overwhelming feeling of kinship.

In The Inquirers we soon found Deneal had a reservoir of interest and background in Eastern religions. We asked him to lead us in discussing Zen and Hindu Vendantism, the *Bhagavad Gita*, and other texts. His explanations helped me see for the first time the wisdom we might find there. I had the feeling that if we could learn from peoples of the east, or just see things from their point of view, and they could accept some of our ideas, many world problems might more readily be solved. Deneal was a mystic, yet practical and vital in a way that provoked real thought. He and Daleen enriched The Inquirers and boosted my morale and confidence. They were life savers for me that winter.

I saw them quite regularly. They often came to my apartment, and we would sit around the kitchen table. I was so enamored with Deneal's mind that I'd often ask him leading questions. He'd listen, lean back, close his eyes, take a deep breath, and then the words would flood out in almost classical language. Often, after they had gone, I would put down on file cards the cogent things he had said that I wanted to remember, or things I liked because they backed up my own beliefs. I still have file cards entitled "DENEAL," with subtitles of "Liberals," "Good and Evil," "Reason," and so forth.

Deneal kept after me to learn to meditate, long before meditation came to be the thing to do to release the stress we accumulate from our complex way of living. I was also invited to their apartment. I wrote Millie and Van describing their austere but practical place—and mentioned a feeling of appropriateness I had felt as I looked up and recognized a portrait of Deneal in a far corner of the kitchen area. It showed a definite likeness to portraits of Jesus. My feelings were an appropriate prelude to the late arrival of a young Catholic priest that evening. My letter said, in part:

"Deneal is a fascinating enigma. He has built up my confidence no end, even though I told him I felt inferior to him and his reasoning/spiritual mind, if all that makes any sense.

"He said he often wishes he could get away from so much verbalization, and that reading thick tomes isn't the answer—that we have to say what's in us to say—not parrot other's ideas.

"He gave a preview of what he wants to talk about at the next group meeting—the strands of Negro protest. He felt Malcolm X's perhaps the most rational! He sees the liberal approach (also Baldwin's) of beautiful intellectual criticism of racial relations in novels, plays and poetry, as getting nowhere, because so few are willing to take a unilateral stand on what they believe, but must wait for the majority decision. That's why he feels democracy can be an illusion.

"The young priest finally arrived and stayed till after midnight. He's sharp too! After his first shyness, he warmed up and included me as 'one who had given our lives to God and so had an obligation to live a holy life!' I was surprised at what he was willing to say and things he's read. We have illusions of the Catholics too. It was a friendly, heart-warming event."

Because I felt comfortable with Deneal and Daleen, we

developed a true intimacy, where one shares ideas and deep feelings to the extent of being vulnerable, yet with the confidence in self to do just that. In another personal quandary in February of 1964, I wrote,

> To D & D
> You came to tell me who I know I am,
> But more important still, that it's all right to be that me
> By offering your you for me to see me in.
>
> I want to ask, "Where did you come from? Why? Just now?"
> And yet I know I need not, for you're here!
> And in your being here
> I have received so much, I have a need to give.
> And now I wonder—so many words to say what can't be said.
> If this is "all" I have to offer, do I need a pulpit?
> Do I have anything at all to say?

Later that month I went from poetry to prose and wrote three pages single spaced, in a kind of journal-writing style, but addressed to Deneal and Daleen. "I needed so much our talk last night. It's always great to talk about oneself—to have others caring and concerned enough to concentrate on one's deepest needs. I suppose this is why people go to psychiatrists and doctors. But when I do this, I've been told by others, 'Do you always have to be so serious?' Anyway, I've thought much about our discussions. Now let me tell you what I've been thinking when I'm by myself.

"I was glad you brought up my single status. This has often puzzled my rational self. I've asked, 'Why haven't I married? Why hasn't the right man come along? I've got what it takes—have I too much in some areas?' I've wondered sometimes whether it's because there was something else for me to do. Surely I wouldn't be in the ministry had I married back in high school days.

"I do have a sense of destiny which sometimes is very great and compelling, and at other times seems downright silly to even think about. But the whole process by which the ministry happened—the coincidences—the technical impediments which would have precluded its fulfillment in most cases and then resolved themselves in mine. I didn't rationally pick it. It just evolved and keeps evolving. So I say to myself, 'perhaps your destiny lies in using your femininity in other ways.'

"I may not know the ecstasies of perfect physical union, but I have had experiences of spiritual union—an intimacy in a kind of creative interchange of personalities along the way, which has not always been entirely divorced from sexual attraction, but sometimes was there because this was held in a kind of animated suspension.

"I've had more social interchange with men than most women who marry. Because of the pattern of positions to which I have been attracted and the freedom involved in my single state, there's often been a special feeling when a certain person entered the room or we talked—that I felt was reciprocated. And I have sometimes cherished (my rationalization or my necessity?) the feeling that I knew if I wanted to, I could promote a relationship into playing for keeps.

"I grew up with many sexual taboos. Now, even if belated, the accelerated liberal education in the three and a half years in Europe during World War II and since, with many lectures and a few lab courses, I somehow feel a pretty well-balanced woman. I sense this partially in a freedom to discuss it without threat. I still think somewhere along the path ahead I'll find the one for whom I'll be 'his woman.' But with the freedom and challenge of my present life, the field is ever narrowed to fewer who could offer more than I feel I have alone. Really, I think I'm being honest with myself when I say this is no problem now.

"But you've brought up the question, Should it be? I often think that even could I choose to live my life again, I wouldn't be willing to give up what I've had in freedom and growth that has come from knowing and experiencing so many and so much.

"And so, if it isn't this, what is it I really want? I've thought and thought, and it always comes back to the example set by my beloved mentor, Easton Rothwell—to be the kind of person that through others having known me it would have made a difference in their lives. This was my second choice way back in Santa Fe, where I'd still had marriage as No. 1. But now I thought perhaps it is my first choice in being minister to many; and if the older No. 1 should come along, I'll have to find the compromise somehow.

"There's a certain selfishness in this, I know, for it's where I gain my satisfactions—my union if you please. This kind of selfishness can be easily misunderstood, but it was a joy in Cleveland to have this feeling in each home I stayed—that in some small way, or large, I left some part of me. I do feel that we cannot have contact with another without each being changed in some way—for better or worse, or in between. Yet in this process I like to think that what I leave is something special!

"In this kind of giving, I seem to gain a deeper knowledge of myself, and of the influence one single person can have through her being just what she is—no more, no less. If we all have need to feel accepted, then my needs have been fulfilled so often that sometimes I wonder if I've not had too much, and all without necessity to pay the piper's price."

It was good to have friends help me explore this question I'd so often asked myself. Richard Kellaway, a compadre in the ministry, once told me that even in honest relationships, most couples at times hide behind all kinds of disguises. They do it to avoid the intimacy. He thought maybe real intimacy could happen only between those who felt strong enough and sure enough of themselves to be open—could expose themselves in a kind of vulnerability by sharing their innermost desires and needs, their deep fears and wild dreams, and not be afraid of losing control or being dominated in the sharing and the closeness. It had something to do with maturity that wasn't related to age. It was saying "yes" to life—"yes" to a kind of spiritual maturity that is more powerful than sex and more intentional than love.

I liked Richard's vision of a "spiritual maturity," and like to feel that that is what I have achieved. It seems tied with the "destiny" I had felt. However, since the sexual revolution, it's not the question it once was. Perhaps for the first time it is okay to live a single life, and many women are choosing just that.

I wondered if it was time to say goodbye to Provincetown. Sometimes with visitors, I felt again the satisfaction that last summer brought, when many people said things that made me feel all I'd said was not in vain. But I knew I couldn't spend another winter in Provincetown. I liked the winter peace, but was beginning to be overwhelmed by the ingrown qualities of old Cape Codders and the aimlessness of art colony residents. I have never been one to run away, although I have felt, too, that there's sometimes wisdom in retreat.

I found out on a trip to Boston that George Spencer had also been thinking of a move for me. He'd had a call from the district director of the West Coast who thought I would be a great minister for the Unitarian Fellowship at Eureka. George told me that he wanted to try to work something out for me where I would be happier than I had been in Provincetown. He said, "You surely have had your trial by fire there." As a result, the department paid my plane fare to go to General Assembly in San Francisco that May.

Once again I felt I was a pioneer as we, in our General Assembly, passed a resolution that henceforth the churches of the Unitarian Universalist Association would show no prejudice in choosing ministers because of age, sex, or race. One evening, after a wine-tasting party, a young woman read my delegate badge and saw that I was from Provincetown. She said in excitement, "Oh, that's where they have a woman minister! Do you know her? Have you heard her?" And then she noted "The Rev." before my name, and shouted, "Oh you're it!" We had a great conversation.

The Assembly meetings were exciting, especially hearing Linus Pauling, who gave the Waring Lecture. Pauling is a Unitarian who had received two Nobel prizes—one in physics—and had the distinct experience of picketing and having lunch at the White House on the same day.

The Eureka Search Committee wanted me to drive back with them to meet their people, though they weren't sure they had enough money to hire a full-time minister. I almost went, just to see that lovely part of California, but later accepted Calgary's invitation to change my return reservation to fly home via Calgary to check them out.

The Calgary search committee took me to dinner on the evening of my arrival. I learned that Calgary was then a city of 300,000. The Unitarian Universalists had started as a fellowship in 1956 and become a church in 1960. They had a membership of 215, with a church school of 225 children, in addition to active high school and college groups. My topic for the service on Sunday was "Freedom for What?" Lots of questions were asked during the coffee hour. Open House that evening featured an impressive display of goodies.

On Monday, I had lunch with Bob McInnes, chairman of their search committee. He told me they had eliminated one of their top three candidates after that minister did a service on his way to San Francisco. Another man in his fifties wasn't sure he wanted to drop his US Social Security and pay into Canadian funds. The third was a Starr King graduate who, of course, was not named, but who had said good things about me and hated to be in competition.

I received much good feedback from my Sunday sermon in which I suggested that in "coming out" from more traditional churches, we offer not just an absence of authority and restraint, but also a fellowship within which to share spiritual and intellectual enlightenment. I especially reminded the congregation that their own personal example served as a personal religious guidepost for their children. I left Calgary with a feeling that my future was taking shape in ways I had not expected.

In the accumulated mail awaiting me at Provincetown was a letter from the Eureka Search Committee, saying that they had voted unanimously to invite me to return at my convenience to talk over our mutual interests. I wrote them back, saying I wanted to wait to hear from another committee. While Millie and Van were up that Sunday, I had a call from Bob McInnes in Calgary that they wanted me to candidate in June. That meant I would spend a full week, including two Sundays, preaching and meeting with groups, after which the congregation would vote. I accepted.

In the reading material in their packet, there was a report of their congregational questionnaire. In the music section, one member said, "If you don't sing hymns, I'm going to go back to the United Church." But another wrote, "If you sing hymns I'll get up and walk out!" I smiled to myself and wondered, "How could any one person minister to this group?" I was to find out, and looked forward to my first real experience of candidating by the book.

The Weathervane of June 7, 1964, carried the announcement that I would be away for the next two Sundays, and Charles Harrel would speak. In the July 5 issue I said, "As noted last Sunday, I have been called as minister of the Unitarian Church of Calgary, Alberta, starting September 1." I added, "When the Calgary congregation said it was too bad I would not be able to be there for their famed Calgary Stampede that summer, I told them 'I'm going back to the Provincetown Stampede, which lasts for two whole months each summer!'"

I had a deep feeling that to the present Provincetown congregation, religion meant "going to church on Sunday." I suggested to the board that they ask Charles Harrell to be their Sunday minister until they could make firm arrangements for the future. Mr. Harrel was a forceful speaker the congregation had enjoyed when I'd been away before. He was not an ordained minister, but under congregational autonomy, the board could make this decision and agreed to do just that. In the same issue of *The Weathervane*, I expressed my thoughts on leaving.

From the Shore to the Mountains

I'm thankful to have started out my ministry in
    Provincetown.
How many times I've said, "I'd not have missed it for
    the world!"
For here you let me try my wings . . .
Here on the Cape, where our big country stretches
    farthest out, with bended arm defying the great open
    sea.
Here I have learned to know some of the salty flavor of
    the life that was and is Cape Cod . . .
The loveliness of spring, with rosefalls pouring over
    fences painted white along the narrow lanes . . .
Excitement of the fixing, painting, getting ready for the
    mobs of summer folk we labor to attract,
But soon resent their parking in our driveways, clog-
    ging up our streets.
They test our patience, even though we're somehow
    glad they're here.

And I have thought how many times I'll say, "And I lived
    just a stone's throw from the beach,

Where clams and scallops, even oysters, are just for
the taking."
But then, perhaps it is in retrospect that we best know
the riches that we had at hand and didn't take
advantage of.

And now I'll leave the shores to go two thousand miles
or more
To trade them for the majesty of mountains that so many
Easterners have never known.
There nature has expressed herself in different ways—
In folding and upheaving of our very earth to make great
sentinels defying man to pass.
These I shall love, just as I've loved the sea,
And I shall love the space that seems to beckon me with
arms that open wide and say,
"Here there is room to breathe and work and grow,
unhampered by tradition."

I'll miss my weekly writing you.
I'll miss our lovely church—a landmark loved by all who
live and come here.
I'll not forget the humbleness I felt each time I raised
my eyes up to the stately tower, before I turned the
key to enter in,
Which stands a monument to those who dreamed and
sacrificed and worked to put it there.
I'll miss my little home which sheltered me from sun
and storms.
But most of all I'll miss each one of you, for different
reasons,
And want you each to know I'm deeply grateful for the
part you played to make my stay the unforgettable
experience it has been!

One night, in the midst of all my packing, I took a break and thought once again about my charmed life: Provincetown was waiting for me even before I wanted to go to work. After turning down Cleveland, I had wondered whether I would have a rugged time finding another church. It seems I had come at just the psychological moment when the Unitarian Universalist Association was ready to promote me as a woman. I hadn't planned to go to San Francisco, but got there all expenses paid, and come home to find not one but two possibilities. And after having had the privilege of living with the splendors of the sea, and now being able to go to another spot where many others hope one day to go on a vacation—I was a pretty lucky woman.

I got out and reread a letter from one of my few younger Provincetown parishioners who had been a sounding board many times. "I have learned a lot from you—more than I can tell you. I have watched with marveling eyes your coping with things here—your steady development. Here you have—or so it seems to me—transcended the institutional limitations and become your own minister. I do not see this development in you as anything dramatic or new, but a continuation of a lifelong habit of opening yourself to influences and then returning to that self. Does this make any sense? As it may not, and I will only get tongue tied if I try to elucidate, I'll leave it at that."

I would keep the letter, for I felt it was thoughtful and insightful and because it came from one who, like me, was just waiting for certain things to happen so she could leave Provincetown. It seemed to validate my leaving and made me feel that with all its unusual challenges, I couldn't have had a more colorful, unforgettable spot for my initiation.

There were several farewell parties. The church gave me a large Dorothy Moffett watercolor of a scallop boat. I had so often mentioned how I loved watching the scallop boats come into the harbor with gulls following for the feast as the men flipped open the shells in an Oriental kind of rhythm. A Bostonian who had summered with us paid to have it framed and sent to Calgary.

The last evening was spent with the Vanderburgs. We did a good job on a fifth of Scotch until it was too late to go out to dinner. Jane said, "It's best this way. I should cook your last meal in Provincetown!"

Charles Harrell ministered to the group for some years. When he left, the church continued with a series of guest speakers and part-time ministers until 1985. Twenty years after I'd left, Provincetown scored another first! The following notice appeared in *The Advocate* on August 22, 1985: "The Reverend Kim K. Harvie, who became minister of the Provincetown Universalist Meeting House in July, describes herself as a 'regular person.' Unlike most lesbians and gay men, the Rev. Harvie never had to hide her homosexuality. 'I have never been closeted. My family was wonderful about it. They said my happiness was what is most important. My lesbianism is one of the most delightful things about me,' she said with a smile."

At twenty-seven, the Rev. Harvie was the first openly lesbian woman to become minister to a Unitarian Universalist church, remarkable even to us back then, and bordering on the miraculous in the atmosphere of the general religious world that was hostile not only to homosexuality but often also to feminism.

I mentioned that at the San Francisco General Assembly in 1964, a resolution was passed resolving that we recruit and call qualified candidates for our ministry regardless of sex, race, or age. Today, more than half the students in our seminaries are women, and we have passed another like resolution including "sexual preference." Our churches are in this new crusade now, with programming for "The Welcoming Congregation."

Although I'm proud of this, I can identify with persons who are uncomfortable with women and gays, especially older members who grew up with a "father image" and without the word "homosexuality" in their vocabulary. For this reason I feel we cannot force congregations to call a woman or someone who is gay. It is a matter of time until they can become comfortable with the idea by seeing it happen for others. I felt privileged to have pioneered as a woman in my first church with a built-in "welcoming congregation."

In Calgary, I was to work with 225 children from good, old-fashioned families, and lots of the young people I had missed in Provincetown. Little did I realize then that the disintegrating family image I had so decried there thirty years ago would spread in an epidemic across our country.

In the Shadow
of the Canadian Rockies

My Canadian ministry began in September 1964 on the way to Calgary from my home in Minnesota. I was to lead a workshop on Sunday morning programming at the annual conference of the Western Canada District of Unitarians at Fort Qu'Appelle in Saskatchewan.

I had been told that smaller fellowships in Canada were often overloaded with social action speeches on Sunday mornings. To prepare for my workshop, I had mimeographed a booklet with definitions and quotations on religion and worship, with the thought that in discussing and clarifying these areas it would help fellowship groups better balance their Sunday morning services.

The black theologian Howard Thurman was the theme speaker that opening morning. I was entranced! His hands were sheer poetry, and his presentation was the best example of what I wanted to emphasize in my workshop. But for those who love to question what speakers say, it was a frustrating experience. You couldn't pick Thurman's presentation apart—it had to be experienced. Our frustrated district treasurer came to me afterwards wondering, "What was that, Vi, a lot of gobbledegook?"

That afternoon our discussion groups met. I started with a written examination, passing out sheets that asked, What is the church? What is religion? What is worship? Is there any place for worship in a Unitarian group? Is "God" a particularly meaningful word for you? If so, why? If not, why not? How do you feel social concerns should fit into a group's programming? I allowed the group fifteen minutes to write the answers. I then collected the papers, redistributed them so no one would have his or her own, and asked several to read written definitions. It was exciting to hear the beautifully expressed answers: religion is a way of life, encompassing our values, philosophy, and approach to daily life; religion is relationship of man to the whole picture of life and his place in it; religion is a deep feeling of a reverence for life—a tolerance and understanding of life, an expressible feeling of belonging to the world we live in, past, present, and future; religion is a combination of values and commitments that make up our standards of behavior, involving every aspect of life.

Their definitions of worship were also provocative and opened a lot of discussion. One particularly intellectual man said, "I was brought up Catholic, and I must admit that every now and then I slip back into the Catholic church just for the ritual!" I couldn't believe my ears as the district treasurer who had described Howard Thurman's words as "a lot of gobbledegook," got up and said, "Now that we're talking about it, I think I had a religious experience this morning! Our president and Vi and I were down at the riverbank looking for dried weeds and things for a big bouquet. They were up a ways cutting cat tails. I stood there all alone looking up the river as a duck flew up from an island and just soared through the heavens. I must admit, I was soaring too!"

That made my day—that and the fact that my workshop on Sunday morning programming was the most talked about at the conference. And ever since, when I move to a new church, I do a Sunday service giving the written exam, collecting, switching them, and having definitions read aloud. This gives me a firm picture of where my congregation stands theologically. Then the next Sunday I use more of their definitions in antiphonal readings, and in my sermon tell the congregation where their new minister stands in each of these areas.

∾

In early November, I wrote family and friends, "My two-bedroom house is rather Cape Coddish in a way, with the VAK touches of Bavaria, Santa Fe, Cape Cod, and the Oriental bit from San Francisco. The mother/daughter who owned the house hope I'll buy it as they move to Vancouver.

"So many times I've asked myself how I could be so lucky as to be ministering to this group. I keep meeting more and more tremendous people—geologists by the dozen, engineers of all sorts, artists, musicians, painters, poets, metal sculptors, teachers, professors, doctors, dentists, architects, city planners, school superintendents, and hospital administrators. And my Provincetown prayers have been answered. Most members are young couples with children. Imagine over two hundred kids from normal families in our church school!

"And it seems I'm really growing on them. I've done two sermons on Thoreau—'Backward and Forward' and 'Spending Money,' and special ones to parents—'College Exit Examination,' and 'Parenthood Entrance Exam.' So many want copies of my sermons that we've started to mimeograph them and have them for sale. With the caliber of intellect here, it's so good to feel you have something to say they want to hear!

"I do three Sunday services a month. A program committee arranges the fourth, often with visiting speakers, when I get the time off to talk to all the kids in our great church school, have outside speaking engagements, or do what I want to. I'll go to Edmonton to do the service there this month, and Red Deer next. We recently sponsored a series of three professors on the 'Problems of Aging' and had a panel on 'The Masculine Mystique,' which was a scream.

"In other ways members seem to like what's happening to the group since I came. Cy Groves, a terrific man, said to me this morning, 'I can't believe it, Vi. You have the gentlest way of inserting the knife so that it goes to the quick, and yet isn't so painful as to create rebellion.' I understand this used to be a group who could take a speaker apart unmercifully, but they've been nothing but kind to me so far! They do insist on a discussion after the service. I've agreed when the subject matter lends itself, but insisted another lead it with me there to answer any questions they may have."

Calgary's comprehensive government worked well. I had a president, immediate past president, three vice presidents, a secretary, and a treasurer, who made up the executive staff that handled much of the church business. Then, under the vice president of administration were directors of property management, finance, and membership. Under the vice president for adult programs were directors of Sunday programs, fellowship and social programs, publicity and newsletter, denominational affairs, social action, and adult education. The vice president of church school had directors of preschool, intermediate and junior high, secretary, and treasurer. All of them made up the full board. In addition, we had a men's club, a women's alliance, a high school Liberal Religious Youth, and college-age Student Religious Liberals.

Not too long after arriving, I received a letter from the assistant to Dr. Dana McLean Greeley, first president of the new Unitarian Universalist Association in Boston. She said Dr. Greeley was to be in Seattle for a meeting and if I wished, he could come back through Calgary and do my Installation sermon. Not often does a minister have such a privilege! I sent an enthusiastic "Yes!" Ministers from Winnipeg and Edmonton gave Charges to the Minister and the Congregation, and the rabbi of Beth Israel Synagogue welcomed me to the community. A huge delegation was down from the Edmonton congregation, our nearest neighbor, over 200 miles to the north.

Dana was quite a contrast to the Calgarians, many of whom had never met a Boston Unitarian. This handsome, born-and-bred New Englander was an impressive speaker with a rather long, traditional kind of sermon. Afterwards, one of our officers, who stood a head shorter than Dana, shook his hand, looked up and said, "Haven't heard preaching like that in a long time, sir. Sure glad you're on our side!"

One of Dana's endearing qualities was his memory of people's names. He called from his hotel next morning to say his plane wasn't leaving until three o'clock and asked if I would have lunch with him. This fledgling minister felt quite a part of the whole show, as Dana said, "Now who would you like to know about? Perhaps I can bring you up to date." He later wrote a warm letter of appreciation and encouragement. The *Calgary Herald* welcomed me with a picture and background story as the only woman Unitarian minister in Canada.

The Unitarian Church of Calgary held its services in the auditorium at Mount Royal College. With our growing congregation, there was agreement that we should have our own building. Shortly after I came, we learned that the Pentacostal Tabernacle, just west of downtown Calgary, was for sale for $55,000. In our newsletter, *The Quest*, an unofficial note read, "Don't judge the building by its exterior appearance. You must see the interior to appreciate the possibilities it would have for the expansion of our program. An inscription across the front of the auditorium reads, Where there is no vision, the people perish!"

At a special meeting of nearly a hundred members, we

voted to buy the building. There were only four dissenting votes. Members were excited, ready to take down the big outdoor sign "Jesus Saves," and move in. But that was not to be. The Pentacostal group decided against us!

Later we found a small Lutheran church that a woman had renovated into a nursery school. Once again, we voted to buy it, ending up with a great celebration party that night—only to have the owner once again change her mind.

Some months later, the next building we considered left me with a vital lesson on handling congregational meetings. It was a large old Presbyterian church building that had great possibilities. We had open house, and the congregation was once more enthusiastic about the prospect of buying the building. At the congregational meeting, after many positive, excited speeches, our church school vice president was recognized. His wife "Jean" was chair of the impressive religious education program. "Paul" was a respected member and good speaker. He said, "Jean and I feel it's quite inappropriate for the church school." His words brought a chill to the whole atmosphere. The motion to buy failed.

I mentioned this when I was guest speaker at Edmonton. Their president (who had been a lawyer in South Africa) cautioned me that at a meeting like ours, we had to be prepared to answer any possible question that might arise—that an unanswered item could change the whole mood and direction. How right he was!

We talked more about congregational meetings, and I learned that if important issues are to come up at a meeting, one should have key people ready to make motions at strategic times, and the president should know his Roberts Rules of Order! That served me well because we had a member who knew the RR cover to cover and gloried in often calling us up short! The Edmontonian's parting words are something I've thought of many times. "Do you know, Vi, sometimes you have to be a benevolent leader and tell Unitarians!"

The 200 children in the well-organized church school was a wonderful antidote to the Provincetown experience. I was eager to talk with parents about their children. In a prophetic sermon entitled "Parenthood Entrance Examination," I quoted Harry Gideonse when he said, "Every generation of adults gets the type of youth it deserves," suggesting that his brilliant prophecy still speaks to us today. "No one can foresee the face of tomorrow, but it is easy to predict that an adult generation as unsure of its basic values as ours will not be able to pass on to its youth an ability to rearrange its conflicting priorities, unless we manage to clarify our own judgment on these matters.

"The most significant thing about a society is its ruling beliefs and values. The most confusing characteristic to youth of our contemporary world is the total chaos in the rank order of the priorities that prevail in our discussion, say, of education in all its ramifications, or taxation, or the conservation of natural resources—or the semantic confusion that characterizes contemporary discussion of the nature of a free society. These are major problems to youth; but they are adult responsibilities."

I followed this with, "We worry more about being able to give our children all the material advantages along the way than we do about preparing them for the years ahead, which are bound to present problems far more difficult and intricate than those for which we ourselves have no answers today. We seem destined to learn the hard way!"

In light of this, I began to think about adult education groups and I learned not to believe first impressions. We provided several sheets on which to sign up for various groups. In light of earlier comments about hymns, I couldn't believe my eyes when more signed for a singing group than anything else. At the very first meeting of the singers, someone suggested we should have a choir. One of our members volunteered to take on the job of director.

That first Christmas, with the choir a large part of the program, we swelled with family pride. The choir became one of the most social, and significant, adult groups. It has lasted over the decades and actually become quite professional, giving yearly, sometimes money-making concerts. In the early days, the social tone of the choir was helped along with a gallon of sherry. We had a special inexpensive but good brand, which we labelled "Unitarian." One seldom stopped at a home in our Unitarian family without sharing a glass of sherry.

We had an active, enthusiastic, high school Liberal Religious Youth group, that traveled hundreds of miles to Edmonton and Winnipeg for conferences. In 1965 we hosted our first crowded Christmas conference in the small home of the advisor. It was so successful, the district LRY voted two years later to return to Calgary. This time we rented the Boy Scout building.

As ministerial advisor to the Western Canada district, I opened the conference by mentioning how cold it had been two years ago when it had been twenty below, and went on, "Much has happened in those two years—in our world—in our Unitarian groups—in our personal lives. Things happen so fast these days. I've wondered whether you feel it more or less than we do as adults? For so many of us, things which for generations we felt we could count on, are all up for grabs and re-evaluation today. We're questioning everything. Whether this is good or bad is for each of us to decide. That's why I feel LRY, and conferences like this, can mean so much to each of us in finding others who have open minds with whom to share our thoughts and concerns, and, in the shelter of a peer group of high schoolers, sort out where we feel the real values lie.

"I'm glad you've chosen the theme 'love.' It's a great big topic, and yet so misunderstood that a Unitarian minister today thinks twice before using it. Partly it's because we have one four letter word to use for so many different kinds of feelings.

"As Erich Fromm said, 'Love is the answer to all the problems of our existence.' This sounds so simple and easy; and yet we all know it's the most difficult thing in the world. But when we take it as he defined it—as care, responsibility, respect, and knowledge of the other person—that's a big order. Harold Panabaker will help us explore this vast topic."

Harold—a much-loved, retired school principal who had a school named for him—was our president. Kids had come over 600 miles from Winnipeg, but we didn't have to worry. Even though we all bedded down in the same building, we had no problems. We could trust the kids, their peer group leaders, and their adult advisors. In looking back in light of today's youth, my pride in these responsible youngsters, with their healthy, fun programs, grows many-fold.

The college-age group of Student Religious Liberals (SRL) was another forte. Much credit went to Bob McCandless, a student at the University of Calgary. To begin with, he didn't get along too well with his folks, but had an apartment in the basement of their home. That's where the group began. By word of mouth, it grew and grew until Bob suggested they didn't need any more members. After joining the group for a memorable New Year's ski trip to Mt. Eisenhower, I received a note from him, "Whatever you may think, you are influencing my ideas a great deal. In reading Neale's *Summerhill* and our discussions with Viktor Frankl's *Search for Meaning*, the emotional and spiritual approach to religion are slowly sinking in. I'm getting my bearings in this crazy society. I doubt that I would have been able to without the inquiring and humanitarian influence of our Unitarian ideas and (especially) people."

Bob later followed many sixties youth in trying the drug trip, spent time in a kibbutz in Israel, found a guru—Kirpl Singh—in India, and joined a group under another guru in British Columbia. There they studied and learned by doing—cutting down trees, making lumber, and building buildings.

Bob has kept in touch over the years, later reporting that he and his folks came to enjoy significant relations.

With the youth groups and with friends, there were skiing trips to fabulous runs near Banff and Lake Louise. I was introduced to the wind chill factor, which is now a part of US weather reports, along with Alberta Clippers. We all had block heaters installed so we could "plug in" our cars to keep the oil liquid. There were times when we would turn down invitations if we couldn't be assured of a plug-in at someone's home.

Our youth and adult groups profited from another UUA fund available to help churches sponsor outstanding speakers as a community service. My high hope of getting my beloved author Loren Eiseley didn't work out, but our request was granted to bring G. Brock Chisholm to Calgary. Dr. Chisholm, a Canadian well-known for his outspoken convictions on major problems facing the world, was to speak on our population explosion and its consequences. He was honorary president of the World Federalists of Canada, a director of Canadian peace research, former director-general of the World Health Organization, and in 1952 won the American Unitarian Association annual award for distinguished service.

One of our members belonged to the plush Petroleum Club and arranged dinner there before the talk. Later, in the auditorium, I introduced the speaker, saying he was the one Canadian I had known of before coming to Calgary: "In this age of specialization it is refreshing to contemplate the man who can see beyond one small segment of humanity or society—look at a man in his world through the eyes of the doctor of medicine, of psychiatry, the military man, the humanist, the prophet."

Following Chisholm's speech, I closed with, "In the isolation of our beautiful setting here in the wide plains of Alberta, in the shadow of the majestic Rockies, we need now and then to be reminded of the world view—that we are not only Canadians, with the problems of our community and our province, but we are also citizens of the world. We thank you, Dr. Chisholm, for pushing out our horizons—beyond the plains and mountains—to become conscious of one of the great problems of mankind today, and also conscious of our responsibility in relation to it."

Just as our bringing Dr. Chisholm to Calgary had been appreciated by many outside our congregation, our church was well recognized among the clergy in Calgary. One of my members, Cob Johnstone, was administrator of the General Hospital, and I was on the Chaplaincy Advisory Committee there, with ministers of other denominations. We sponsored a ten-week clinical training session with lectures from doctors on different diseases, followed by rather intimate discussion in group sessions. At lunch afterwards, the climate was warm and informal. Several asked questions about the Unitarians. An Anglican minister poured out problems and later told me how much he envied my freedom. Johnstone had made the ministers a part of the "healing team" in his hospital, and they all loved him for it.

I also attended meetings of Calgary's Inter-Faith Community Action Committee. Two members (a Catholic priest and a rabbi) were known as "The Bobbsey Twins," because they were often off to legislatures in Edmonton or Ottawa to push some issue. In May the meeting was to be special. We were invited to Father O'Byrne's cottage, Casa Gondolfo, at Bragg Creek in the Rockies. As I was to learn, the Catholics always made provision for good physical, as well as spiritual, relaxation.

One didn't have to read only the religious page in *The Calgary Herald* to learn about my speaking engagements and sermon topics. My being the first woman minister in Canada in modern times brought special newspaper coverage: "Calgary Minister Speaks Out—Abortion Laws Condemned"; "Cleric Outlines Funeral Co-op"; Minister Says Funeral Plan Avoids Excesses." One article, "Minister Spoofs Prime Minister

Diefenbaker," began, "A city minister has taken a mild run at politics in general and the party leaders specifically," when I criticized the Prime Minister for being involved in a questionable association.

I was featured twice in the *Calgary Herald's* "World of Religion, Our Churches Speak." One topic was "Religion for Our Age," which set out my Unitarian beliefs, beginning with what today seems a prophetic pronouncement. "In a world sick with the paranoia of anti-Communism, the profit and progress psychoses, where the only answers seem to be "bigger and better" schools, hospitals, churches, wars, cars, planes, and rockets—where, at a peak economy, with more wealth of time, money, knowledge, know-how, we live with little real satisfaction or enthusiasm, and with more fears, anxieties, and less security—where human values are blurred, where we are rushing headlong on all fronts, but don't even dare ask where we are going—it must be said that if humanity is to survive, what the world desperately needs today is a religion for our age.

"A religion—offering not childish discipline of reward and punishment in an age when we need mature, adult, forward-looking decision—and not courting allegiance by offering to relieve man of his own responsibility for himself, his neighbor, his world.

"A religion—which welcomes the inquiring mind (be it theist, atheist, agnostic, humanist) and is not defined by belief or church attendance, but by the necessity for individual freedom of belief and responsibility for decision and action.

"A religion—which is a headlight out in front, lighting the way as it exposes rocks and pitfalls and even man-made barricades—instead of a taillight to the status quo, the present mixed-up world, trying to avoid disaster by signalling danger from behind.

"A religion—which offers supporting fellowship of other seekers after truth and meaning, wherein man may find a vertical dimension, to rise above this bulldozed, cluttered, horizontal age with a dimension of height in the wonders of nature and in the celebration of life—and a dimension of depth, of sensitive awareness and concern for human values, a dimension which measures thought and action in every field of endeavor, and within all fields of knowledge."

In the second "Our Churches Speak," my topic, "World Problems: A Church Responsibility," began, "Not Christianity, but the Christian church and its people, as guardians and champions of human values and human dignity, must accept responsibility for many of our world problems today." Other *Calgary Herald* articles included "Pastor Urges Abolition of Capital Punishment," and, as we were fighting about religion in the schools, "Broad Religious Teaching Urged": "Religious education in schools should not focus on sects or dogmas, but rather stress the broad concept of man's common experience, Unitarians were told Sunday at a service in Mount Royal College auditorium. Rev. Violet A. Kochendoerfer said the recurring controversy of religion in the schools 'is a perfect example of the inability of our generation to rise above the rigid indoctrination of our childhood. We fail to see what our children themselves comprehend—that one's religion arises out of one's individual experience and has nothing to do with words spoken to a captive audience. It is in this area we need most to break through rigid selfish beliefs, to stress not our differences, but how much we have in common.'"

The first time I was guest speaker in Edmonton, the newspaper article lead was "Female Minister to Speak in City." Sermon titles featured, "For Whom the Bell Tolls," "The Masculine Mystique," "The Church is Dead!," "Long Live the Church!," "The Ordeal of Change," "A Look at the Bible," "The Historian's Approach to the New Testament," "From Judaism to Christianity," "Unitarianism—the Now Religion," "The Battle of the Sexes," "Of Art and the Future," "It's All Right to Be You," "College Exit Examination," and "A Case for Trial Marriage."

I often think of that last title. It grew out of a discussion group at my home, mostly of young couples, but included Bob McCandless of the SRL. I often did sermons in series and had made "A Case for Marriage" and "A Case for Divorce." This was back in the days when parents' concerns centered mainly around pre-marital sex.

In our discussion, Bob mentioned that two couples he knew were living together but were not married. He thought that they both would eventually marry, and maybe would have a better chance for a good marriage. This gave me the idea of adding a third sermon to the series, which turned out to be "A Case for Trial Marriage." I had quite a list of pros and also a list of cons. Back then, unbelievably, it disturbed some of the Unitarians. How often I've thought about it, when not a decade later most couples I married would have been living together! And now, another decade later, we're just beginning to question aspects of our sexual revolution.

❧

Calgary was an education in many ways. One was through knowing members from the Dominion countries like England, Scotland, South Africa, and Australia. I loved the dialects, especially the "Scottish," and learned to say that instead of "Scotch." Calgary was the oil capital of Canada, and I had geologists and geophysicists by the dozen. Many of these were interested in a study group organized by a member who moved to Calgary from Toronto.

Jim Ramsey, sponsored by the Schalkenbach Foundation, led groups in Henry George Economics, one especially for Unitarians. George's basic concept of "Progress and Poverty," was eerily prophetic as it inquired into the cause of depressions and of the increase of want with the increase of wealth— so descriptive of the world we see on all sides today.

Henry George, known as the Single Taxer, felt we made a

mistake by emphasizing taxation of improvements on land, instead of taxing land itself, which produces all wealth—our natural resources—food, shelter, minerals, energy. Because land is limited, it becomes a matter of speculation and should be controlled by quality assessment and taxation. Today, we emphasize taxation on the improvements we make on the land—our homes and buildings. I felt his principles (shrugged off by many people as idealistic) could revolutionize our world's problems, and suggest why, with our great progress and wealth, we still have great poverty. With the economic crises around the world, one can but wonder!

"Jim," one of the congregation's vice presidents was a geologist with the Alberta government—a delightful, sharp chap. He fell into the category of those who seemed uncomfortable with what I liked to think of as the religious dimension of human values as well as feelings of heights and depths. We had had a rather violent discussion on just such points, and I had dropped a note to explain my feelings. On March 30, 1965, I received a letter from him.

The sermon he mentions in his letter was entitled "Rethinking Work and Leisure," from around the time "cybernetics" became a part of our vocabulary. I often think of this sermon today, for I'd said that with computers added to automation, the time would come when there would not be jobs for everyone as we thought of them then—that if, in our wisdom and wealthy economy we planned right, we might be able to divide things up so that each could have work, say, four days a week. However, I wasn't sure we were ready to cope with all that time off from work. I shared a deep-felt concept of seeing leisure, not as merely time off from work, but rather time in which we could do something we enjoyed doing. I encouraged the congregation to look for work they did enjoy, and quoted a fellow student at Starr King, who said, "If someone wants to pay me for what I enjoy doing, so be it!"

Jim wrote, "Just a note to repeat that I enjoyed your last Sunday's sermon immensely, and that in this, I had a lot of company. In the course of the meeting (and I am twitting you here) I had reason to reflect that two of my pet windmills, at which you used to tilt pretty regularly, are spared your attention lately, and seem likely to remain scatheless. May I name them?

"The 'mature liberal.' I think that you have discovered that (a) you, too, are an immature liberal, or (b) we've all been mature liberals all along. Have it either way, but I am glad to see that your response and mine to something manifestly wrong are just about the same, which did not seem likely back in Sept/Oct.

"The discussion period: I suspect that your fears of this bogeyman have subsided out of sight. At least, I think they should have, because all of the discussions I have attended this year have been most worthwhile, and no lapse of absolute good taste has occurred in my hearing. Mind you, the congregation has adjusted to a much better concept of the discussion period than formerly."

Jim hoped our current open-ended discussion would continue, for he felt we surely had a number of people who had ideas to add to sermons equal in point to what the minister said.

"Joe" was another geologist. He was adamant in his feeling that the minister should "never mention politics from the pulpit." As a congregation, we were accustomed to hearing his repeated complaint, would listen, but not pay too much attention. Then I wrote an open letter to President Johnson that was printed in *The Calgary Herald*. In speaking of the conflicting statements about our position in Vietnam, which was known as the "credibility gap," I mentioned that I was an American citizen living in Canada—that I wanted to be proud of my country, but questioned how this was possible when I couldn't believe the statements from the White House. This letter infuriated Joe.

Timed to coincide with a march on Washington, two bus loads of Unitarians from Edmonton were coming to Calgary to demonstrate on the Vietnam issue. Not knowing just when the buses would arrive, I said I'd meet them at the Consul General's office building. Large pictures appeared that evening in the *Herald* showing the delegation marching down the main street, the leaders carrying a sign, "Edmonton Committee to End the War in Vietnam." On the sidelines a small group were carrying a sign that said on one side, "Down With These Communists." On the reverse side appeared "Three Cheers for the USA!"

Because it was Saturday, the Consul General was not at his office, but the group made a cordon around the building. At four o'clock, leaders of the Edmonton group, a university professor and I, drove with police escort to the home of the Consul General to take our letters. We had coffee for the Edmontonians before they left for home, and, since I was to go to a dinner with them on the north side and lived in South Calgary, I was invited to the home of Phil Davidson, a member of my congregation, until it was time to leave for the dinner.

Just as we were leaving, the phone rang. Phil answered and said, "It's for you, Vi. Jim Butler calling." I smiled, thinking Phil was kidding. Jim Butler was the host of a television show on Saturday evenings after the late movie. I had been his guest on two occasions, and we had talked about memorial societies and religion in the schools. Photos of our delegation at the home of the Consul General had appeared on the evening television newscast, and by calling around, Jim had found me and wanted me to go on his program that night.

He was persuasive enough that I finally agreed and was told a cab would pick me up at midnight. I left the dinner party early to do some homework. Jim met me in the station lobby. Going upstairs to his office he said, "We were fortunate to get Alice Tyler to join you on the program. I hope you won't mind. She's waiting in my office."

Miss Tyler was a teacher who, with a group of her students, had displayed the anti-Communist sign. When Jim started fielding practice questions (as he usually did before broadcasts) I said to Miss Tyler, "Now when we get on the air, I'm going to ask you your definition of a Communist." Even with this advanced notice, she didn't answer my question—just wrung her hands, saying in a high-pitched voice, "Oh, everyone knows what a Communist is!"

It was four in the morning when I got home. I was awakened at eight by a phone call that the guest speaker scheduled for our eleven o'clock service would not be able to come. I had a program chairman who was in charge on the one Sunday a month I didn't speak, but I felt I couldn't make this her responsibility.

Then I remembered a tape I had. I had sent it to Phil Hewett, our minister in Vancouver, to get a recording of a speech my theology professor had given at a conference there. When the tape arrived, on the reverse side Phil had taped his sermon "A Conscience on Vietnam." It was a great sermon, which has been entered in our Congressional Record and in a like document in England. I felt good about my congregation hearing it, but it infuriated Joe as he also read in one *Herald* article, "A delegation of eight, including three Calgarians, then drove to the Prospect Avenue home of J. L. Hagan, US Consul General, to deliver three letters—two addressed to him and one [mine] to President Johnson. The press was barred from the presentation, but afterwards it was learned one letter came from the Edmonton committee, one from an assistant professor of sociology on the U of A campus, and one from the Rev. Violet A. Kochendoerfer, pastor of the Unitarian Church of Calgary."

In another article, it said, "Rev. Violet A. Kochendoerfer, Unitarian Church of Calgary pastor, is also presenting her letter to the Consul General as an individual and as a US citizen. Although she believes many Canadians support her views, she feels they are reluctant to criticize the policies of their neighbor, even though decisions in Washington do not affect them. 'Because these persons have no individual recourse to express their concern,' Miss Kochendoerfer says, 'I, an American citizen, would speak for the concerned group.'"

Joe and some fellow geologists went to the congregation's executive of the board, demanding that I be fired. When the executive refused, Joe's group wrote a letter to the full board. Though not all on the board agreed with me, they did agree that I had "freedom of the pulpit," and again refused Joe's request. But Joe and his group wouldn't give up. The next step was an open letter to the congregation, which finally resulted in a congregational meeting that brought out a record crowd.

A letter to Joe from Harold Panabaker said, "Every opportunity to discuss this issue will be given at the meeting. I would hope that the matter can be discussed without bitterness or malice and settled finally in a fashion that all will regard as conclusive.

"If I may venture a personal word, I suggest that you will be on stronger ground if you confine your remarks to a presentation of your own uneasiness at the contents of the minister's remarks and the nature of her actions. This uneasiness I can accept and respect, though I do not happen to share it. However, I feel that if you try to fault Miss Kochendoerfer on the ground that she has violated the constitution of the church, you will get nowhere. The fact remains, no matter how she was identified by others, that she did not at any time claim to be speaking or acting on behalf of the church. And this, in my view is the constitutional point at issue."

During part of the discussion at this congregational meeting, I said I would leave the auditorium. Sitting back in the faculty room with one of our officers, I smiled and said, "This is just like candidating all over again." The congregation expressed a vote of confidence, and I wrote Harold Panabaker, "How can I thank you! Your note of support and advice, given in your own inimitable way, is part of the reward of the ministry! This has been a crucial year; but I feel that largely through your mature leadership, we've met the enemy and they are ours. And if we can build a climate within which we no longer feel we must take sides, we can use our precious energy for a positive program for the group, instead of fighting among ourselves."

After a few weeks things seemed to settle down, though Joe was unhappy after the *Herald* chose to print excerpts from my sermon "The Courage to be Imperfect." I had mentioned the Premier of Canada and said in part, "Out of our Christian heritage in the west, we have built a perfectionist world of perfectionist people. Pharisees that we are, we can't be good all by ourselves. We must insist that everyone else be good too, and we self-righteously judge everyone who does not agree with us. For, being perfect allows no room for criticism, improvement, learning from others, or even trying to understand them. Being perfect, we must protect the status quo at all costs—by foul means as well as fair; and if anyone disagrees with us, we must make devils of them. Only then can we relax in our perfectionism.

"And built into this is the adult success image, which we insist our children fit into. It may take work and frustration to fit into a square pattern of success if one's a round, fat circle sort of person, but parents know best. They know from experience it will be worthwhile in the end. And, 'Thou shalt honor thy father and thy mother, that it may be well with thee.'

"But all is not well with our children; and I have a sneaking suspicion that even if children try to keep this commandment, it isn't very easy at times, because fathers and mothers and adults just aren't always honorable. Take right now, for instance. Without even asking what young people think, adults are taking them out of school and sending them half way around the world to get involved in killing people (which another Christian commandment tells them they're not supposed to do); but if you mention this before you get to be an adult, you're labelled a 'peacenik.'

"Others are stealing gold bricks from the government pouch. And even our very own government in its highest offices is all mixed up in a sex scandal of all things, and big grown-up men are calling each other names their folks didn't give them! Do we really want our youth to honor this?

"I was thinking how refreshing and lifegiving it would be if we could really see ourselves as we are, and laugh at ourselves for our shortcomings—find the courage to be imperfect. If Lester Pearson, our Premier, could pick up the phone one day and say, 'John, isn't this last go-round a bunch of silliness. Let's get together and look at ourselves and laugh at ourselves before we have the whole world laughing. They used to respect us, you know.'"

And speaking of children, the Alston family was a perennial source of pride at Christmas time. Each year, their family picture would appear in the *Calgary Herald* with their twelve children—two of their own and ten adopted, ranging from nine months to fourteen years in age. In order to adopt in Canada, couples had to be members of a church, and two couples joined simply for that reason.

The Alstons, however, were staunch members, and at the time they adopted their last child, I was invited to lunch. There were fourteen at the table, including Native Americans from two different tribes, a Japanese teenager who wasn't going to get dessert if he didn't eat his vegetables, and tiny black Amy in a high chair. Don said they'd have to stop adding to the family because there wasn't room at the table for more. After the meal the family was going to the Winter Sports Center, and the kids were on the floor seeing which skates would fit whom as they were passed down.

In another family with three sons, the mother was chosen as Mrs. Chatelaine of Canada, her portrait appearing on the cover of the national magazine. The joy of achievement and busy life was tempered by the husband's affliction with multiple sclerosis. In another family, the husband won a sabbatical on an arts award, while his wife took leads in theater groups. The Centennial Planetarium, of which the *Calgary Herald* said, "gem of a job," was designed by still another member; and our metal sculptor received a commission to do a large piece for the Expo in Montreal.

I could go down our membership list with great stories about countless other members. Many, who have remained friends over the years, helped make my Canadian years in Calgary the vital, special ones they were.

∾

My Canadian experiences stretched well beyond Calgary. I received a letter from a member of the Regina Fellowship, who hoped they could one day have a minister, asking me, "What does a Unitarian minister do?" In my answer I attempted to give them an idea of my usual activities.

"First of all, every spare moment I have, I read! I can't just be reading for the next Sunday's presentation—I must be reading ahead and around the edges, keeping my eyes open for possible sermon topics, readings, appropriate music, new ideas. And in putting a service together, I make endless phone calls about music to be taped, arrangements with the choir, getting script off to those who may help read, etc. Then Friday I begin putting the Order of Service on paper, type it, and cut the stencil. Once that's done I jump into the Ghia and run it over to the mimeographer.

"I have an average of two board or committee meetings each week, and a weekly evening discussion at my home, which requires preparation, hostessing, and cleaning up. I feel guilty taking an evening off, for there's always visiting to do. Unitarians are such busy people and I like to visit evenings when the whole family is home. I try regularly to visit our older members who don't get out.

"Some members come by for regular formal counseling. Much is done informally as they drop by, or over the phone. Ah yes, the phone! Some days you expect to get at a project and the whole day goes by and you wonder what you've done. About a third of the calls are from non-members, and many involve something to do.

"I spend too much time, it seems, reading mail, some of which has to be passed on to others; and at least a couple of mornings a week answering official correspondence. Like writing you now! Waiting to be answered is another request from your very own fellowship about what you should do if a member dies. There's another from one of three Unitarians in Pincher Creek wondering when I might visit them. An emergency request I have to do today came from your LRY advisors. As Western Canada LRY ministerial advisor, they wish me to write all LRY presidents, advisors, and ministers explaining the informal meeting planned for Fort Qu'Appelle over the long weekend—that there will be chaperones, etc. Another inquiry about memorial societies.

"I attend regular meetings of committees, organizations, ministers' and study groups in the community. I've had talks with several couples who want to get married. If there's a death, one drops everything.

"In between, one works on the presentation, getting something down to say on Sunday. Sometimes a topic just takes off; sometimes it doesn't come together, and one starts over. And believe it or not, it's more difficult to give a short sermon than a long one.

"Then there are the trips away, always pleasant, but they entail extra material to prepare, arrangements to make, and correspondence. I can't just say to a secretary, 'Please get me a plane reservation to Vancouver; and while I'm gone. . . .'

"Actually, ministers in small churches have a far heavier

load without secretaries, janitors, and assistants; and no matter how many hours one works, the job is never done. Instead of an eight to five job, mine runs usually from ten A.M. to two A.M., for I'm a night owl. I find I can get more done when I get home from a night meeting than I often can during the day. And most times it's been seven days a week. Does this give you some idea?"

In my letter to the Regina Fellowship, I mentioned a letter from Pincher Creek. It was from a family who had taken their children out of the United Church and belonged to the Church of the Larger Fellowship (CLF), which sends printed material to isolated Unitarian families. Joan Turcoat (Mrs. GA) talked about what they liked in CLF and asked, "We would very much like to have you come down to Pincher and show you some of the lovely country around here. I can't very well ask you to come and speak to the Pincher Creek congregation (membership three!) but we've never met a real live Unitarian minister and would enjoy getting to know you, and would like some of our friends to meet you as well. I do hope you consider this a sincere invitation and let us know when you are free to come."

I accepted the invitation and immediately fell in love with the foothill country just thirty miles north of Waterton National Park, which is the Canadian part of Glacier. This was the beginning of a wonderful friendship that has lasted over the years. "GA" was Garth Turcott, a lawyer and first National Democratic Party member to be elected to the Alberta legislature.

Going in another direction, I was on the Unitarian Western Canada Regional Board. Our meetings were often in Saskatoon, Saskatchewan, where I'd be a house guest of the Baileys. Alan Bailey was a professor of neurology at the university there, and Mary, his wife, was a psychiatrist.

One time Mary said, "I'd like to take you to lunch tomorrow, but I'm using LSD with a patient and have to be with him for an eight-hour stint." She felt she'd had some real breakthroughs using LSD with patients. Mary is a person to command one's respect; and on the basis of her observations, I mounted a crusade that brought me speaking engagements in Calgary. When I spoke to the Knights of the Round Table, the *Calgary Herald* lead read, "Fear 'Motivation' for LSD Control."

I asked Mary about this years later. She said, "I used it with over a hundred patients. It's a great accelerator in depth of involvement and therefore saves hours of psychotherapy. However, the cost is prohibitive in therapists' time, and, because of the later street abuse, its use was eclipsed." Experimentation in Canadian clinics had corroborated all this.

That spring, the Edmonton minister and I flew to Vancouver to join two other ministers at the Pacific Northwest Ministers' Institute. We were driving and then catching a ferry to Rosario Lodge on Orcas in the San Juan Islands of the Olympic Peninsula of northwest Washington—the resort we'd discovered on our Starr King spring trip.

It was 1965, a year in which we were to elect a new president of the UUA, and that evening we had discussions about whom we should back. With the help of libations, discussions got heated and scary. One minister swung his weight around—wouldn't listen to others, and often would interrupt as others spoke. I was furious with him, but afraid to get into the fray. This was during the days of encounter groups, when frontal attack was encouraged to provoke expression of personal feeling. I felt the process was often exploited by self-serving persons.

During free time next afternoon, we gathered in a cottage on the shore where this interrupting minister was host. We had drinks and got into hot discussions. At one point, one minister called a greatly overweight man by name and said, "I'm ashamed to have you as a colleague in the ministry." After a gasp of silence, the accused tried to defend himself, when the host rudely interrupted him. Without thinking, I burst out, "Will you shut up and let him talk!"

Then they turned on me, and I ended up in tears. The accuser and the host put their arms around me and said, "Vi, you know we could just ignore you. We wouldn't do that—you're one of us! And since you are, you'll learn to take it the way we do—sometimes the hard way." Their words helped me dry my tears. Later I was thankful for the whole experience—of being accepted in such a concerned, earthy, and equal way.

∾

After a month home in Minnesota, I returned to Calgary in time to drive to the Pacific Northwest Summer Conference at Seabeck on Puget Sound in Washington, where I was a discussion leader.

The theme was utopias, the idea of planned communities, which, for better or worse, has turned out to be prophetic in our controlled suburban pattern around large cities. Each of us were sent copies of Huxley's *Island* and Skinner's *Walden II* as bases for discussion.

The Wolfes were a resourceful couple from Argenta, British Columbia. They were members of an intentional community that reflected their concept of human values. It had been formed by families from Los Angeles who didn't want to bring up their kids in that rat race and had sent scouts to find a suitable location. They found it in the ghost mining town of Argenta on eighty-mile-long Kootenay Lake in the Selkirk Mountains.

The Wolfes were there to tell us about it. Argenta was only eighty miles out of the way on my way home, so they invited me to spend the weekend. I accepted, to see for myself the idyllic location they had described.

It was late afternoon as I rounded the north tip of the lake and started down the eastern side. About four miles down I read a scrawled sign on a big sheet of plywood nailed to a tree, THIS IS ARGENTA. ARE YOU LOST OR ARE YOU CRAZY? The road went down a steep slope to a log lodge on the shore. There I was given directions. "Continue on to a switchback, and in about half a mile or so you'll come to the Wolfe's."

I found a large, sprawling home-like building in a picturebook setting, designed by ex-architect Wolfe to also provide rooms for the community school. Like the Wolfes, the other Argenta citizens, many of whom were Friends, were fascinating. Each family took responsibility for providing a needed service or supply.

In addition to the families, I met a charming white-haired gentleman—father of the editor of *Macleans Magazine*. The Wolfes had been fascinated with my poem, "Credo in Driftwood," and asked me to read it to him. The long drive back to Calgary brought me home with all too little time to get things ready for the new church year.

The Canadians had their own national meetings. The theme of our 1965 Annual Canadian Unitarian Council meetings in London, Ontario, was ethics—in political life, in business, in personal life, and within the community. I was the speaker at the Sunday service on "The Human Side of Humanism." The Order of Service described my presentation as a creative service that combined elements of folk music, readings from e. e. cummings, and some challenges to the adult Unitarian movement recently voiced by the continental Liberal Religious Youth.

I opened my presentation with the following phrases from e. e. cummings's *Six Non-Lectures*: "a fanatical religion of irreligion, conceived by sterile intellect, and nurtured by omnipotent non-imagination . . . a spiritually impotent pseudocommunity enslaved by perpetual obscenities of mental concupiscence . . . a sol-disant free society, dedicated to immeasurable generosities of love; but dominated by a mere and colossal lust for knowing."

I pointed out that e. e. cummings might well have been writing about us, because he was a Unitarian. I went on to say that we have a tendency to say about any outspoken liberal, "He's a Unitarian without knowing it," as though we had some kind of monopoly on all free-thinking people.

Back home in Calgary, I joined the College Women's Club largely because they were studying the history of Canada that year. I was surprised to find how young Canada is as a country. The grandmothers of some women there were the pioneers! At another meeting we drove south to meet with the Lethbridge College Women's Club. Luncheon there was served by Japanese women who had elected to stay there after their Canadian internment during World War II. While there, we viewed the authentic Japanese garden that had been the Lethbridge Centennial project.

In attending meetings from Vancouver to Toronto and Montreal, the mileage went into the thousands. Many times it was necessary to fly, but I loved trips on the Canadian Pacific Railroad. Going east, it was possible to have two nights and two days of peace and reading time. I now prize a dictated letter confirming train and sleeping car reservations on a railroad no longer providing Canadian transcontinental travel.

That fall I received a letter from our beloved Laile Bartlett, wife of the president at Starr King, who was writing a book about Unitarian fellowships. She wanted to know what I thought about women in the ministry and about Canadians. On the woman question I said in part, "I entered the ministry as a woman, but expected to be accepted as a person. I do not feel I have to prove anything. I am not a feminist who feels the need to demonstrate. I look to the ministry as a mutual endeavor—that of fulfilling my own personal needs in a life of service to others, while at the same time hopefully helping others realize more of their human potential.

"If asked on a questionnaire, 'Do you want a woman minister?' I can readily understand those who would say, 'No.' But the real question, I think, is 'Do you want Vi Kochendoerfer as your minister?' In this context I feel those who do not want a woman minister might vote for me if they had an opportunity to meet and to know me as a person.

"On the other hand, I do not discount the feminine fortes. I feel we often have a special caring quality. I say this out of experience of many significant relationships with men and women in every possible kind of situation—from the experience of a heartwarming acceptance at Starr King by a male student body; the acceptance, support, and encouragement of persons in churches; and especially of many women excited to find me as a model.

"Any feeling by men against a woman minister is mitigated in our Unitarian congregations by the fact that the minister is not an authority figure, and I rather expect to find more difficulty with older women who may still have a father-image in the pulpit.

"Now about the Canadian Unitarians. First, for our own group. One big problem I sense is that they know little about Unitarianism in the larger picture. Most joined because of the freedom of thought idea, and know only what they have seen here. We're so isolated and far from other groups that it's difficult to look outward, so there's the tendency to look inward where problems can arise in a cramped perspective.

"In general, I can see a need for a real Canadian identity. They keep emphasizing their ethnic origins. In applying for a marriage license, they can't just say 'I'm a Canadian'—they must say, 'I'm a Scottish Canadian' or 'Ukranian Canadian.'

"I must admit, however, that Canadians know far more about us then we do about them. Newspapers and newscasts give excellent coverage because what happens in the States does affect Canadians. On the whole I feel they are constructively critical of the USA."

∿

I returned from the 1965 General Assembly in Boston and speaking engagements in Brewster out on Cape Cod to find a stack of mail. I was up for Final Fellowship and had to send a special delivery letter to the chairman of the Ministerial Fellowship Committee to report on what had happened in my third year.

"In every way, Calgary is the exact opposite of Provincetown. First of all, I'm working with people who are liberals because they chose to be and not older ex-Methodists looking for a new home. The predominance of our membership here are young people with families, which makes for a vital church school program of over 200 children! Members are eager and sharp, ready to take issue and express opinions on just about everything—better versed in US problems and politics than most Americans—a tremendously organized group that really works. A large percentage of the group is responsibly involved. Tremendously busy people give hours each week to their church assignments.

"As much as I wanted to shed tradition in Provincetown, I would like to add some here. I'd also like to add a dimension of depth to the 'intellectual stimulation' approach quite a number insist they want, for there are those less verbal who have missed a religious dimension here, and feel the need for an atmosphere of warmth and personal consideration.

"So, still no blocks for this woman in the ministry! If I can attribute it to any one thing, I feel it's my hopefully honest, forthright, warm approach. As several persons have said to me in this past year, 'If you can meet them in person, Vi, you're in!'

"Over all, I just don't know how I could be so lucky. The board here is a minister's dream! There's still the excitement of the fellowship spirit, but with many of the corners rubbed off. Calgary's a growing, live city, and I have a feeling our church will grow with it!"

Later, when the official letter came from the Fellowship Committee that my Final Fellowship had been voted on, the chairman added a penned PS, "Your example and devotion is an inspiration to all of us on the committee. We shall miss your letters. Congratulations!" I was pleased.

That same year I wrote a long letter to George Spencer, who was still director of the UUA Department of Ministry. I told him I had just read Lester Mondale's book, *Preachers in Purgatory*, with his idea that perhaps two-year stints in fellowship churches should be the rule, and since I felt we were a fellowship church, perhaps I shouldn't try to push it beyond three.

To be ready for a possible change, I decided to bring my papers in Calgary up to date. I then went on to describe the ups and downs of the past two years, where we had come to terms with pledging and faced buying a building. I explained our problems with Joe and his following who had forced the special congregational meeting, and closed with personal considerations, mentioning the isolation.

"It takes a train or plane to go most anywhere. This is part of the group's problem too. Most of them have never been inside another Unitarian church or met other Unitarians. Western Canada District hasn't helped a bit. Phil is a great old man and I love him, but he's done absolutely nothing to help. There's no one to talk with professionally outside of Bob in the Edmonton church, and the Pacific Northwest District Ministers Institute once a year in January. Financially, we Americans take a beating. Even though my salary is $7,500 (and the Canadian median $9,000), those dollars are worth only 92 cents US! In addition, I have to drop US

Social Security, but must pay into Canadian Old Age and Retirement Funds, which won't be of any benefit. And then there's customs and two tax returns."

I said I wanted to be on the list if exciting openings occurred and I'd prefer the Southwest, the Northwest, or West Coast—anywhere except the LA area. And with all their problems, I'd prefer a fellowship church, small enough so I could get to know everyone. With all their built-in problems, I liked their vitality and felt I understood their dynamics. "My greatest strength is on the one-to-one level, where I feel I can be most helpful."

I had an answer from George, "Thanks for your good letter. I'm beginning to believe in telepathy because during the past few weeks I've been thinking about you and wondering if you really desire to stay in Calgary much longer. Then comes your letter explaining your desire to move. I can understand your reasons for wanting to get out of there and every one of us feels you have done a grand job. Of course I shall be willing to assist you all that I can."

Each time I thought about a move, I had a sense of adventure, wondering just where I might end up and how. It was easy as a minister, and especially as a single person, to move to new parts of the country and have a ready-made family of friends.

I got a letter, this time from Jo Bartlett, asking for my reactions to my experience so far. He was working on his own book about Unitarian fellowships called *A Moment of Truth*. My answer had a judgmental tone, since my Calgary Joe and his small group of followers had not been able to accept the congregational vote of confidence and kept creating an unsettled climate, much like some of the hundred case histories in Mondale's *Preachers in Purgatory*.

I felt Joe's constant verbal critique was part of what I thought of as the Fellowship Syndrome. Unitarianism all too often encourages membership by merely "signing the book."

This offers freedom without requiring any individual or group responsibility and provides an easy, ready-made haven for unhappy people to spout off with us when they can't do it against their boss, their spouse, or someone else. I had checked this out with several of my clergy friends, who agreed.

I mentioned my early days in Calgary when "pledge" was a dirty word, and only one or two were allowed to know who pledged what. When the vice president of administration moved and another took over there, he said to me, "This was a real eye-opener. The ones who are on your back for one thing or another are exactly the ones who don't pledge, or pledge and don't pay." Perhaps it's a kind of guilt process. They pick and complain so they can say to themselves, "If only Vi did or didn't do this or that, perhaps I'd pledge."

I mentioned this in a letter to Jo Bartlett, "Most of the time I know darned well that this is where I belong, and that although Unitarian Universalists can be the most frustrating breed to work with, it's still a great privilege to minister unto them. Overall I've found the ministry a continuation of the great opportunity I felt in your letting me 'in' at Starr King— to grow myself, in helping others to realize more of their personal potential.

"In my ministries I try to challenge the falsity of the smug image I sense we all too often have of ourselves as we feel we're out on the cutting edge. We prize individual freedom for ourselves, but find it difficult to allow this to others, and dissipate much time and energy in discussion that could be put to good use in implementing as a group the great things we say we stand for. This is the kind of image I'd hoped to build here in the Bible Belt of Calgary, where I have found a couple of United Church ministers and an Anglican with whom I can speak almost as fellow Unitarians."

I thanked Jo again for what Starr King had provided in helping us understand our crazy, wonderful fellowship movement. He had made of us not scholars, but real people ready to serve. I said, "I know I have something to give, and all I can do is give as best I see it, and let the chips fall where they may."

∾

When I saw that Tallahassee, Florida, was on the vacant pulpit list in 1966, I told George I'd be interested, since the South was a place I'd never lived. George sent my papers. On November 8 the phone rang. As I picked it up, an unfamiliar masculine voice said, "Miss Kochendoerfer? Happy Birthday!" It was Homer Still, chairman of the search committee in Tallahassee. He said he'd called the day before, right on my birthday, but I wasn't home.

This said something to me about him and about Tallahassee, so I accepted the invitation to pre-candidate on November 25 in Atlanta. Because there weren't a lot of churches around Tallahassee, Atlanta was the best place for me to pre-candidate. I eagerly looked forward to getting the material that was on the way. In a letter, the district executive said, "Gene Pickett [the Atlanta minister] was nigh ecstatic when I told him the rare variety of Unitarian minister that would be filling his pulpit." I was excited to speak in the big new church in Atlanta.

When the material arrived, I avidly read the notes on the Unitarian Church of Tallahassee. "Location: Capital City of Florida. Population about 60,000. Primarily a governmental and institutional town. Little industry. Florida State University—13,000 students (to 25,000 by 1975). Florida A & M University—formerly all Negro, now integrated. 3,500 students (to 6,000 by 1975). Something of a cultural oasis in West Florida.

"History: Started as fellowship 1953. Built chapel 1958; burned mortgage 1962. Membership today 135.

"Organizations: Church school enrollment about 70, attendance about 50. Liberal Forum—college students—strong on social action and achievement from time to time. Has sponsored major lecture series on campus. Active LRY, high school students, adult discussion groups, Women's Alliance.

"Membership: Majority university connected with state employees, a few representing business. Racially integrated. Now about ten percent Negro. 135 total includes goodly number of graduate students and a few undergraduates, all highly educated and intellectually oriented. Sunday morning attendance averages 75 to 80. Theology, strongly humanist."

Florida State University was negotiating to purchase its chapel for $26,000, which was located on the edge of the FSU campus. Although the church owned a two-acre wooded suburban site with architectural plans for a future building, the congregation had unanimously ratified a board's vote to give priority to first obtaining a minister.

That was quite a picture. But again, it looked as though in Tallahassee I would not get away from an isolated location.

The district executive wrote that there were some questions about a woman, but I had expected that. Because Homer Still had said the congregation was strongly humanist, I started adapting the sermon I had used at the Canadian Unitarian Council.

The new Atlanta church was exciting. The sanctuary was like a small football stadium in the ground, with elevated seats making a bowl. The pulpit was a movable gate-enclosed box that stood in one of the entryways. Gene Picket (who was later to become president of the Unitarian Universalist Association) was gracious and helpful. When the pulpit rostrum seemed low for me, we found a huge old Bible to put under my manuscript. I said, "When I come in the gate, I can take off my shoes!"

Atlanta had double services, so I spoke twice. Special music for the first service was a harpist, who went on and on, to the point where Gene said to me between services, "I'm afraid you'll have to cut what you say, Vi. The harpist took too much time." Shades of Provincetown! Once again, I was reminded that musicians are pros too and often act the part in unhappy ways.

We left Atlanta right after lunch, because I was to return to Tallahassee with the search committee and it was a 260-mile trip. One car had gone ahead. I was to drive halfway in the other car with Homer Still and Arthur Kidd, another member of the committee, until we could meet and I'd switch cars so I could talk with all of them. "Marjorie," one driver, said that she would share the driving with a passenger, Ellis Rasmussen, so she could get some work done. She was to take over driving with me as a passenger on the second lap.

At one point along the way, Homer Still said, "I wish we had more time, Vi. I'd like to drive off the freeway so you could see Warm Springs. It's a lovely little town." Shortly beyond there, the road went downhill and we could see far ahead. There were lines and lines of cars along the road. We gathered there had been an accident and traffic was still moving slowly. I'll never forget Homer's voice as we passed the accident scene, "Those are our people!" He drove ahead until there was space to get off the highway. Homer and Arthur walked back. When Arthur returned, he said, "I think Ellis is dead."

Marjorie had said Ellis would drive the first lap, but for some reason she was driving. As a car ahead braked to make a turn, she had slammed on her faulty brakes, which swung the car to the left, right into the path of an oncoming car. Ellis, who was sitting in the passenger seat, was killed instantly and his body crushed. Marjorie's legs were mangled, and "Jane," another passenger who had been sitting in the back, also was injured.

We waited in the rain for ambulances. Hours later, we were all back in Warm Springs. When the hospital decided they couldn't handle the women, we followed another ambulance to Columbus, Georgia, where they were hospitalized. We finally arrived in Tallahassee at six in the morning. I stayed for Ellis's funeral on the following Tuesday. I've often thought of how I might have been the casualty had the plans put me in that car first.

Weeks went by and I hadn't heard from Tallahassee about the position. I had decided to write them just as I received a letter from the chairman of the search committee at Brewster on Cape Cod. He was most excited with the news that I might be available and spoke with others on the committee who knew me and who shared his enthusiasm. But before that could go very far, Homer Still's letter arrived.

"As chairman of the pulpit committee of the Unitarian Church of Tallahassee, it is my pleasure to invite you to candidate for the ministry of our church. My apologies to you for the delay in corresponding. Our committee took its action over two weeks ago, but I referred the question of whether or not there were objections to candidating a woman minister to the board of the church. The poll of those worthies was held up to await the return of some vacationers. We would be happy to set the dates as soon as your convenience would dictate—perhaps the first part of February?

"Both Marjorie and Jane are out of the hospital now and doing well. Marjorie must wear her cast for some months, of course. They both appreciated your notes. Sara Rasmussen [Ellis's wife] will prove to be a woman of strength and resource, I believe, in the really difficult life readjustment necessary for her. All of the committee send you their warmest regards. And Happy New Year!"

When I arrived that February afternoon, the scheduled program was a sightseeing trip to Alligator Point, which turned out to have an exciting "dirty" beach—one with shells and lots of fascinating beach combings. The maid at the hotel was amused when she found the bathroom floor covered with sea shells!

In my first candidating sermon I spoke of "A Unitarian Trinity," in which I said, "The trinity is one of which each of us is a part—the trinity of Congregation, Minister, and Church. Each has its own role, and yet they are all interdependent. As Jack Mendelsohn, minister at our Arlington Street Church in Boston, observed, 'The future of the liberal church is almost totally dependent upon two factors: great congregations (whether large or small) and skilled, effective, dedicated ministers.' Then he emphasized their interrelatedness, 'The strangest feature of their relationship is that they create one another' in becoming a church."

The service was followed by a week of meetings with committees, boards, neighborhood groups, luncheons, dinners, and open houses. On the second Sunday, my topic was "Unitarianism—the Now Religion," a religion I suggested "will speak to the 'now generation,' who before too many years will be replacing our generation in policy-making positions."

After a successful week of candidating, I was voted to be their first minister, starting in September of 1967.

Back in Calgary, I received flowers, cards, and letters from Tallahassee members. A letter from Dorothy Spoerl at Boston headquarters said, "I'm glad you decided to go to Tallahassee. It will be a lot harder work, but I also think it will be more stimulating, and you can do far more good there (both for the denomination and for the cause of women in the ministry) than you could at Brewster, though I can see how a return to Cape Cod would be enticing and it would be nice to have you in the neighborhood again."

Cliff Hoffman, the Florida district executive said, "You were elected because you were the best candidate available to them and they're fortunate to have you." He did mention two influential women who had had problems with the thought of a woman minister.

Having spent most of my first trip to Tallahassee with Armenta Still, Homer's wife—an outgoing Southern woman—I'd sensed a reserve when I went back to candidate. When I called her after the first service on Monday to get her husband's office number, she said, with seeming reluctance, "You pushed me way over yesterday!" That broke the ice, and we talked of her feelings about a woman minister.

Later, when I called her husband, he laughed and said, "It was really funny, Vi. When I announced to the board that we were asking you to candidate, I also had to announce the resignation of my wife as social chairman, because she said, 'If I'm going to vote against her I can't be arranging all the parties.'"

I realized that she had wanted to write me off as a woman, but liked me as a person, when she said, "I wish you weren't the kind of person you are." Another time, she said, "This will sound utterly inane and illogical, but one reason I feel as I do is that I can't stand the thought of a woman burying me if I die!" She'd told this to the district executive who had said, "Well, you can let Vi come, and, should something happen to you, I promise to do your service!" So, Armenta voted for me, though she did push for a written ballot, so shy persons could vote "No" if they wanted to! She also stayed on in charge of social occasions.

The other congregant who had reservations about a woman minister was an older woman everyone seemed to love. After my first service, she sent a bouquet of red roses to the hotel with a lovely note welcoming me to Tallahassee. I liked her when I met her. I didn't learn until after the vote that she, too, had said at one time, "I don't care if she's J. C. incarnate—I couldn't vote for a woman." But after that first Sunday, she said to Homer Still, "Well, now I can understand why you had to ask her here!" She sat next to him at the meeting, filled out her ballot by writing, "Yes, with great enthusiasm!" and showed it to him.

When I returned to Calgary, there was a letter waiting from Rabbi Stanley Garfein of Tallahassee. "My wife, Vivian, and

I were delighted to hear that you accepted the call of the Tallahassee Unitarian Church. We look forward to meeting you when you arrive in August. I'm sure you will find much to challenge you in this community. It is by no means a monolithic one, and the extremes are likely to pull you in two directions. The Ministerial Association manifests the varying ideologies, and the members of it look forward to your active participation in its deliberations. Until we have the opportunity to get to know you better, stay well and warm in your northerly climate, and prepare to live in a most beautiful natural setting."

With that warm invitation to my new home, I could settle down in Calgary to finish my ministry there. In the early March issue of *The Quest* it said, "Controversial moral issues will be the fare for April as Miss Kochendoerfer begins a four-part series: Suicide, 'To Be or Not to Be'; Euthanasia, 'The Right to Die'; Abortion, 'The Right to Preclude Life'; and Homosexuality, 'The Need to Condemn.'"

I did my usual series on Eastern religions (Hinduism this time) and a series on the Bible and Unitarianism. Some rather tongue-in-cheek titles included "The Gospel According to St. Marshall and St. Timothy" (McLuhan and Leary that is) and "A Battle of the Sexes" or "Total Extermination of the Male."

My sermon "Education for Leisure" was given at a time when we had too many students in Calgary and too few buildings. I told Paul Goodman's story of the second grader who reported to his daddy, "Today we learned how to plant seeds. We ran out of dirt, and the teacher chose me to go out to get some more. I was out there all alone, Dad. Do you know, I could have escaped!"

In my sermon I suggested that if kids felt school was a prison, and we didn't have enough buildings, why didn't we say, "Okay, kids, you can choose to go either morning or afternoon, when we'll concentrate on your learning how to read and write and do a bit of arithmetic. For the other half of

the day, there will be places with books and art stuff or musical instruments, or barns with old cars, and adults who love
to paint or make music or maybe just tinker with car engines.
You can choose whatever turns you on. If you'd rather do
nothing that half day, that's okay too. Many of us need to learn
how to loaf."

In the next issue of *The Quest*, I had a long article entitled,
"Too Far Out?" and said, "When I spoke on Education for
Leisure and suggested a hypothetical situation which eliminated grades and rigid requirements and schedules, some of
you felt it was pretty far out. May I quote from a recent article in *Time* magazine which started, 'All over the US, colleges and universities are scrutinizing the value of lock-step
requirements and, to a surprising degree, are dumping them
in favor of letting students form their own educational patterns.'" At the end I said, "You may say, 'This may be all right
at university level, but . . .' For those who would like to explore further this approach at lower levels, I'm starting a study
group at my home based on Neale's book *Summerhill*, which
tells of an exciting forty-year experiment in this field which
has worked."

One Sunday, after I'd spoken about the Hutterites (a com-
munal group that had a colony near Calgary), a whole cara-
van of members accepted an invitation to visit there. As we
arrived, the church president's wife said, "Did you read in the
paper about the plane with sky divers that crashed into the
mountain? We had the radio on coming out, and one of those
killed was Neil Brown."

Neil was not a member, but his wife Doreen was, and his
son regularly attended church school. I also knew that there
was an Anglican clergyman in Doreen's family. This occupied
my mind the whole afternoon as we were shown around the
colony with the little girls who looked like miniature adults,
dressed in long skirts and bonnets.

Before I could call Doreen, she called to ask me whether

I would do a brief service. "Even though he didn't come to church, Vi, I do feel Neil was a truly religious person." It was almost a joy to write with all the imagery of mountain climbing and sky diving. In the eulogy I said in part,

> He knew and gloried in the wonders of his world,
> As most of us can only wonder at the courage—spirit
> of adventure—in one who'd conquered mountains,
> and flew the currents of the air.
> His was the challenge of the soul—the inner need to
> rise as high as limbs and wings can fly
> To find a freedom from the smaller self that most of us
> can never know, but only guess.
> In this he leaves for us the heritage—the vision of the
> heights we can aspire to . . .
> If we but find the courage to reach out to all of life
> with fearlessness and adventure.

There were fifty at Neil's private church service. One wife of a sky diver, who was Catholic, said she had to have a copy of the service. Another Anglican woman talked about her mother's funeral. "She was a pillar of the church, but there was no eulogy. What was said could have referred to anyone walking down the street." Doreen later wrote a note, "I really can't express to you how very wonderful your service for Neil was for me. It gave me a great deal of strength and peace within myself. I truly felt Neil's presence so very strongly. It was as if we had been brought closer together instead of being separated. He would have approved."

In the March 1967 issue of *The Quest* (largely because Joe's group still couldn't accept the congregational vote of confidence on the Vietnam issue and kept stirring things up), I did a service on the constructive use of controversy. I received many notes and letters after it was then announced that I would be leaving. One spoke for several: "I want you to know how I feel about your leaving. I couldn't help but think yesterday during the service how I'm going to miss your sermons. I've also felt you'll go a long way in the ministry just being the way you are. Then of course I start getting mad at a few people who don't seem to appreciate the thought and effort you put into these sermons for us.

"I remember that confirmation meeting. There were so many who got up to speak on your behalf; but it seems that even though these troublemakers are such a tiny minority, they're the noisy ones. That's been our problem all along. I find myself not wanting to be a part of it all; yet why should I quit since I'm the one I feel is Unitarian.

"But I did want you to know how much it's meant to me and John, too, I know, to know you; and please don't go letting that group's escapades change you. I don't suppose you can keep in touch with everyone; but I'd like to if you feel you could. I feel I'm losing a real friend as well as a fine minister."

I felt again that negative part of what I see as the Fellowship Syndrome, in taking advantage of our touted individual freedoms. This constant confrontation often keeps significant people from joining us and may be a significant part of why we don't grow. This was expressed in another member's letter addressed to our president, with a copy to me.

"It's been something over a year since I joined the Unitarian Church of Calgary. Being one of those rare lifelong Unitarians, it was a logical affiliation for me. However, since that time, and even before, I have been concerned about the feuding factions and the struggle for power within the church. The situation seemed to stem from the fact that one faction had to have the last word. For that reason, I never made a pledge to the church—the first time I have ever failed to do so.

"In my opinion, this feud reached its culmination in the treatment of Miss Kochendoerfer. I don't think a church ever existed where the congregation was one hundred percent behind the minister. In the time I have known Miss Kochendoerfer, I have found her to be a hard worker, extremely loyal and interested in the success of the Calgary church. I am personally very much ashamed to see this devotion rewarded in this manner.

"I have always spoken proudly of being a Unitarian, because I felt that Unitarians put religion to work. I'm not so proud any more.

"[At the bottom of my copy he penned], I hope you'll remember, when you leave, that all but the few were very much for you."

In the June 24 issue of *The Quest*, I said in parting,

I'd like to leave some word of wisdom as I go back
    home,
But know that no mere words can say the way I feel—
    which is the most important after all.

I see our group here as a microcosm of the whole wide
    world,
Our high ideals and unaccomplished goals,
Our samenesses and differences, and what we do with
    them.
I feel so strongly this is where we must begin to solve
    our problems,

So thanks for letting me share you and Canada for a
    while,
Now I can see me and my own United States in larger
    view.
My fondest hope is that you'll learn from our mistakes,
To set example on your wide frontiers, in giving brave
    new leadership to all of humankind.

I've always felt that my three years as a landed-immigrant in Canada were a rare privilege. When my check from the Canada Pension Plan comes each month, I'm reminded of friends across Canada with a feeling of fondness, remembering it was my home for a while.

As I returned to the United States, I was once again fulfilling a dream of finding new experiences to expand my understanding of my country and my life. Born in the Midwest, I had lived twice on the West Coast, once in New England, and once in the Southwest. Now I was to add to my life experience by exploring the deep South. How fortunate I was to be doing it as a Unitarian minister with a ready-made family awaiting my coming!

My Years in the Deep South

Each move is an adventure, but this one was new and different. To this mid-Westerner who had lived in most every other part of the country, and even Canada, the thought of making a home in the deep South was both exciting and promising. I felt no fear or apprehension, remembering the ready-made family I'd already met, and the touted "Southern hospitality." During the long drive I thought of future sermon topics and remembered what one member had said in a note back in March, "Yesterday's service at the Unitarian Chapel was an interesting one, with Kazantzakis as the topic; but the Finners and I agreed that it needed you to give it the special quality of—perhaps it's dignity and rounded-out-ness that we crave. Anyway, you will be warmly welcome when you return to us in the fall."

This warm Southern feeling was reinforced as I drove into Tallahassee, past scores of homes, each in a spacious park-like setting. And further on, in less posh neighborhoods, smaller homes had individuality and privacy under huge live oaks whose spreading branches seemed to offer a graciousness that said, "Welcome! Please stay and we'll protect you!"

I was to report in to my church president, Herb Taylor, at his home on Hilltop Drive. I found it tucked away in a ravine, hidden from the city all around. His wife Shirley came to the door with apologies for Herb, who was off to Australia to chair a genetics symposium at Canberra. I learned later that Herb was one of the world leaders in molecular biophysics—devising a way to label and follow the behavior of individual chromosomes through several cell divisions. He obtained the first evidence that DNA in chromosomes is replicated by a template mechanism, which was the beginning of what is surely becoming a revolution in modern medicine. I later told him I'd questioned scientists playing around with genetics; but knowing that he was a vital part calmed my fears. I learned to love and respect the Taylors, working with Herb as president and Shirley, who was in charge of our church school.

Shirley accompanied me and a real estate agent in searching for a home. When rentals turned up nothing interesting, we started looking at houses for sale. We were just about to call it a day when the agent said, "There's one more on Monticello Drive. I have the key." We went in and on the mantle of a fireplace in the living room was a note, "To the family who decides to buy our home, we hope that you will enjoy living here as much as we have. Sincerely, the Holroys—Don, Dorothy, David."

I knew this was to be my new home! The lot was wide on Monticello and 250 feet deep with a special private back drive, which gave me my own park, complete with a small pond. It was an older house, which I'd always wanted, and had been there long enough to have not only large live oaks, but tall pines, Chinese elm, magnolia, holly, pecan, dogwood, and fruit trees, but several varieties of camellias and budding azalea bushes twice as tall as I was and a fire-red hurricane lily in bloom. Until furnishings arrived from Calgary, I lived in Eleanor Moore's lovely home until she returned in September. This gave me time to explore and spend time on the beaches at Alligator Point.

When I was settled in, I wrote a note of introduction to my new church family: "Your Minister's Idiosyncrasies: First off, please feel free to call me at any time on matters of importance; but I'm a late stayer-upper (usually 2 A.M.) and a slow starter in the morning. So 10 A.M. to midnight will be a safe range for an intelligent conversation. Since ministers do not work a forty-hour week, I prefer not to announce a special day off, but to take time for personal recreation as opportunities arise and schedules permit."

Armenta Still insisted on a formal reception to introduce me to the community. Invitations went out to more than 300 for the lovely occasion at the Still's home. Something like 150 came, including the president of Florida State University and his wife. It was a gala occasion. As a hostess, Armenta could be Southern formal, but combined it with a gift of informality that was genuine and "made" any occasion.

The Fellowship had been meeting in the small building at the edge of the Florida State campus. When the growing University felt they needed the ground and building, it was sold and the money used to purchase property in a lovely residential area of Tallahassee. We had permission from the University to keep meeting in the building, but it became inconvenient and we made arrangements to hold services at Temple Israel until our new building was ready.

I'd had a call from a newspaper photographer that he'd like to take my picture near the large sign on Meridian Road, which said, FUTURE HOME OF THE UNITARIAN CHURCH. The photographer had a telephoto lens and shot the picture with me in the middle of the road between passing cars. Then he said, "Let's take something more interesting." He had me drive the Ghia around in the sun and shot me getting out. And, of course, this is the one they used in the paper!

My opening sermon was based on Loren Eiseley's *The Immense Journey*. In "Words for Gathering" on the second Sunday, I said, "There is always a kind of magic about beginnings—like the beginning of a new year, where there is a sense of wiping the slate clean again, ready for new commitments and new proclamations. Last Sunday I spoke of our ancient beginnings as man, and the wonder of our immense journey to the twentieth century. This is the second Sunday of beginnings—the beginning of a new and closer relationship with our Jewish friends, who warmly would lend us their roof until we can be under a shelter of our own. So, let us rejoice in these beginnings—these new experiences—and find in them an inspiration to greatness."

The Tallahassee rabbi, Stanley Garfein and his wife Vivian (who had earlier that summer welcomed me to Tallahassee by letter) lived across from the Stills in Waverly Hills. Shortly after I arrived, they had a dinner party for me in their lovely home. With an evening of many stories and much good laughter, Stan and I agreed to exchange Thanksgiving Day services. He said, "I want my people to meet you, so you do it this first year at the Temple." We were featured in the Temple Israel newsletter when they announced my Installation, as well as the Thanksgiving service.

Rabbi Garfein had proudly presented me earlier at the Tallahassee Minister's Association monthly meeting. He seemed excited to have me as a liberal compadre among the more staid, conservative Southern denominations. I tasted this climate as I admired an impressive Bible collection at a Methodist church. In my conversation with the minister there, I mentioned a controversial article I had just read on the Dead Sea Scrolls. The minister cut off the conversation with "Oh, the author is an atheist!" That settled that! But I did make another good friend.

I was invited to dinner by a young Episcopalian minister and his family. We met when he invited me to a conference they sponsored at a gulf resort to consider social issues. We talked with several state officials to learn how the churches could help in the poverty issue. Closing the evening at the conference, following the prayer, Jim said, "And now the Camp Weed ritual includes going over the bridge." This meant driving about five miles to a coast nightclub for late evening imbibing. This is where I began a long friendship with Jim, who, like the Anglican minister in Calgary, admired my many freedoms.

My Installation as the first minister of The Unitarian Church of Tallahassee came shortly after Thanksgiving. It was my third, and the best! Armenta Still started it off with an Alaskan crab dinner for our board and out-of-town guests. At the Temple we robed for the procession, and came in with the congregation standing and singing the impressive processional hymn "Forward Through the Ages."

The rabbi gave the opening words and welcome with such warm eloquence in talking of me and "us," that none was left untouched, and many fought back happy tears. Eugene Pickett, minister of the Atlanta church, delivered the Charge to the Congregation. Cliff Hoffman, our Southeast district executive, gave the Charge to the Minister, saying he needn't charge me, but went on saying complimentary things and ending up by giving me a big hug.

Chaplain Wellborn (a Southern Baptist minister) caught the spirit and welcomed me from Florida State University, and Chaplain Hudson spoke for Florida A & M University. Herb Taylor, our president (who was again away at a Denver convention) had turned over the actual Installation privilege to Lew Allen, our finance chairman, whom we all loved. Toby Van Buren, a Starr King buddy I'd asked to do the installation sermon, did a great job; and since I had only to give the closing words, I could relax and fully enjoy the whole occasion.

It was one of those times when the affair really came off. Everyone (including guests from Jacksonville, Panama City, and

Marianna on the gulf coast and Valdosta and Atlanta from Georgia) seemed touched, happy, and proud to be a Unitarian. It was early in the morning when I returned from festivities at the Dorlags.

As I sat by myself thinking about it all, I had the feeling Eric Hoffer had expressed in his "Passionate State of Mind," "I got more than I deserved!" There had also been letters and wires and flowers. As one member wrote, "It would be difficult to tell you how thrilled we all felt at the Installation. Everything was perfect and we have a lasting memory. We love you!"

ॐ

Plans were completed by November of that first year for a new $80,000 building. Bids came in at $117,664, with plumbing and mechanical at $25,000 and glass at $10,000, so plans and specifications needed drastic revision.

We broke ground in February of 1968 with a congregational picnic. It was a nippy, sunny day and the kids had a ball playing Tarzan on all the sturdy vines that hung from high branches of the towering pines between the magnolias and dogwood of the three acres of heavily wooded land.

That spring and summer were involved in the building, which was reached by a lovely circular drive through tall trees from Meridian Road. I was excited, watching the evolution of our new home built on hexagonal modules with no right angles. Both sides of the sanctuary were window walls, and large windows in front made a lovely tree-lined picture to frame me as I spoke from the pulpit. Each room of the religious education section was a small, glass-walled hexagon attached to the next in a tail back into the woods.

Seating consisted of forest green stacking chairs that could be cleared easily to make a lovely room—great for our series of gourmet dinners which came to be much talked about. It was superb for concerts or even drama, with near-perfect acoustics. Lovely hanging chandeliers of cherrywood were delightful at night as the window walls reflected and rereflected them far into the woods on each side.

At the dedication service the beginning of my second year, Herb Taylor introduced the architect and turned over the keys to Dexter Easton, the new church president. I opened the service with these words, "I think I speak for each of us when I say I find a real delight in being here each time I come, which somehow says to me we planned and built it right! We built with wood and block and glass that spells out integrity and honesty and unity, yet with an openness of spirit which closes nothing out, but lets into our lives the beauty and the ever-changing outside world—with clean and simple lines—uncluttered walls—to help us shed unnecessary burdens from our weekly lives.

"Do you remember what we said a church is—just about a year ago—when each of us defined that word? These are just a few of the things you said: 'A church is a group of people organized for the purpose of searching for truth, and aiding the development of the whole man toward the fullest life possible.' 'A church is a group of people in search of better understanding of themselves and their relations with each other.' 'A church is a group of persons holding certain common goals, who gather to get strength from one another.'

"So, a church is people—you and me in fellowship with one another—who add the warmth and color, life, and growth, without which these four walls would have no meaning."

Herb Taylor led us in the formal dedication:

At the place we meet for worship in our common quest for what is great and beautiful and true . . . to look at life in large perspective, and find commitment to the high adventure of a liberal faith,
We Dedicate this Church!
As our home away from home, wherein we find com-

munity of fellowship, and in this larger family share together the deepest celebrations of our lives,
        We Dedicate this Church!
As a structure with sheltering roof, protecting walls, and
space where we may grow in spirit with each other, and
host newcomers in honest fellowship of understanding
and concern,
        We Dedicate this Church!
As a place from which we may go out to our community with better understanding of ourselves, our families and our fellowmen,
        We Dedicate this Church!

At the beginning of that second year, I started a tradition
of thanks to Herb Taylor for his major part in building our
new home on Meridian Road. I presented him with a flam-
ing chalice to pass on to Dexter Easton as the new Keeper of
the Flame for the next two years. I also suggested at that meeting that we call our newsletter *The Meridian*, which it still is
more than a quarter century later.

Ꮼ

Each month I drove 500 miles round-trip to be with eight of
my colleagues in Orlando—a central point for the big state.
I'd drive down on Thursday, we'd meet Friday, and I'd come home
on Saturday. This gave us two overnights and much time to
be together. Once again, given my isolation, I looked forward
to these meetings, where I was warmly accepted.

That first year I often heard my colleagues mention
"Mentone," and it seemed that interesting things happened
there. It turned out that the Jacksonville minister had a cottage in the mountains of northeast Alabama to which he invited all the men for an unofficial informal retreat a few days
each year.

They had known I was coming to Florida that first year, but since it was a one-bedroom cottage and they slept in their sleeping bags on the living room floor, they'd felt they couldn't have a woman there. After they got to know me, they said, "You've got to come to Mentone next year, Vi."

I wrote the host and said, "Surely you have a kitchen area where I could put my sleeping bag, or perhaps someone will drive a station wagon and I can use that as my boudoir." He replied, "Oh, we'll settle that when we get there." He was right: his cottage was on the side of a steep hill with a large living room and sliding glass doors leading to a huge deck. I picked the deck for my bedroom and came in each morning to line up to use the one bathroom.

This was the time of the first encounter groups. The Jacksonville church had a taped ten-part series, which we ministers condensed into three days to make for an unforgettable encounter experience. I was pleased when one mentioned later that having a woman there made the whole thing more balanced and normal somehow, and far more significant for him.

That spring we Florida ministers joined the ministers from the district north of us for an official retreat on Jekyll Island off the south coast of Georgia. Because it was off-season with few tourists, we had a whole motel to ourselves right on the beach. I shared part of this meeting with the congregation in *The Meridian*: "I wish some of you might have been at Jekyll Island the afternoon and evening some twenty high school LRYrs from the nearest Unitarian church joined us to share in an experiment of communication between teenagers and ministers.

"In giving us their backgrounds, there was only one brother and sister who were from a home where they seemed happy. Their parents were foreign-born. Far too many were from broken homes. There was one boy who had two fathers and two mothers and whenever he talked about them he had difficulty trying to explain to us which father or mother he was talking about. One bright girl's recently divorced mother was marrying the divorced father of the boy sitting next to her. She said, 'I do so hope that this will make him happy.' The boy had his doubts.

"When asked what they most wished for their parents, what came through most often was, 'I wish they wouldn't work so hard and have time for other things and for us.' Realizing that much of this incessant work was to provide themselves with their education and personal demands, one of two sisters whose parents were divorced, said, 'I wish my dad would either make a million dollars, or forget it and cut us off so we could go it alone somehow.' All this recalled a prayer I'd read in the newsletter of the Community Church of New York City, which said 'We are thinking of our young people this morning. We are struggling to understand them. They want so desperately to tell us something—something important about themselves and their hopes and dreams—something about a confusion that overwhelms them—that has to do with us—something about our blindness and why they don't like this world we have put together for them at so much trouble and work and battle.'"

The next January, our Institute was in the other direction— in New Orleans at the Bourbon Orleans, one of the oldest hotels in the French Quarter, parts of it dating back to 1813. We discussed abortion, sabbaticals, summer programs, pulpit exchanges, and LRY. On the way to New Orleans, I did a service in Mobile about redefining religion: "Religion is a way of looking at birth, life, and death, and is involved in the human effort to search for the meaning of existence. Worship (the Old English 'Worthship') is the celebration of those things we feel of highest worth—the sharing of sorrows and joys and aspirations. Liberalism is not an antonym for conservatism and shouldn't be confused with political or religious views. It has to do with our relationship with others—a willingness to have our own beliefs, and to allow others their freedom of thought and affirmation." I concluded with these thoughts: "Yesterday does not belong to us, nor does tomorrow. The only time we have is now. Let us use now to learn to love and work for brotherhood."

One has no way of knowing the influence of one's words or actions—for good, or sometimes not—until one read about it or one was told. I thought about this as I received a letter from a girl in Afghanistan. She'd become acquainted with one of our former students in Tallahassee, who had given her a copy of one of my sermons about Asia, "The Blessings of Backwardness." She said, "It meant so much to me; but, alas, I lost it. Could you please send us two more copies? We're over here with the Peace Corps."

I had another request by mail for a copy of "When a Man's a Man," after I'd done a service in Augusta, Georgia. Both local papers had lead articles and one said, "Her sermon, entitled 'When a Man's a Man,' will concern the changing roles of men and women in today's world. She feels that her subject is one of the basic problems in contemporary society." I'd written the Augusta church's program committee, and they quoted me verbatim in their newsletter, "I've chosen this topic because I feel that the changing roles of men and women are one of the basic problems in our confused world today. It's not to make a case for 'women in the ministry.' I may not even mention that in so many words. But the fact that I am saying it should give it some significance. I intend to be a bit rough on the men; so, if you want to tell them that, they just might come prepared!"

I began the sermon, "In a way I wish I had titled this morning's presentation, 'A Delicate Balance,' suggesting that 'A Man's a Man' when he can live both sides of himself simultaneously and in balance—his masculine and feminine, his child and adult, his rational and irrational." On the back of the Order of Service, I had them print, "A Take-Home Examination for Husbands," with questions about how they saw themselves in relation to wife, children, job, etc.

Receiving requests for copies of sermons began our publication practice, made easy by the fact that I used a manuscript in my presentations. The rabbi gave us an old IBM electric typewriter and we found a volunteer typist to duplicate my sermons and have them available.

Because I was the only Unitarian Universalist minister in the Florida panhandle, I also ministered to several fellowship groups. The fellowship at Eglin Air Force Base at Fort Walton Beach was 150 miles away on the Gulf. In between were Panama City and Marianna. I spoke regularly at Marianna the first Wednesday evening each month, spending overnights with one of the families.

The Schultzes, with whom I frequently stayed, were an unforgettable couple—both pediatricians with their own children's hospital, which they closed for a time while I was in Florida so that they both could fly to help the starving children in Biafra. They were the parents of eight children, the owners of a private menagerie in a large pasture, home not only to goats and sheep, but also to ostriches, a lion, a giraffe, several llamas, plus pelicans, in addition to Dick's collection of Rolls Royces, one of which was the hearse that took Queen Mary to her final resting place! I looked forward to those monthly meetings with the Schultz family and other interesting Marianna members.

∾

The summer conference for all of us that first year was at Brevard, North Carolina. Bill Kunstler, the well-known liberal attorney, was theme speaker. Whenever there was an unpopular cause that most lawyers wouldn't touch, Bill Kunstler seemed to show up as defense counsel, so it was great to get to know him personally. This we did as he was billeted in our cottage, and we shared hours of libations and great conversation in the late afternoons. Kunstler was an easy person to be with; it was possible to admire his audacious courage as well as realize that this was exactly what brought him publicity—both adulation and discredit.

I had no way of knowing what a memorable summer it was to be. I left North Carolina in early June to drive to Minnesota where my mother had just recuperated from surgery. We had a great week in Winona, seeing relatives and friends in the area before taking off for Duluth. We spent a super week there with all the grandchildren and great grandchildren before Mom died of a heart attack.

It was terribly sudden; but in another sense it was so right. I'm sure if Mom could have spoken to us from her little pink cloud, she'd have said what she always did, "Everything happens for the best."

I shared memories of my mother with the Tallahassee congregation in *The Meridian*, "I wish each of you might have known my mother. She was a simple soul who impressed unforgettably all who knew her with her joy and love of life and of people. Her enthusiasm was contagious. Even the physician who knew her for one short final day was deeply impressed with her insight and courage. Her intuitive knowing and sensing of others' feelings, her awareness and concern for them, are the stuff that healthy living is made of. Even though she lived her whole life in the home in which she was born, her life and example have touched the lives of many across the continent. I shall leave our homestead in Winona this summer with that 'lost' feeling of no longer being able to say, 'I'm going home!'"

I've often said that I have known scores of PhDs—even psychiatrists—but that I would willingly set Mom up aside any of them. Though she had not gone beyond the eighth grade in school, in her simple, intuitive caring for people, she surmounted all the intellectual jargon and professionally described maladies suffered by so many.

～

On April 15, 1968, for the second time in my short ministry I had to scrap an announced sermon topic to write another memorial service. In Provincetown it had been the sudden news of Kennedy's assassination. Now it was Martin Luther King, Nobel Peace Prize winner in 1964, who had given the Ware Lecture at our General Assembly in 1966.

A general sense of chaos followed his assasination. Florida A & M (a black college) was closed for a week after sniping and one fire bombing in which a young student was burned to death. One could sense the tension at a Martin Luther King memorial service on campus. Three of our members were on the faculty at Florida A & M, and one, Louise Blackwell, who was white, was known for helping integrate restaurants in our area.

The next Sunday was Easter. In a letter home I said, "My Easter sermon really took off. You know those times when you can just feel it. My topic was 'Profile of a Dropout.' Easter and Jesus aren't easy to talk about with Unitarians, many of whom have disavowed the theology of Christmas and Easter. But I talked not about the immaculate white-robed Jesus of Christian Sunday school days, but a Jesus who reminded me of our very own teens, with long hair and sandals, living in desert country without showers and laundromats That made him a more human, down-to-earth person we could more easily identify with, and even listen to, as we needed to listen to our youth.

"I've mentioned Lew Allen, my black finance chairman. His mother and brother were in church the next Sunday. She's most attractive—about my age I suspect. She was so impressed with my sermon, entitled, 'Immortality is Now,' she wanted a copy. This amazed me, since Lew told me she used to call him and argue over long distance about joining our 'atheistic' group. She told me that he had written that they now had a minister, but had not said I was a woman, so she was truly surprised. She, like me, thought, 'How nice he didn't feel he had to make such a distinction. It's almost like not having to say another is Black.'

"And I wanted to mention that our junior highers have made friends with a group of Black kids at a community center near here and they've done things together. So the mothers of our kids thought they'd like to get to know the mothers of the Negro kids and have had several get togethers. Then the Black mothers thought they'd try to make a bit of money; and just last week had a fish fry to which we all went. One of the women who does the most work has ten children. Their home is unbelievably tiny. Yet she's always pleasant, with a big grin which shows she's lost most her teeth."

The UUA Black Caucus General Assembly was in Cleveland that June. It was an unforgettable experience—the Assembly itself, and on both ends of it in Atlanta! Any flight from Tallahassee went through Atlanta, and I wanted to see something of that big historic city which people here love as they do San Francisco in California. So thanks to Helen Pickett, the minister's wife, I had a tour of Southern mansions, Cabbagetown, and Vine Street (poor sections segregated into white and black) and followed the line of march of the Martin Luther King cortege.

Seeing old friends from Cleveland and Calgary was the high point of the Assembly for me. There were more than a 150 blacks, who were part of many evening parties and room sessions. After years of significant work under an astute leadership of men like Hayward Henry, chairman of the Black Unitarian Universalist Caucus, this GA was truly a time of decision. The historic Ware Lecture by Mayor Carl Stokes of Cleveland helped put into perspective what we had to face later.

Good liberals that we are, we got emotionally involved and voted a million dollars for the Black Affairs Council, to be raised over the next four years. Some of us wondered how we could ever explain to our people back home because one had to be there to experience the peak experience we all shared in voting for the unrealistic figure, which was never raised. On my return, I was asked by the Tallahassee Human Relations Council to speak; my topic was announced as "Black Self-Determination—A Report from Cleveland."

On the return trip from Cleveland, a Unitarian member of the Atlanta City Council took me to lunch and gave me a tour of the downtown, complete with a description of their plans for underground Atlanta. It reminded me of a Baptist service I had attended in Tallahassee. We had arrived late. The church was packed. Those in one pew squeezed together to make room for us, and a couple in front of us turned and offered us fans. The Wakulla choir, dressed in white, was up front singing and swaying in unison. During the sermon, I put myself in place of the locals, for whom the words "Jesus will take care of you" has a meaning I feel we Unitarian Universalists little understand. All, especially women and children, were proudly dressed up, many with white gloves. I thought of how they lived during the week in small crowded houses provided by the owners of the large tobacco fields. But this was their fancy home on Sundays and they loved it.

I was reminded of another event that had happened one evening at my own church. About a third of the way through the Christmas service, I noticed a dozen young people—white and black—all well-dressed, walking along the window toward the entrance. After the service I found they were all from Leon High—a group called "We," who do things together and had decided to go to church.

They were there because they had picked First Baptist as their first choice, only to have the ushers there tell them that no blacks were to be admitted. I wrote a letter to the editor of *The Democrat* suggesting that it reminded me of Mary and Joseph and Baby Jesus being turned away because there was no room for them in the inn. Today, I proudly boast about my Tallahassee congregation because ten percent were black!

As I tell that story I often suggest that many Unitarian Universalist congregations feel guilty for not being integrated and work hard to attract at least one or two "token" blacks to salve their own consciences. In Tallahassee, we had our "token non-intellectual!" "John," a retired fisherman, had never gone beyond eighth grade. A perennial philosopher, he openly spoke his mind with no awe of the PhDs in our group.

I also think of one of our black youth, a handsome, outgoing young man. He had asked me to join him for lunch one day, because he wanted to talk. He said that his father was a janitor at the University. "He's so proud of me; but often, Miss Kochendoerfer, I feel I'd like to slip off to Canada, where nobody knows me. I could worry more about myself and not be expected to spend my life fighting for my people." He was a part of our youth group, a group that would make any church proud. I've often wondered whether he accomplished his dreams.

❧

After that spring so filled with the race issue, I found myself shifting to other concerns. In June I received a letter from the Rabbi Garfein thanking me for the words I'd written for *The Tallahassee Democrat,* supporting our opposition to school prayer. It had been forwarded to them on their vacation. He said in part, "Though this is more than a Jewish concern, being basic to our American democracy, it's been interpreted even by liberal colleagues as 'the Rabbi's resolution.' . . .

"In a different area, we both have experienced the kind of negative obstructions that come from the displaced old power structure of a congregation. Anyone who respects himself cannot allow such a group to abuse him. How to turn their garbage into something constructive is the difficult question. By the way, professors from the University tell me that similar pettiness exists in the hallowed halls.

"Many times I've wished colleagues would lend more than non-directive sympathy to my congregants who run to tattle when I don't do as they please. We all need to be more constructively helpful in each other's ministries. And we could all use more humor. What a delightful story could be created out of our vicissitudes."

Stan Garfein and I had turned out to be best buddies. I didn't realize then how prophetic Stan's perceptions were and how important his support would prove to be. But it did remind me of a concern I'd had as "Hazel," one of my congregants, tried to make me her protégé. She was a wealthy widow and started taking me to plays and operas, until soon it was expected that I would be her companion.

I tried excuses, but that tactic didn't work. I finally declined her invitations, explaining to her that I didn't feel comfortable with the situation. This she couldn't accept and began to find one thing after another to be unhappy about. Finally, formerly one of the church's best supporters, she withdrew her pledge and used her money to do things that would give her congregational credit (such as buying a new movie projector for the church school), but her refusal to pledge added to problems with our building fund and budget.

When a congregation calls a minister it is like a marriage. After the honeymoon, it often turns out to be the little things that bring on the power struggles. This was especially so in a group that had done their own thing for years, with their own ongoing leadership who had kept the show on the road.

In utter contrast was tiny, bird-like Lucy Johnson, one of the oldest members both in age and membership. Lucy was in a credo group at my home. This was her credo: "Though I realize that my most productive years have passed, and that those I acted significantly among are dead or old, and that whoever is still remaining is far away, I still find inner peace in doing the simple tasks that may contribute to the well being and happiness of others near me, and by using the little influence I can exert in promoting what seems just and humanitarian. If the causes I work for meet with success, or people are appreciative of what I do, I feel grateful for the pleasure it gives me, but I am not dependent on such pleasure for an incentive to keep on with my endeavors. The work itself is the important matter. Honors seem infantile like paper stars given to children. I am always glad to have them go to others to whom they furnish encouragement."

Lucy understood from dire experience what a true power struggle was. I had once encouraged this eighty-two year old to write about her experiences in California politics. When Upton Sinclair campaigned for governor in 1934, California was solidly Republican. The Republicans had precluded the Democratic party from renting any convenient headquarters, so Lucy had spent days finding an old building for them to use. She single-handedly hauled in tubs of water in order to spread wet newspapers around to keep down the dust as she made the building habitable. For all this, she was to be in charge of Democratic headquarters. Then at the formal meeting, someone else was named to the position; she couldn't believe it and cried that evening. Then she tried to think it all through, "But what should it matter to me? I was not concerned with anything personal, but with electing a governor. Only my hurt vanity could suffer, and I would go ahead with the work as if nothing had happened. I made up my face with care to obliterate the tear stains. All were angry for me, but I told them to pay no attention. It was all in the family. Then I realized that I had a tough hide."

Part of Lucy's secret was that she had kept her childlike qualities, and when I think of her, I also think of our many young members in Tallahassee. Our college-aged Student Religious Liberals, called the Liberal Forum on the Florida State campus, had an active membership. When important issues were at stake, it sponsored campus speakers that attracted huge crowds. I remembered our college-aged group in Calgary when I got a letter from Bob McCandless. "Alan, Carol, and I have dropped out and are hitching around Europe and North Africa. Right now we're living very simply on the quiet little Greek island of Kythera. We've traveled since the start of September, hitching across rural roads of Europe. We avoided hectic cities altogether where people are indifferent. Found the rural friendliness and hospitality amazing, especially in Italy and Greece. I think the stories of poverty and misery must be myths. I have never seen happier people.

"Soon we'll hitch to Istanbul if we can get into Israel from Arab land. We've applied to work on a kibbutz for two or three months. (Used you as a reference, incidentally!) We're doing the Zen thing, partly because a calm acceptance of reality, undivided, unjustified and unconceptualized—has great emotional appeal, and partly because it's just natural. Why hassle? Why invent problems? Don't question it. Just accept it. You don't like it? You don't have to like it! Hippie talk!

"We have you to thank for turning us on to the spiritual, nonintellectual thing when you were in Calgary. I've ordered *The Three Pillars of Zen* from Beacon Press to add to our 20-book library of Ionesco, Laotsu, McLuhan, Goodman, Hesse, Fromm, Dylan Thomas, Alan Watts. We've also benefitted from the mind-expanding effects of the New Alchemy. I had a terrifying, beautiful rebirth experience with LSD, which convinces me that my problems are strictly of my own creation, and the way to mental health is simply to stop thinking there is a problem and simply do what Nature directs. Kingdom of God within—where else?

"Many of my grey memories are bitter. I have a horror of our education system—a physical prison until age sixteen and a mental prison for benumbed grey minds from then till one's BA. I could never go back, unless it were to some place like Goddard in Vermont, which respects individuality and gives the student a say in his education. I can make enough money in six months driving a Caterpillar, and spend the other six exploring myself and this groovy world we live on.

"What many of us from LRY would like to do within the next few years is to try to set up a farm commune somewhere in British Columbia or Alberta. I think we have the mental and emotional resources to do it. For the next couple of years Alan and I plan to visit communes and farms (Kibbutzim, Hutterites, Quakers, 'Heads'). We may fail, but the sun will rise while we sleep." I was so pleased that Bob had kept in touch, for I felt deeply that we needed to listen to our youth.

We had a great LRY of mostly junior highers who would be with us for three years. I was proud of them and the responsibility they assumed. One time as we were talking about budget problems, these kids, believe it or not, contributed $250 from their treasury and pledged $500 more. At one meeting I had Lucy Johnson speak to them. They loved her! We opened by singing the LRY hymn,

> We would be one as now we join in singing
> Our hymn of youth to pledge ourselves anew
> To that high cause of greater understanding
> Of who we are, and what in us is true;
> We would be one in living for each other
> To show mankind a new community.
>
> We would be one in building for tomorrow
> A greater world than man has seen today.
> We would be one in searching for that meaning
> Which binds our hearts and points us on our way;
> As one we pledge ourselves to greater service
> With love and justice, strive to make men free.

The kids were frequently off to many conferences and beach parties. When one advisor said she didn't want to be responsible for them on overnight parties, we founded the Youth-Adult Advisory Committee, YAAC for short. Kids were asked to write down all the rules they would live by, to be discussed at a meeting with parents.

The "co-ed sleeping" point was most open to discussion. It was solved when all agreed that there could be a coed sleeping area at LRY overnight functions, provided an advisor or chaperone was present in the room. Violators would be sent home, with a telegram to parents that LRY advisors would no longer accept responsibility. Curfew was from 2 A.M. until 6 A.M., with no one allowed to leave the quarters. In addition, there were the usual "no firearms, no alcoholic beverages, no drugs." I was proud of our group.

I had a challenging, almost scary invitation from one high-school principal. I shared it with our parents in *The Meridian*: "I recently received a call from Mr. Parker at University High School asking whether I would participate in a panel with the rabbi, a Catholic priest, and Protestant ministers for a two-hour session in the auditorium as a wind-up for their class, 'Religion in Twentieth-Century America.' He said to me, 'You really must come, because in deciding which denominations to ask, Unitarian was underlined on several papers.' Some students know who we are!

"Perhaps you'll be just as amazed and pleased as I was to learn some of the questions they intend to have us discuss. These are what I can remember from the long list. There was some statement about the accommodation of science and religion, and 'What is your opinion of the Pope's stand on birth control? Why hasn't the church been more active in social reform? What do you feel about the hippie's religiosity? How literally can we interpret the Bible? Why are sacraments necessary in the church? What is the real purpose of religion? Is the church simply another institution bent on maintaining itself? What is your church's stand on racial matters? Abortion? Pre-marital sex? What has been your involvement in the Arab-Israeli conflict? What about taxation of church property? What do you think of the theory that no man can be reconciled in

God until all men and all institutions are reconciled?' I'll let you know how it all comes out!"

It was quite an experience—easier for me than for some of the other ministers. I could have wished that some of our adult members were as much interested in asking such basic questions.

With college students, I was deluged with draft counseling. I did a service based on Michael Ferber's historic sermon, "A Time to Say No!" The UUA had issued a pamphlet stating that the Association had passed resolutions opposing draft registration and calling for support for young people who opposed participation in the military because of conscience. As I first opened it, I read "This pamphlet is not meant to be an explanation of opposition to military service, but is an explanation of options available at this time for young people who may soon be facing draft registration. There are three basic options: 1) military service, 2) non-cooperation with the Selective Service System, 3) alternate classification such as conscientious objection (CO)."

Under "Conscientious Objection" it said in part, "Because the Selective Service System will require CO applicants to justify their claim, it's important to act now. Ask yourself questions, such as, 'Do you oppose nuclear war? Do you think a major conventional war could be kept conventional? What about your own part in both kinds of wars? Is it all right to be a medic but not a missile repair technician? Is a nuclear war worth the destruction if it preserves the United States? Can such a war preserve any country involved in it?'

"The UUA has a Registry of Conscientious Objectors. This is an important way to show you have held objections to participation for a period of time. You should also take time to speak out at your church or school on your feelings, as well as gather letters of support for your position.

"Any Unitarian Universalist who wishes to place on file a statement of conscientious objection to war is invited to write the office of the executive vice president. The statement must be accompanied by a letter from the minister or an officer of the society to which the person belongs, certifying membership. Statements filed are then provided upon request of the writer, when necessary, to appropriate government officials."

It was difficult to write local draft boards and try to explain conscientious objection without using all the religious terms. After mentioning the respect I had for the board's difficult position and heavy responsibility, I said in part in the case of a graduate student, "I have nothing but admiration for the deep personal integrity of David. He is the kind of member one feels honored to have in her congregation. . . .

"I am deeply impressed by the fact that a mind like his, intrigued by scientific theory, is mature and whole enough to encompass not only knowledge, but wisdom—to come to the great realization that there is a religious dimension of man—his love, his honor, his courage—his life itself, that lies outside the realm of the factual considerations of scientific inquiry. It is in this realm that David finds his commitment to God—a commitment which he cannot violate because it is a higher commitment than that required by other men.

"David has talked with me at length about his commitment and his concern; and I feel sure you must feel about such a young man as I do—that we should feel honored we have young people with the depth of personal belief and commitment to an ultimate concern which will allow no compromise without a violation of his own person."

I also helped three young men "escape" to Canada by making arrangements with Canadian congregations to help them get settled in a new home. I can still picture myself sitting on the floor of my living room with a young man and his girlfriend pouring over a map. It was helpful that I knew Canada and where our relatively few congregations there could best offer lodging and help in finding employment. That evening, after much discussion, he decided on Vancouver. Many years later I received a letter from Washington, DC, from the girl. She wrote to tell me she had never heard from him, but had read about his involvement in an accident as a bush pilot in northern British Columbia. It seems she had been carrying a torch all these years, hoping to hear from him, not knowing he had married. The other two young men are also still there and are now Canadian citizens.

And speaking of youth and marriage, the new church was made for weddings! Early the next year there were two, which brought me young friends who were to enrich my life over the decades.

Jeanne Miller's father was a retired military man. She was an army brat who had lived in place after place, until her parents had retired to Tallahassee. Her madonna-like beauty belied her quiet, rebellious spirit. In a discussion group where she was the one young person, she shocked many of us at one point as she straightened in her chair, raised her chin and said, "No one can ever hurt me!" I'd felt she had built a kind of armour of rebellion to protect her from hurts involved in having ever-broken relationships as the military family moved from place to place while she was growing up.

Jeanne, to her parents' dismay, had joined picket lines when employees were striking at Alberta Box and Crate Company. Even this wedding was part of that act of rebellion. Years later, after the marriage had failed, Jeanne told me, "Vi, I wanted you to stop me. I wouldn't have let you, but I did want you to do it." "Tom," the son of a Florida State professor, was a conscientious objector. This may have been part of the attraction for Jeanne.

They had planned most of the ceremony. The music they chose set the atmosphere: "Children of Darkness," "Today," "Bridge Over Troubled Waters," and "Be Not Too Hard." At the conclusion, Jeanne and Tom took big armloads of carnations from two huge vases and passed one to each person there.

A large newspaper article, "An 'Uncommon Wedding'

Unites Couple in City," included a photo of this lovely young bride handing a long-stemmed carnation to Lucy Johnson. It was a classic picture I still love. No one could guess from the picture they had so much in common.

Word seemed to get around that Unitarian weddings were personal and meaningful, and we had requests from non-members. After I married Mike and Terry McGee, they joined our church. At the time, we needed a leader for junior highers in the church school. Many adults shy away from working with junior high schoolers, but Mike and Terry said, "We'd like to do it." They had the kids write a script about human values, got a movie camera, and the class shot their movie all around Tallahassee. The kids loved it and wouldn't miss a Sunday, and finally presented their completed show to their parents.

I spent quite a bit of time with Mike and Terry that year, after which Mike decided he had to become a Unitarian minister. He applied to Starr King but was not accepted. The next year, they volunteered with VISTA and were off to Arkansas.

The following summer, just as I was about to visit them, they were given a commendation, after which they were asked to leave. They moved back to Tallahassee. One day I picked up the phone to hear an excited male voice almost yelling, "Guess what! We just had an Airmail letter from Starr King. We're accepted!" They used the little they'd saved from VISTA to buy a second-hand car for the trip to Berkeley. Mike eventually graduated from Starr King and became one of my protégés in his climb to the ministry of one of our outstanding Unitarian Universalist congregations at West Shore in Cleveland.

❧

In November of 1968, I flew to Berkeley for an unforgettable two weeks of continuing education at Starr King along with ten former students. The "continuing" was a shaking experience of becoming caught up with frontiers of learning—so necessary for the future growth, not only of my ministry, but of our nation. And of course, it was great to be back at the old stomping ground!

I had been eager to learn more about group therapy with Mike Murphy, director of Esalon, for we'd sponsored a sensitivity/encounter group in Tallahassee. I had brought in an outside professional to lead it, but I sat in. It seemed exciting, did bring several into the church, and seemed to solve basic problems for some. Yet, it surely wasn't for everyone. I sensed the need for caution and questioned the uncontrolled use of "encountering."

For an introduction to cybernetics, we spent an evening on the Cal campus with Dr. Hegget, who was then in the forefront in this field. We were fascinated with playing around with computers, not believing then that they were to be such an integral part of our future.

I mentioned to the men at the conference that I had never even tried "pot." They couldn't believe it and said, "We can take care of that, Vi." And so they did, the very next evening. When I came home from visiting my friend Elsie, I found eight of them sitting in a circle on the floor in a dimly lit room, passing around a marijuana stub clamped in a little brass holder. I joined them, took my puff, inhaled, and held my breath. Nothing happened! Apparently, this was often true the first time; but at least I could go Bill Clinton one better—I had inhaled!

On the homebound plane, I felt as though we had more mind-blowing experiences in those two weeks than I had expected or even wanted. It was a relief to come back to Tallahassee where things filtered down more slowly. Then after a few weeks, I began to realize how fortunate I had been to have a taste of these history-making innovations. Little did I realize then that the mind-blowing experiences I had as a grown-up would turn out to encompass the lives of our youth from kindergarten to the grave.

That brave new world of our youth forever emblazoned itself on my mind after the 1969 General Assembly in Boston. After a visit to my beloved Provincetown, and a guest speaking engagement in Brewster on the Cape, I spent eleven days at the Statler Hilton. Assembly sessions were electric, in support of the Black Caucus program we had started funding the year before.

I did check in at headquarters and the Department of Ministry, since there was the feeling that I just might be making the decision to move. Then an old Red Cross friend I visited in Townshend, Vermont, had arranged a guest-speaking engagement at the Brattleboro church. After the service, I had quite a talk with one of their younger members. "Bill" had met me the past summer and came specially to hear my sermon, "Of Us and the Future," sharing thoughts of Henry Miller from his *Wisdoms of the Heart*. Bill invited me to visit him before I left.

The next morning the phone rang. It was Bill. "Vi, I have sad news. My sister Barbara, who was up from Miami for the summer and in an apartment in Brattleboro, was on an acid trip last night and jumped from a fourth-story window. Can you come talk? Would you be willing to do a memorial service?"

I hadn't brought any material with me, but I was flattered that even though there were three Unitarian Universalist ministers in the area, Bill felt he wanted me to do it. It was an extended commital service at a lovely hilltop cemetery with dulcimer music. I hadn't known Barbara, but Bill said she was a straight A student in math, who had coached college students and had been voted the "most outstanding student." It seemed such a waste, but was a sign of the times.

∾

That third year in Tallahassee I dealt with a new issue—abortion. The present law allowed abortion only when a woman's life was in danger. I soon discovered that legislation to liberalize the law (to permit abortions when pregnancy might impair the mother's physical or mental health, might result in serious physical or mental defect to the child, or was the result of rape or incest) had been introduced by my dentist, Miley Miers, who was also a legislator. Miley's efforts for some years had been to introduce liberalizing legislation, so just before leaving for a monthly ministers meeting in Orlando, I put a copy of a sermon I'd written on abortion in the mail to him.

At the ministers meeting, we talked about Dr. Mier's bill, comparing it with another I'd brought along that had been introduced by Senator Shevin. We felt the Senator's bill was better. That week we had planned a pulpit exchange. From Orlando I went to Fort Lauderdale to do the Sunday service. During the coffee hour, the phone rang. It was Dr. Miers. There was to be a legislative hearing Tuesday morning in Tallahasee and he wanted me to be there for a strategy session Monday evening.

I had made other commitments with friends staying in Key West, but Dr. Miers offered to pay for my airfare to make this possible. It was a long drive even to Key West, where I could leave my car and jump on a plane to return to Tallahassee. I was to ask to sit with a Dr. Mixon at Miami and speak to Dr. Ingram who would board at Tampa. At Tallahassee we were taken immediately to the home of the president of the Florida Medical Association, who I then found out was paying my traveling expenses.

A crowd had gathered—doctors, legislators, lobbyists—and I realized that I was to be a card-carrying lobbyist myself! As we were having drinks, Dr. Miers said he wanted me to start off at the hearing and to relate parts of my sermon. The group was scheduled for a radio interview and as I waited for the others, I had a long talk with Dr. Sackett, another legislator who was chairman of the Committee on Health and Welfare.

Although he was a devout Catholic and disagreed with abortion, he still felt as a legislator he must serve all the people.

I hadn't eaten since breakfast, and at nearly ten that night, we went to Joe's Steak House for drinks and dinner in a private dining room. We were there until after one planning legislative strategy for later that morning.

I recapped the discussion from Orlando about Senator Shevin's bill. Anticipating opposition, the group revised Dr. Miers's bill to provide heavier penalties for violation, requiring the abortion to be performed in an approved hospital, and adding a voluntary conscience clause that would allow any hospital, doctor, or medical worker to refuse to participate in an abortion case. I got to bed about 3 A.M. after doing my homework.

Because I was to start off the program, I was taken immediately to the hearing room when I arrived at the Capitol the next morning. I presented the resolutions we ministers would recommend and in further testimony used the word "existential," which one committee member didn't understand and questioned. After my testimony I was taken immediately to the airport to be flown back to Key West on a tiny executive airline.

After two relaxing days in Key West, I returned to Tallahassee and wrote a letter to all Unitarian Universalist congregations in Florida. I urged writing key legislators (including the Speaker, a firm Catholic), telling them that the Florida Unitarian Universalist Ministers Association had gone on record as supporting House Bill 11 and Senate Bill 208, urging their passage.

My testimony resulted in a flurry of news coverage. The *Miami Herald* wrote: "A Tallahassee woman minister, urging adoption of a liberalized abortion bill, told a legislative committee today, 'I want every child born to be a wanted child.' Rev. Violet Kochendoerfer of the Unitarian Church said that making abortions illegal no longer 'scares' young women into morality. 'Our young people are telling us that our 'thou shalt nots' are for another generation and we can no longer build a strong moral code on fear,' she said. 'Ninety percent of the protest often comes from the Catholics,' she said. 'Why should the majority who want reform be blocked by the minority who do not?'

My prize clipping is an editorial from the *Orlando Sentinal*. "The Unborn Have Rights. There are various arguments being made in Tallahassee that we should make abortions legal, that we should rid our minds of any objection to the killing of an unborn child, be its mother willing.

"Lady ministers and obstetricians and others are telling legislators what a better world this would be if a mother, or would-be mother, could avoid bearing an unwanted child. The Rev. Violet Kochendoerfer of the Unitarian Church in Tallahassee, for example, told a committee that she wants 'every child born to be a wanted child,' that the penalty for abortions no longer 'scares young women into morality,' that we can 'no longer build a strong moral code on fear.' Others agree with her.

"But we would ask her, and the others who agree with her, what has that really got to do with it? What about the rights of the unborn, and courts have ruled that it does have rights. Though it may be unwanted by its mother, what would it have wanted? What about the wishes of the father? What if Martin Luther had been unwanted, or Abraham Lincoln, or Joan of Arc, or you or I?

"And if the penalty for abortion no longer scares young women into morality, would removing it induce them into it? And if fear as an ineffective factor in building a moral code has anything to do with it, does it follow that we should remove the penalties for murder and robbery?

"There may well be selected cases in which abortions could be justified. But the fact that they don't scare girls into being home by ten doesn't even come close."

Later, the headline in the *St. Petersburg Times* read, "Tallahassee Minister Asks for Abortion Law Reform," with a long article that said in part, "'Law is no basis for moral decision. You can't legislate morals.' The view is that of the Rev. Violet Kochendoerfer, minister of the Unitarian Church in Tallahassee and active lobbyist for the reform of the Florida Abortion Law. Miss Kochendoerfer was the Saturday luncheon speaker for the annual (Thursday through Sunday) meeting of the Southeastern District of the Unitarian Universalist Association at the Princess Martha Hotel. . . .

"'Abortion is a matter to be determined between a woman and her physician, not by law,' she told *The Times* in an interview. . . .

"Miss Kochendoerfer advocates abolition of abortion laws, except for making it mandatory that anyone who performs an abortion be medically licensed. 'The present law makes lawbreakers of otherwise law-abiding citizens and breeds disrespect for law. This puts many doctors and mothers in an untenable position.' . . .

"Emphasizing the need for women to be concerned for other women, Miss Kochendoerfer says, 'Women must face the issues and work for women, because it is women who face the problems while men make the laws.' She adds with a smile, 'Some say the solution is to elect more women legislators!'"

As a legal lobbyist, I had to file a statement verified under oath of all expenditures paid or incurred and by whom. Dr. Miers's law was defeated.

In addition to the abortion issue, there were other concerns that I felt at times should be brought to the attention of the general public. I sent to the editor of *The Tallahassee Democrat* a statement of a problem that was to grow out of control in a matter of decades: "I so wish our country could shift from a curative to a preventive society. We wait until leaders are assassinated to think about gun control. We get more excited about transplanting hearts and kidneys than keeping them healthy in the first place. And there's pollution and so much else; and now the president has appointed yet another commission to study the subject of violence.

"Erich Fromm (who wrote perhaps our most definitive book on the subject of love) states that 'love is the only sane and satisfactory answer to the problems of human existence.'

"Instead of 'violence,' I'd like to see our president appoint a commission to inquire into the nature and promotion of love—perhaps to replace other subjects from nursery to graduate school for one year—and all Americans concentrate on learning how to love; for, as Robert Kennedy said at a memorial for Martin Luther King, 'When we have learned to love, our country will have then fulfilled its promise and its destiny.'"

Just after my abortion days were over, we faced our annual financial drive. I spoke out to my own people in Sunday sermons and in my column in *The Meridian*: "To Our Old Members. As a colleague said in his Clergy Column, 'I took my spiritual temperature last Sunday and found I was high on enthusiasm for what is brewing in the church!' I've had this feeling too, what with phone calls to say how excited new people were about a service, to ask whether we have a college group to join, etc.

"It seems the past two years of ground work are beginning to pay off; but we need to bottle and cap into membership this brewing enthusiasm. I know how easy it is after the long push to get a minister and build a building at the same time, to want to relax for a while. But if each of us could set a goal of bringing in one new member, then that would be possible budgetwise!"

In another issue of *The Meridian*, my column spoke out to remind us of how decades ago we were concerned about some of the same problems we still are not validly facing today. I wrote, "'Now is the Time for All Good Men to come to the aid of their planet,' said *Time* magazine. 'With all we know, what we don't know about the earth we live on not only can hurt us, it can kill us.'

"Last Sunday we dedicated nine of our children with ages ranging from eleven years to one week, when I asked you to dedicate yourselves to providing the kind of atmosphere (!) in which these children might grow to their greatest potential. As it was going on, I wondered whether it was quite fair to ask you to say, 'We do,' to something which it might be eminently impossible for you to do—in that rather schizophrenic way we have of facing problems these days. For some ecologists feel we have gone too far to reverse the processes of destruction. Others feel we could save the world if we begin now to fundamentally change our way of life.

"Last week two young friends stopped by to talk in the concerned way students do these days. One, who recently graduated at FSU in biology, said, 'Perhaps we'll become human carp that can exist on the filth that kills all the other fish.' I can't quite forget that, and keep wondering why we accept predications of doom with such equanimity, and go merrily on following the Pied Piper of Profits and Plenty."

∾

In June of 1969, the feeling that it was time to move on was in my blood. Just before leaving for the summer, I wrote to Rabbi Garfein, who proved to be my best confidant, and shared some of my problems with him. I said in part, "I did want to stop by to talk since you know the persons involved. Seems this duo, rather knowing they can't do any more harm than they have by cutting their pledges, sort of realize, I think, that they have 'shot their wad.' But I do have the feeling that if they want me out, they'll accomplish this one way or another.

"I don't know whether or not I told you, but I agreed to have written into my contract the fact that at the end of three years, the congregation would have the right of review—in light of the fact that I was their first minister and also a woman. So this is their next point of attack, except I think they must feel that by then they may have even less power.

"The latest I heard is that they wanted to present a resolution to the board that I be allowed to stay this year if I'd agree to leave at the end of the church year. Their move has been handled very well by key people, and won't even come up at a board meeting. Most people won't even know about it. But even though we know they don't have enough power to really sway a vote their way, they, or some of them won't leave, but will keep things stirred up in new ways. I can't help feel that they may try to use the summer program to help promote the 'back to fellowship days' climate, on the basis that our budget can't afford the new building and a minister. And surely this case can be made!

"I talked with three key people this week. They have agreed with my decision to set the wheels in motion to find another job. I've never had any difficulty so far; but it can take a long time, especially if there aren't any openings where one would like to go. So I'm doing it partly as a 'hedge'; for I like Tallahassee and like what's happening in our group. I feel I still have things to give and to receive.

"Usually this kind of thing is jealously kept from the congregation. However, my mentors now feel that though it not be officially announced, it not be kept a strict secret. They feel that if people knew, they might begin to think of the fact that if I leave, it will be sometime before they're financially able to have a minister. The kind they want isn't going to come for peanuts."

And that's surely what my salary would sound like today! My beginning salary was $8,100. In November I wrote my sister, "There are rumblings, led by the very two gals who played such a deeply rosy part when I came. They say they want the group to grow, but when it does, the complexion changes, others take over, and they don't have the power and adulation, and having things the way they knew as a fellowship. In one sense I can understand this, but it's something we need to work on. . . .

"As I told our district director [about one of the women], 'If she decides this is what she wants, she'll do it one way or another.' Part of the trouble is that the director is one of her and her husband's best friends, and finds it difficult to separate himself from this friendship. So she uses this and him, even though he tries to be fair.

"It's funny, though; for I still like her and I feel she likes me, though not in my present role. It's a kind of schizophrenic relationship I sense when we're doing things together. There are so many things we enjoy in common; but that old feeling she said she had about not wanting a woman to do her funeral is still there.

"Anyway, all is quiet now, but I'm sure at the end of the year (since my contract calls for a review by the congregation) it will all come up again. In many ways I wish it had come to a 'vote of confidence' last spring. This might have settled things sooner. Many good solid members have no wish to go back to a fellowship, which is what the opposition wants.

"Part of it was that I asked for a raise at a time I knew wasn't a popular move; but since they haven't lived up to their contract agreement for an annual review of salary, I wanted to remind them of this. And even though the money isn't there, I'd like to have them agree that they should be paying me more (in light of the Ministers Association Guidelines). All this, because as a woman I don't want the men thinking that I'm holding down standards. At any rate, all that's over within my thoughts now, or at least for the time being. But it's I who have to make some decisions.

"Three men on the board agreed with me that for my own protection and bargaining power, I should start looking for something now, which you know I did in a small way last summer. Remember I wrote you that Caribou, Maine, would have put me right to work if I could have said 'yes' back then. But I told them I still felt I had unfinished business here, and my contract calls for three months notice.

"After the first of the year, I'm thinking of announcing my proposed resignation, perhaps giving three months notice as of June 1, which will carry me through till September. This would give them something solid to work with, and at least put me on the initiative. For many members I know would leave if I did, and they can't afford another minister. It would in all likelihood be a man, perhaps with family, and they'd have to up their salary sights quite a bit.

"On the other hand, as Claire (one of my members with whom I can talk about things) said, 'You should do what's best for Vi, without thought of the group here.' She's right. Deep down, I know that if we ever needed what real religion stands for, we need it today like never before. But as with so many things, it's become irrelevant for many; or, like you and Frank, they find they can be religious without the formal trappings of the church.

"But my ministry has been meaningful to many, especially to young people here who flock in. That's part of our problem, and may be what bugs some older members. Many of those who have joined are graduate students, or undergraduates who don't have the kind of money that makes up a solid share of the expenses. You know that permanent residents here are pretty much traditionally churched, which suggests why our membership is largely Florida State and Florida A&M faculty.

"My one-to-one relationships are most satisfying, both in the congregation and with the other ministers here in Florida. And I do get around! Just last Monday a reporter for the two Sarasota newspapers, who's doing a new series on the abortion question (and I've become an authority around the state!), spent over two hours here. When we were through with what he came for, we got into other discussions. He's in the big wealthy Episcopalian church at Sarasota, where they have a big healing program—huge plant, plus three curates. We got to talking about that and other religious stuff and he was so excited with my story he didn't want to leave.

"Speaking of abortion, there's a clergy counselling service for Florida being organized so FSU can send students to us. We're to have medical outlets to send gals to (some out-of-state) with counseling before and after. This could be dangerous but rewarding. And as I told the Sarasota chap, I don't think I even want to work for the same abortion bill my dentist Miley Miers is going to try to get through one more time. With all the stories I've heard about the unbelievable happenings in illegal abortions, it doesn't begin to touch the problem where it really lies. I feel I'll be for repeal of the law.

"But even with all of this, I do enjoy the work. I love putting together sermons, because I know I do a specially good job. I'd miss the university climate too. As a generalist, I rather enjoy taking pokes at the many specialists we have. Many are physical scientists; and, being what they are, there isn't a place in their mindset for anything but logical, rational approaches. I smile too, because I have no degrees at all, in (I'm pretty sure) a congregation with more PhDs per capita percentagewise than anywhere else.

"I'm getting a lot of mileage on my sermon, 'The Other Reality,' which touches my feeling that the important, and actually 'religious' reality of things like beauty, honesty, courage, love, cannot be proved by repetition in the scientific experiment, but are in another realm of 'reality.' And to their credit and my gratification, many are like my beloved Herb Taylor. I can see his wry smile, when I feel I can say sometimes at coffee hour, 'This wasn't your cup of tea this morning, was it!' . . .

"One more thought. I remember that many times before when I've been in a quandary, if I just quit trying to find answers, something happens, often way beyond anything I could dream of. Then I know what I must or want to do. It's just a bit of a different twist to Mom's 'Everything happens for the best!' There are many times when I do feel we're our worst enemies, and the best thing we can do is to get ourselves out of the way (my version of a Christian friend's 'Let go and let God!'). But right now I feel I need to take some kind of initiative, except that hasn't come quite clear as yet.

"Then with all this ruminating, I also realize that at my age I'm not likely to change from what I am or have been. I have had and still have a pretty exciting and enriching life; and get far more appreciation than most people do. I should feel fortunate. Most of the time I do!"

I did write George Spencer in Boston. After reviewing some of the above, I said, "It's really a classic—the growing pains for a fellowship with its first minister—the lack of definition of roles—the unwillingness to become 'organized' so the right hand knows what the left is doing. You do remember that we moved into a lovely new building last September; so this group, with less than fifty pledging units to begin with, did well nigh the impossible, though financial short-fall is now part of the problem.

"We're just getting settled in, and I feel we've had a truly great year, largely because we're pulling in young people— even at high-school age they're coming to know about Unitarians and ask for us. I've spoken to classes in three of our high schools. Consequently, because older residents here are pretty much Christian or Jewish churched (or templed), many of our fifty-five new members are young graduate students, who can't help much financially. So I can understand how some of the old guard who have been keeping the show on the road for years might feel.

"Even so, we have a great LRY, and I do believe we have the best youth-adult relationship of any group in our district. What the church has meant to several new families has been heartwarming. One said, 'We spent three years in St. Louis vegetating in the church there. We haven't been here six months and we're part not only of the church program but the community. If anyone would have told me I'd be spending most of my Sundays at the church and loving it, I'd have told them they were dreaming.'

"Well, it seems there's a group which always comes through in the pinches and did in the last go-round, which in a way was just what we needed. We now have a psychologist, who's an organizer of all things, and seems an answer to our needs! Another plus is the fact that the supporting group doesn't feel the need to take sides or draw lines, but keeps thinking of ways to let the others keep face and be happy. It's unusually admirable in that way, since this is what we talk about from the pulpit and hope will happen.

"So I really feel we have a great year to look forward to; but I also feel that perhaps within that year I should find another spot for me. As I sit here typing at home, where I've just gotten really settled, watching several varieties of birds flit around on one of our perfect days, I hate the thought of leaving. But I do mean it. I don't want to get into the rat race in July, though I wouldn't mind talking with some people if you feel it wise. I'd like to do something with the timing we did here, where we finally wound it up in March for me to start the next September.

"My Preferences. I don't want to live in a big city. In fact I won't. Even though isolated, I enjoy a smaller community in a part of the country where I can explore and where there's natural beauty. Even though they usually have built-in problems, I prefer a fellowship church with a youth orientation; for our youth are the future of our world! Well, you'll probably want me to fill one of the forms. . . ."

I did offer my formal resignation February 28, 1970. The Board accepted it with my stipulations that it become effective June 1. I would then continue to serve through the church year until June 30. Since my contract offered two months vacation, my salary would then continue through August 31. I was also to have freedom to candidate for other churches during this time.

Through all this, I felt the group knew little about professional ethics and didn't seem to want to learn. Because of this I knew another minister in the future would have to go through some of the same problems.

I received a note from one my members, Shirley Taylor, who sensed this. She and husband Herb had risen far above the specialized PhD stereotype I'd so often railed against, to be the kind of quiet mentors from the start. We wouldn't have had the new building if it hadn't been for them; it came about with their quiet oversight all the way. Yet, that was now part of the problem, where we could just about make the mortgage payment to the bank, but had no money to pay off members who made loans. This created the situation where all the clout was on the side of the unhappy. Shirley said she felt our incoming president was a great ivory-tower scientist, but just wouldn't be able to handle divining women of which we had two too many.

Her note continued, "I don't really know who can, frankly. I'm of the opinion we need to learn to live and work together as a group without a minister for sometime before we've any business looking for one. What we've done—or not done— the way we've blundered—is evidence enough that we must grow up some.

"In hind-sight, our 'matriarchy' finally was our undoing. We didn't fully appreciate our situation. That must be changed; and obviously the only way we can alter part of it is to begin paying off some of the money invested by members like you know who. We should never have let her put in so much we now see. And I say that knowing that we'll be lucky if we can pay off the mortgage with the bank, let alone the member loans, or get another minister.

"Please don't leave us feeling that we feel you've failed. It's more like a dose of psychological assault-and-battery perpetrated by some members, and the rest of us unable, or unwilling to read them out of the meeting. You've offered us your best; and you know it's been widely accepted and so appreciated by most of us."

There were many, especially new members who had come in since I had been there, who just had not known what was happening, or what they could do. One said, "I can't believe you won't be here. If we got enough support. . . ." Another letter in the same mail was from a wonderful woman, Annelle Sterk. She was a Quaker, but since there was no group here, she became a member of St. John's Episcopal. Her husband was Catholic, but since I was here she came regularly to hear me, and I performed a wedding for their son. They have a lovely farm on rolling hills with big live oaks covered with Spanish moss.

She wrote, "Dearest Vi! I want to express to you the feelings that I am sure you already know the Sterks have for you, and our deep regret over your leaving the pastorate here. We feel that the church is losing a valuable spirit in you, and that the community will be the poorer. We need your insight, your tolerance and wide understanding, your acceptance of modernity and its ideals and problems—your knowledge. But also we need just you—for you are special—and we like you so much! Steve Jr. and Kay send their love and regrets. All of us shall always be grateful to you for the beauty of their marriage ceremony."

In a letter to my sister, I said, "One may have lots of heartaches going through these times with churches; but there are also the great rewards. One was little Lucy Johnson. She's in her eighties—a little bird-like gal—and one of the greatest 'liberals' in our group. I wasn't at the congregational meeting last night, but Terry and Mike came by with several others to fill me in. They said that Lucy stood up and said, 'The youth today will be our salvation. Vi has a way with them and has attracted this great young congregation. I think we should do everything we can to keep her here!' They said there was a long silence, 'cause some of the other older members don't quite like so many young people around."

I heard from my Florida colleagues. "John" from West Palm wrote, "This is a rough game we're in, but almost everywhere I look these days I fail to see a sense of sustained commitment to the issues of life. For those who do have it they too often are chewed up. Just now I'm also more drained of emotion than I like to admit. Nevertheless, I'm concerned—for you."

"Charles" in Jacksonville wrote, "In this note it would be impossible ever for me to express the scope of my feelings. The best I can say is that I think you have proven something for yourself and the congregation by insisting on some dialogue and some setting up of machineries. With all of this, something has been accomplished in the overall balance of the Florida ministry. I shall be interested in your plans. Do keep in touch."

The Liberal Religious Youth group, bless them, tried to help with fund-raising when the opposition tried to use the budget issue in their "back to fellowship" movement. After their fund-raising effort, I wrote the kids, "Please let this be a secret between us; but if I could pick whose trust and championing I cherish most, I think you know it's you. Today I can say, 'Vi, how lucky can you be!' You-all have made these past few weeks seem worth the while and more. I'm proud to be your minister and thank you for the trust and championing. For what I am—my faults and strengths together—are not entirely divorced from you. You minister to we grown-ups in a way we can't forget."

On June 10, 1970, I wrote home, "Last Sunday night, round about ten, the minister's home was invaded by fifteen LRYrs and their advisor. (Remember they're our high-school group.) They were bearing gifts—a luxurious white long-haired bear rug for beside my bed they said [and it's still there!] and a mobile delicately balanced with individual works of art, strikingly incorporating expressions of love and appreciation and thoughts of the past and the future—something from each of them. 'It's for your study, wherever that may be, so you can think of us and know we love you.' I was overwhelmed!

"There were times when I could bash their crazy heads together, and then they turn around and make me so proud I could bust my buttons! This was one of the button-busting times, which was worth the whole three years in Tallahassee.

"In addition to the lovely gifts, I thanked them for listening to a need I had and doing something about it. They'd collected a huge supply of super-sturdy liquor cartons in which I can ship my books. Midst hugs and tears and many fond farewells the last contingent left with invitations to visit wherever I settled down again. I'm sure some of them will!"

Several church members put their thoughts on paper. One wrote, "Dear Vi, with the help of a gin and tonic (which I wish belatedly you were sharing), I'll put on paper how sickening I think all this business is. Is it perhaps a reflection of the country as a whole? The silent majority are really frightened people, frightened mostly of the young. Do you think the people who have been longest in the church, and who have built up that lovely physical property, are afraid of our young ones who may now be in the majority?"

I have letters members wrote for me to use in seeking another church. One of my favorite older members wanted this to go with me: "To Whom It May Concern: Intellectually and spiritually, the ministry of Miss Violet A. Kochendoerfer at the Tallahassee Unitarian Church has been a challenge and an inspiration. I speak, to be sure, for myself alone, yet I know many others who have shared the life and the illumination provided by this exciting minister. Alive to the news, responsive to urgency, she has led us to participate to a greater extent in social change.

"On another level she has deepened for me, and for others, our awareness of the meaning of religion—conveying what Lewis Mumford calls 'a sense of the mystery that encompasses all life.' Through her, too, we have been introduced to many great minds, past and contemporary, and this has been an enriching experience.

"I'm seventy, and definitely an elderly member of our congregation. I feel that Vi Kochendoerfer is my friend—but so too do the young people of our church, the high school and college age young people, many of whom have become members since she came as our minister. She does, in fact, seem able to relate to all ages.

"Over the years, I have visited many Unitarian churches and those of other denominations. It is my often-expressed opinion that Miss Kochendoerfer rates in the top rank. It will be our loss, and a great one, when she leaves us."

Annelle Sterk sent another long letter she thought might help along the way. I especially liked the paragraph that said, "She is the kind of person with whom one can be honest and quiet, and from whom inspiration and nonsentimental self-acceptance will always be realized. In her personal life she has shown she can meet difficult situations with poise and clarity of thought. Her sermons, her marriage and memorial services, are stimulating and thought provoking."

Our finance chairman said, after mentioning the financial days ahead, "Personally, I find Vi to be a very fine individual. She interacts particuarly well with the younger members of the congregation and encouraged get togethers which have led to a good rapport between age groups.

"Vi has been especially interested in Sunday programs. Her sermons certainly rank toward the top of those in Unitarian churches. She has a remarkable imagination and a good feeling for what makes an appropriate and effective presentation. By no means would she expect anyone to agree with all she says. On occasion her aim is to be provocative and to encourage thoughtful reaction.

"Vi has a good understanding of the ministry and has many ideas worth paying attention to. We are all indebted to her for helping us make the transition from Fellowship to Church."

Our church treasurer, a professor of chemistry, wrote, "Your departure from Tallahassee has for me an ambivalent aspect. I feel that the decision for you to leave was correct. This does not imply failure on your part, but instead, it reflects the stresses and strains that must be anticipated in the type of church that we have. At the same time I regret the fact of your leaving. You have made obvious and valuable contributions here. That we have the interest of significant numbers of young people is evident to all, and may prove to be difficult to maintain. But perhaps more important and less obvious—your personality, expressed in the unique context of the ministry, has made a lasting and beneficial impact upon me, and I suspect upon most others with whom you have had contact. As you enter this new phase of your life, you carry the warm regards of Dorothy and myself and our wishes for your happiness."

And finally, Lucy Johnson, bless her, after describing once again my success with our youth, seemed to have clearly sensed a part of me I liked to have remembered. "She seemed to me all that the minister of a liberal church should be—a mind well stored with knowledge of world religions and human problems, together with love of the poetical and emotional aspects, which to an individual may be more important than understanding."

I delivered my last sermon on Sunday, June 7, 1970, and attended a farewell picnic at the president's cottage on the Gulf.

I had planned to drive to New England up the East Coast, since I had not seen most of it, until a good friend suggested I visit her friend in Charleston, South Carolina. This friend, who lived in a huge white house with a columned entrance in the historic Battery section, was an unforgettable privilege to meet. Over tea on a back veranda, I learned she had studied at Wood's Hole and became the first biology teacher in the State of West Virginia back in 1904. When I showed an interest in a stack of *The Suffragist* magazine dated 1918, I left with a copy as a souvenir.

In Boston, I left my car with a Red Cross friend in Marblehead and flew to General Assembly in Seattle on a charter flight, which was chummy and fun. I found there was a much longer list of ministers seeking churches than there were openings. Even so, it was a fun time. And because Starr Kingers had rebelled at the cost of drinks the previous year, they'd arranged to rent a large excursion-type boat that handled 150 people. On a perfectly beautiful evening we cruised around Lake Union and Lake Washington from 6:30 to 11:30. We arranged for our own food and drink and got two jiggers for a dollar, had roast beef, French bread, green salad, red wine, all for five dollars!

I returned to Townshend, Vermont, to visit another Red Cross friend. After a week I was joined by a Minnesota friend for a trip to Nova Scotia, returning to find mail and messages. Pennsylvania State College had called twice, and I had an invitation to stop by.

I did stop there on my way west. With the university setting, the many professors in the group, it warmly reminded me of Tallahassee. At one evening meeting I was going on and on about the single tax economist Henry George from my Calgary experience, only to find out later I had been talking with a professor of economics who happened to be president of the group there. This explained a kind of twinkle in his eye and a bit of a smile. It made me realize that (at least in the Unitarian groups I'd been part of) no matter what one talks about, there's bound to be some specialist there who knows a lot more about it! Still, I like my role of generalist! It was in State College I found for sure that there was a long list of ministers looking for churches—the beginning of much white-collar unemployment.

I was also asked to pre-candidate at Beverly/Chicago, where my Starr King friend Hunter had been minister. But just thinking of living around Chicago was not for me and I turned that one down. I was looking forward to the summer at home, where I could unload my crammed Kharmann Ghia, relax, and wonder about my next stomping ground. I might mention here that Tallahassee was to survive without a minister for the next ten years.

My Last Church

I mentioned going home, forgetting for that moment that since mother's death there was no "home." As I visited Winona and stood before 318 East Fifth Street, the roots were still there; and I cried out to myself, "Why did they change that side entrance I designed! . . . It's meant to be a white brick house, not gray!"

Later, I felt fortunate to have had those roots throughout my early life, as I thought of the itinerant children of today. I found a new home base in Duluth, Minnesota, where I had a sister and her family. This was the beginning of the seventies, and I spent the next several months there. This was a new experience for me—to be a part of the beginning of unemployment for professionals as well as working people.

George Spencer wrote from Boston, "There's no substantive improvement in the situation. The number of churches seeking ministers remains dangerously low, and the number of ministers without work and looking for a church is terribly high. It's a nervous year, especially with large graduating classes of theological students this spring. But we shall continue to do the best we can."

The UUA had unanimously passed the Resolution on Equal Employment Opportunities for Women at the 1970 General Assembly. For fun, I sent a letter to UUA President Bob West, a Starr King compadre, and suggested we place an ad in *The UU World*, "Does your congregation need a token woman to make you an honest group? You can get one cheaper!" I told him I wasn't looking for special consideration, or wished to undercut ministers' salaries, but did share feelings that I'd been called by congregations because I was the best they could get for the salary they were offering. His chatty reply suggested that were we to put the ad in *The UU World*, we would indeed get some interesting responses and that, although many congregations continued to have their prejudices, the Association surely would do what they could to help. He closed, "Please do not give up the fight, for we need you!"

I wasn't exactly unemployed. The Duluth church had had a difficult separation with their minister and decided not to replace him that year. In the fall, after I'd done three services for them, they felt they should take advantage of my being there. At the January annual meeting I was called as a half-time minister/consultant for the last half of the 1970-71 church year ending in June.

I also had a commitment with the Virginia, Minnesota, Fellowship for one Sunday a month, and the Fargo-Moorhead Fellowship asked me to come as a consultant for two Sundays and the week in between. A Duluth group, in starting a world affairs council, was interested in my becoming their executive director, but I decided I wanted to stay with the ministry.

That feeling was reinforced by a long letter from young Bob McCandless of my Calgary days. He wrote on return from his "hippie drop-out" trip around the world. Bob had tried the drug route, lived in a kibbutz in Israel, and found it all wanting. In returning to Canada he made up with his family, and said, speaking of the Calgary church, "The seeds you planted here are beginning to sprout. We've finally bought a building and have a home of our own." Later, when he learned I was without a church, he sent a card that actually labeled me as a pioneer. "Congratulations! Hope you're a bum for a while and love it. Doesn't take much money to live cheap—but it takes guts. What is a minister anyway? Just a human, but a bit of a pioneer I hope. I don't wish you contentment and security. Rather hassle, expansion, internal revolution, rebirth even. Life's too short to be even in a minister rut."

Early that summer I'd received a letter of interest from the search committee at the church in Kent, Ohio. With the help of the UUA Department of Ministry, I'd been asked to pre-candidate by groups in Tempe, Arizona, and West Hills in Portland, Oregon. I told Kent that if neither of these came through I'd get in touch with them.

I couldn't have planned a more rewarding summer vacation to old stomping grounds. Tempe let me change my return plane reservation to stop over in Santa Fe where I had spent eight wonderful years, and I returned to Minnesota just in time to leave for the Portland, Oregon, of my Reed College days. I wasn't called at either church. The chairman of one committee said in his letter, "Our job had been made especially difficult because we had so many good candidates to choose from."

While I was working with the church in Duluth, and not facing the possibility of working in other fields, the idea of having no degrees began to take on importance. I discovered that some institutions had begun to offer credit for experience in meeting entrance requirements. I mentioned this in a letter to Starr King and learned from Bob Kimball, who had become president, that they had indeed changed the rules in awarding the graduate degree to some persons who had not held an undergraduate degree.

His letter continued, "I am not certain where this leaves the school on the matter of a retroactive degree to a person who graduated more than ten years ago; but the faculty recommends degrees to the board of trustees; and we might pursue the matter." I did, enclosing a three-page, single-spaced letter of my background and experience, together with my arguments supporting my claim to a degree.

On March 24, 1971, I received the following letter, "Dear Vi, At the meeting of the board of trustees on March 14, the board accepted a recommendation from the faculty and voted to award you the Bachelor of Divinity degree from Starr King School for the Ministry to replace the Certificate of Completion awarded you in 1963.

"Our changes in protocol here seemed to make this a fair thing to do. If the law schools can give JD degrees to people who formerly had LBs, we felt the change in nomenclature was appropriate. When we have diplomas printed up (which will probably not be until fall) I will mail your diploma. In the meantime, the action is official and you are now an honored Starr King BD. Warmest congratulations!"

The degree was later changed to MDiv (Master of Divinity). The diploma did indeed come as Bob had said, without my reminding them. Ten days later, a second diploma arrived with a letter explaining that the engraver realized it said "completed his" on the first one; so he had made another one for me. I tell everyone now that I have two master's degrees, a "his" and a "hers."

I wrote Bob to express my gratitude to the board, saying it was good to know that the spirit of Starr King still reigned— that Unitarian Universalists could rise above legalism and choose the values where they lay! I had the same feeling I'd had ten years earlier when the director of the Department of Ministry had said that even though I had no degree, he felt the Fellowship Committee would accept me on an equivalency basis.

Because I was involved in the Duluth area, I had not written the Kent Committee. In September, just as I was talking with the Virginia Fellowship about an ongoing commitment,

I heard from Kent. Paul Cox, chairman of the Kent Committee, wrote me to describe their group of just under a hundred talented members who met in an historic old building. When I read that half of the membership was affiliated with Kent State University, I felt right at home to begin with!

Cox felt the Kent church had great potential and needed a "minister who can help us focus our efforts, use our talents, and give corporate expression to our mutual attitudes of openness, experiment, and willingness to accept challenge." It sounded great!

I answered, saying how impressed I was with their talents in music, art, and drama, and the extent to which their building was used by other groups. I liked what I saw in enclosed copies of sermons, orders of service, newsletters, and such. It mentioned an agreement to share me with the fellowship in nearby Canton one Sunday each month as part of their outreach program.

I agreed to pre-candidate for the committee at the Akron church on October third, with the sermon topic "The Triumph of Triviality—What the Church Can Still Do Best." Gordon McKeeman, the Akron minister, was quietly helpful behind the scene. I was asked to candidate.

Because of my Minnesota commitments, we set the candidating dates for the week of November 14 to 21. Paul Cox responded with the schedule for the week. I always enjoyed meeting a potential new church family at lunches, dinners, and neighborhood groups while candidating.

As they mentioned their history, I was surprised to learn that I was to be the third woman minister of the Kent church. Mrs. Abbie Danforth served from 1889 to 1891 and 1898 to 1900, Mrs. Carlotta Crosley from 1903 to 1916. Marge Fessenden, a charter member of the church, was the first baby to be born in Kent. She told glowing stories of growing up in the church, and said young people loved Mrs. Crosley. "At parties we didn't have pot to smoke, but we did have snuff to sniff!"

I was called. There were several congratulatory letters from my former church members and compadres. Especially pleasing was a letter from Bill Schulz, who had just spent a year and a half as student minister at the Kent church. His letter came from Chicago where he was continuing at Meadville/Lombard Theological School. He wrote, "I can only hope that you have as personally rewarding a sojourn with the people of the Kent Church as I did over my year and a half with them. I found them to be as exciting, open, and flexible a group as I have found anywhere, with a real appreciation for life's most touching moments."

On his way home to Pittsburgh, Schulz usually passed through Kent and suggested we meet. He came in January and we had lunch together. From stories, and copies of his sermons, I'd been intrigued with his imaginative approach at Kent. He shared helpful information about special persons in the congregation, and we smiled at a picture he shared of his robed self in action behind the rostrum of that old building he said he'd come to love. Little did either of us dream then that one day he would be president of the Unitarian Universalist Association!

As Paul Cox had said, the building was old but practical. The original church building at Kent, dedicated in 1838, had been traditional in design. Sixty years later its interior was completely rearranged with the sanctuary lengthwise across the back half, so as to provide office space and rooms for a church school. Along the way, pews had been replaced by blocks of opera seats. In trying to form a circle, they came out a long diamond with the pulpit at one apex.

The room used for coffee hour was in the center—small, windowless, dungeon-like, two stories high with balconies around three sides of the second floor. With fixtures two stories up, the only daytime light came from two tiny lamps on low tables.

The interior decorator in me rebelled, and we made *The*

UU World with a picture of its redecoration. Ceiling lights were lowered with two huge Japanese lanterns, the walls were painted white and papered high on one whole end with Wayside Pulpits—framed blocks of white with outstanding sayings in bold black letters. An innovative hanging of bright red carpeting accented another wall.

We established the Joy Committee (named after the member who was a compadre in the project) to approve any further aesthetic changes. This project was just the beginning of refurbishing the entire church, which was all ready for my fourth Installation in April.

Mine was a Kochendoerfer ceremony. Ministers are usually given the privilege of selecting their Installation speaker and visiting ministerial friends to give the Charge to the Congregation and Charge to the Minister, and the church then covers expenses for their travel and accommodations. I decided this wasn't necessary. With the thought of saving the church money, I chose three church members, each from Kent and Canton, to say what they expected of me and three to share what they hoped to do for me.

At the service, after Paul Cox's opening words, the Rev. Bill Jacobs of the Kent State Campus Clergy welcomed me to Kent and the Kent State community. Then the president of the Kent congregation said, "What I want to contribute— and I hope it will speak for you—is to allow Vi to be a complete person, to allow her to be genuine and human. I want to be able to share her abilities and her mistakes, her dreams and her disappointments, her thrills and her doubts. I want to be a caring friend when Vi is impatient and frustrated, as well as enjoying her good times and her laughter. I will try to be open and receptive to all that Vi is."

"Hale," an officer of the Canton Fellowship, encompassed briefly what responsibility he felt members should feel toward me, "a willingness to cooperate, an interest in the projects that you present, constructive criticism and friendship, with open mindedness and creative ideas . . . a growing together with you in the appreciation of others, in freedom from fear, and in a love for life."

The service was even more memorable for the outstanding presentations of our choir. Asked for my favorite poem, I chose "Disiderata," which a composer in the choir had set to music. On my living room wall today is a lovely framed rendition of the poem they gave me at the reception.

∾

I began my Kent Sundays with two services of the written exam I'd first tried so successfully in Canada, entitled "Ever on Sunday I & II." Once again I was surprised at the great, succinct answers they shared on big areas like "religion," and "worship." I also continued my practice of exploring the world's religions each year, which members seemed to appreciate. I started with sharing thoughts from Edmond Taylor's *Richer by Asia*, taken with his premise that there can be no understanding toward world government without a melding of Eastern philosophies and the learning of the West. This brought a sermon, "The Classic American," which shared the earthly wisdoms from the Native American, whom I'd come to know more closely in Canada.

To continue speaking for the often misunderstood, on Mother's Day, women loved my sermon on "The Suffering Servant," and especially appreciated my "Fall of Man and Rise of Women," which even the men approved of! Each service was enhanced by our superb choir, sometimes performing selections especially written by one of the members.

My contract included conducting two monthly Sunday services at Kent and one at Canton, with the fourth Sunday off. It was less than an hour's drive to Canton, where, in addition to the Sunday service, I spent an extra day in counseling and working with committees and youth. The services there were held at the YMCA, and I had a lovely office at the home of a parishioner with whom I stayed. Joyce Geler was one of our special contacts there, and I was to marry a son and daughter of that family.

∽

A highlight of my four ministries as a modern pioneer was my acceptance by the ministers of other denominations. My ministry in Kent put the frosting on that cake!

Bill Jacobs of the United Christian Ministries on the Kent State Campus was a good friend of the congregation. That is why I had invited him to welcome me to the campus at my Installation. And I imagine it was Bill who put me on the mailing list of the Kent Ministerial Association. I was pleased not to have to take the initiative, for I had found in church files a newspaper clipping with the headline, "Minister Charges New Council, Creed Eliminates His Church."

The former Kent minister Peter Richardson had said, "We cannot, of course, require a creedal affirmation from members." The clipping said that the Protestant and Roman Catholic bodies represented on the Council insisted that the following sentence in the preamble of their constitution be a condition of membership: "In the Providence of God, the churches of the Kent, Ohio, area desire to witness their oneness in Jesus Christ as their Divine Lord and Savior."

At any rate, I decided to accept the invitation of the Association, and it turned out to be a heartwarming experience during my years there. It didn't take long to find that I was not only their first woman member, but also, for some, in their friendly acceptance, (and because of the absence of their theology in our church) their token atheist!

At their request, I led a celebration for women at a meeting of the clergy of Northeast Ohio, which attracted over sixty ministers. The service was partially adapted from a celebration by the Presbyterian Task Force on Women, whose reports I found impressive on paper, though not yet in practice.

After a call to worship, we sang a song of sisterhood entitled "One Woman's Hands" (adapted from a Pete Seeger song) followed by a prayer of confession in unison, which had a Christian opening and closing, but did say, "We relegate our women to the Martha role, and rob ourselves of their sensitive counsel." Some men said later that this was the first time they had heard a woman in the pulpit!

That spring all Kent clergy had an invitation from Glenn Olds, president of Kent State, for a Sunday afternoon coffee so we could meet his longtime friend Olga Whorrel, a spiritualist healer. Although I knew Olds had been formerly a Christian minister, my first reaction was, "Why does Glenn want to even admit that he knows someone like her?" That said more about me than of Glenn and proved to become a lesson I've not forgotten.

Olga was a delightful, old-fashioned, bosomy woman in a black satin dress. Her speciality was a "laying on of hands." She felt she was "a pipeline for God"—that the healing came not from her, but through her, and said persons described feeling the warmth from her hands. She told a delightful tale of an invitation to meet with skeptical scientists, who asked her to "do her thing." Then, when it seemed to work, they wanted her to do it again to make it scientific!

I later bragged about having met Olga because both she and her husband were well-known people. In a roundabout way it made me rethink my sometime feelings of superiority to other organized religions. This feeling was expressed at a luncheon meeting at a Presbyterian church when a member said to me, "This is the best ministerial association I've ever belonged to!" I could agree with him, for I was not only accepted by the Kent ministers, I felt privileged in their special appreciation of my pioneering womanly role.

After Tallahassee, where the congregation was made up largely of Florida State and Florida A&M professors, Kent was like coming home. In addition to professors from widespread disciplines on every board and committee, the chair of our religious education program was a nationally known specialist in junior high education.

It always feels good to be singled out in a positive way. I had this chance at Kent State not only as a woman, but also as a Unitarian Universalist minister. A professor in women's studies asked me to explain Unitarian Universalism to her class. I was especially pleased when I learned this was at the request of students who were impressed by the fact of my being a woman in the ministry. I said in part, "In our denomination of Unitarian Universalism, our basic premise is in individual freedom of belief and interpretation, which can then change with the times. Though we recognize the Judeo/Christian as the heritage which defines and gives meaning to our lives, we also value teachings of all the world religions, as well as meaning we find through our own experience and learning in our secular world.

"So, to avoid confusion, in what I say this morning, I will be thinking of religion in a somewhat different way from the traditional concept. For me it's what one *is* which defines [his] religion, rather than a set of beliefs. Beliefs strongly held, will, of course, have much to do with what we are; but I feel we should be consciously aware of how our stated beliefs square with the way in which we live our life.

"I think of a definition of Ralph Waldo Emerson, who was himself a Unitarian minister. 'Religion in the mind is not credulity, and in the practice is not form. It is a life! It is the order and soundness of a man. It is not something else to be got—to be added—but is a new life of those faculties which we have. It is to do right. It is to love. It is to serve. It is to think. . . . It is to be humble.'"

Another time I was speaker for Bill Jacob's experimental college class on "The Many Faces of Religion," where a different religion was considered each week. It was always a challenge to introduce Unitarian Universalism to people who had never heard of us. Of the fifteen students, three were avid questioners who even stayed after class. When I said "I hope I didn't shock anyone," one answered, "I'm sure you did, but that's what this course is all about. Don't worry. Next week we have the Latter Day Saints!"

That fall I started on the faculty of the experimental college at Kent State. These were pass/fail credit courses, and students could choose one each quarter. It all started when I first attended meetings of the Campus Clergy. A young Lutheran had also just come to Kent and was at the same meeting. George Gaiser was loud and brash, and I was unimpressed.

Don Shilling, president of Campus Clergy, was a Methodist and had just agreed to open a course on death and society. When more than forty students signed up, he told me he didn't know what to do with that many students. I had completed two sermons on death and offered to help. George also called him, and Don suggested that we all get together to see how we could work it out.

That was the beginning of five years of a heart-warming and eye-opening experience for me. I came to love these two men. In my book they were "liberals" in the best sense of the word—in that we have a right to our own beliefs, and allow that same right to others. In long sessions with Don and George after classes, I found I could almost accept their theology as they shared it. I wondered sometimes whether, in their denominational premises, they didn't have more to offer on the search for ultimate meanings than we did as Unitarian Universalists with our wide-open "individual freedom of belief."

In our class, as we considered the care of a dying person, many nursing students shared actual experiences, mentioning that often terminal youngsters seemed to have a mature "knowing" of impending death—even offering adults strength in the process.

We invited local professionals to help in our discussion of the doctor, fatal illness and the family, and preplanning. A class on the care of the dead involved field trips to a cemetery, crematorium, and funeral home. We also spent time on grief and discussed traditional funeral practices.

All three of us felt deeply rewarded when Roy Nichols, our grief specialist, said one day, "I've heard what I feel is a tremendous compliment to you three. One student said to me, 'They call this course "Death and Society," but I'm learning more about life than I have in my whole nineteen years of living.'"

The Kent Ministerial Association asked the three of us to sponsor an all-day session for area ministers on the subject of death. It attracted over a hundred clergy of all denominations. In my group I started by suggesting that death isn't easy to talk about in our society—that the three things we have in common as human beings, sex, the bathroom, and death, are the very things we can't talk about without using euphemisms. I quoted Shakespeare, when he said, "We owe God a Death. Death is a tax the soul must pay for having had a form and a name." This suggested statistics that one in one dies; and yet it is impossible to conceive of ourselves as not being, "Like the man who said to his wife, 'When one of us dies, I think I'll move to Chicago.'"

This conference followed an appearance of Elizabeth Kubler-Ross at Kent State, for which the auditorium was packed to overflowing. Kubler-Ross was a pioneer in the death scene with her famous five steps—denial, rage, anger, depression, and acceptance. In a workshop with her that helped me to face the actual concept of death, I listened to an attractive woman who had had a recurrence of cancer and decided against further chemotherapy and a woman who had been diagnosed as terminal, but had decided she would live to see her daughter graduate from college several months ahead.

Don, George, and I led the Death and Society class for five years. Although Don has moved on and up in the Methodist hierarchy, George continues what we three started at Kent, so each year I get an update.

In a file I've kept, there's a letter from a young man whose fiance was killed in an auto accident. He discovered that she had been in our course and had written some papers for me, which he asked me to share with him. This led to long-term counseling by mail.

I kept another letter from one of my students that I felt significant enough to send on to the college paper *The Stater:* "Musings on Taylor Hill—Today I was sitting on Taylor Hill and thought to myself, 'What is life? What is death? What do they really mean to me?' I sat there for some time contemplating, and to tell the truth the roar of the 'cat' and the other implements of destruction and construction were so loud I could hardly think.

"Finally I felt, 'Hey, you're alive!' What a joy I felt! I thought of all the times I'd been unhappy about some irrelevant thing, like a class schedule or dormitories—things that are secondary to the greatest joy anyone can hope to ever experience— life itself!

"Then I thought about what had happened here on the hill just a few years ago. What was this thing called 'death?' Death means a lot of things to different people. Some fear death, others romanticize it; but this is avoiding the issue itself. Finally I said to myself, 'Death was here!' Regardless of all I've written, I'm glad the gym will finally be built here. Death is not something to be memorialized, but neither is it to be forgotten."

He was speaking, of course, of the happenings that forever put Kent State on the map of people's minds. It began on Thursday, April 30, 1970, when President Nixon announced over national TV the invasion of Cambodia to drive out North Vietnamese forces. Rallies began in downtown Kent and on campus the next day. At this time the mayor of Kent declared a State of Civil Emergency, requesting the National Guard to be put on alert and the city put on curfew.

That evening, a rally on campus against the Cambodian invasion attracted over 500 students. An American flag was burned, which led to the burning down of the ROTC building. This brought in the National Guard, who used tear gas and bayonets to disperse the crowd.

The next day, students mingled with guardsmen on campus. Armoured personnel carriers, jeeps, trucks, and armed troops were stationed on every street corner in town and patrolling the entire campus when the governor of Ohio arrived. After touring the campus, in a press conference he spoke of students as nightriders and vigilantes, worse than Brownshirts and Communists and threatened to eradicate the problem. He told university authorities to keep out of the situation, and said he'd put two guardsmen in every classroom to keep the university open if necessary. He threatened to declare martial law, but didn't. After a sit-in, when students were told that university, city, and National Guard officials would meet with them, they were once again tear-gassed, chased, and bayonetted. Fifty-one students were arrested as they neared the campus for the meeting.

On Monday, May 4, 1970, classes went on as usual with many of the students who had been away over the weekend unaware of what had happened. At noon, two thousand students gathered at the victory bell on the Commons to protest not only the Cambodian invasion, but the National Guard invasion of the Kent State campus. Several thousand other students were spectators. The National Guard commanded the group to disperse, but they wouldn't. Amid tear gas and milling students, who thought this was a victorious showdown because the guardsmen were beginning to retreat, a single shot was fired. Two more shots, then a volley exploded, cutting down thirteen students, killing four and wounding nine others.

Bill Schulz was then minister of the Kent church. That Friday, the Unitarian Universalist Church of Kent held a symbolic memorial service for the four slain Kent State students in protest of the mayor's refusal to either grant or deny the church permission to hold such a service. In a statement to the press, Schulz said, "Actions and decisions of Mayor Roy Satrom during the last few days have in my judgment seriously impaired the principle of church-state separation, and endangered, if not ignored, the constitutional guarantee of free religious assembly for the purpose of worship. . . . The citizens of Kent, Ohio, must not be denied their constitutional rights of religious assembly—particularly at a time when hundreds have need of such community."

The shootings at Kent and massive student strikes caused many colleges and universities to close. Kent State closed for the remainder of that spring quarter. Sixty days later troops were withdrawn from Cambodia.

Every May 4 for years thereafter, classes at Kent were canceled to commemorate what had happened. Speakers included Dr. George Wald, Julian Bond, Jane Fonda, and Judy Collins. There were candlelight parades and all night vigils at the cordoned squares where the four students were killed.

∽

My arrival on campus two years after the Kent State massacre was historic in a different way. Because I was on the faculty, I was included in a Russian winter festival and seminar sponsored by the Study of Socialist Education at Kent State with Ford Foundation money. University president Glenn Olds and his wife led two planeloads of students, faculty, and staff to Russia over the Christmas holidays, where we participated in the colorful 50th anniversary of the USSR.

I returned with enthusiastic feelings about Russia. We had spent a whole day at the University of Moscow, as well as a day in schools where second graders were writing English script. In the seventh grade we each had a student to talk to because they could speak English. From talking with Russians, I felt their sense of pride in a country with clean streets and shiny, clean marble subways. I thought of all this on the plane home as I read a London newspaper. I did a double-take when I read the lead article of the "This Is a America" section. Entitled "Where Murder is a Way of Life," it described Detroit with 692 homocides for the year!

The next year was 1973—Watergate summer. I was on a trip to Ireland, but did see Nixon resigning as I sat watching a live broadcast on Irish TV at 2 A.M. As I looked back at that history-making episode at Kent State and the Watergate summer, I realized I'd been ministering during years of historical events we would commemorate in years to come.

In each of these history-making situations I felt a pioneer, and was pleased to be used once again that same year to make the feminine point in another field. A new member of our congregation had moved to Kent to become a professor of pharmacology in the new School of Medicine at Northeastern Ohio University. As an experimental college, they needed a human subject experiments review committee; and "Ed" delighted in appointing a woman minister to join the other doctors and lawyers.

I was fortunate in having a creative congregation who were eager and active. It was important to me to communicate regularly with all my members, and I felt the newsletter (which we named *The Gougler Gazette* for our address on Gougler Street) was a good way to do just that.

I kept discovering more and more things about our

church—historic and otherwise. In March of 1976, in celebration of our bicentennial, we attached a bronze plaque that made us an historic building.

The *Kent Record Courier* let us share this history with the whole community by asking me for an article. They featured us with the headline, "Meet the Unitarian Universalists—It is One of the Oldest Churches." I began the full-page article by setting forth our entire history on the continent and in the States, and went on, "The Unitarian Universalist Church on Gougler Street, just opposite Brady Leap Park, was founded as the First Universalist Church of Kent in 1866. Old residents recall how large a part the church played in the early religious and social life of our city.

"It is of interest to know that John R. Buchtel, founder of Buchtel College (now the University of Akron) was a member of the church in 1870. Included in projected Bicentennial plans is a reenactment of the historic Election Day Dinners in November, commemorating a practice that for years brought many of the voters of Portage County to the church next door to the old City Hall." This article led to our reinstituting the election-day dinners, which turned out to be a popular annual affair in the Kent community.

We also made *The UU World* with the headline, "For Kent Unitarian Universalists: Tapestry is the Tie That Binds," featuring a picture of the colorful hanging we had dedicated one Easter Sunday. Families were allowed a one-foot square of burlap to design and embroider in commemoration or expression of their feelings of liberal religion. The colorful result was huge and heavy. One night about midnight the phone rang in my apartment. Bill Jacob said, "Vi, I'm here alone hanging the tapestry. Want to come help?" I grabbed two cans of cold beer from the refrigerator and dashed to the church for the special hanging! This added the finishing touch to the tremendous paint job of the sanctuary that we had done ourselves. At the service, we celebrated with an original song composed for the day.

This was the second church I served with a preponderance of university people, which may have colored my judgments of the ministry. It demanded quality, challenging sermons requiring wide reading and cogent presentation. Nevertheless, I felt fortunate to have a congregation who could articulate their views and provide such lively discussions. It also gave me an opportunity to verify feelings I'd had about teachers.

I had always questioned the merits of tenure, and admired one member (who I understand was an outstanding teacher) who did not receive tenure because he refused to publish. It was my opinion that publishing might be a valid requirement for research professors, but had little to do with making a good teacher.

The church did not have a professor in the finance and business area, and though professors seemed to be forever fighting for salary increases, when it came to the minister's salary, it was something else again, even though I felt I was on their professional level. I then learned that salaries for women on college faculties were lower than those of men.

I had started at Kent in 1972 with a package of $10,000. With deductions for parsonage, travel, etc., I was left with a cash salary total of $3,750! When I brought my need for a raise to their attention, my package was increased to $12,000 a year before I left in 1977.

Though I never made a crusade of it, I regularly reminded boards that especially as a woman I had to uphold ministers' salary standards. Even though I was aware that women still seemed doomed to work for less than men, I didn't want Unitarian Universalist ministers to feel I was ignoring the schedules they had set for themselves.

During my third year at Kent, I wrote home about an episode I'm proud to list among my many "firsts" as a woman minister: "Last Sunday I had quite an experience. St. Patrick's (our big Catholic Church in the next block from my apartment) was having visiting ministers for Octave Sunday. At the

Kent Ministerial Association meeting one of the young priests asked if I'd take a service. I'm not sure John knew what he was doing in asking a woman to do the homily, but he suggested the big 9:30 A.M. guitar mass.

"I dashed over fifteen minutes early. In meeting the moderator of the congregation, I said, 'I'll bet this is a first for St. Pats!' He smiled and said, 'Yes, Rev. Kochendoerfer, that's true; and I'll just bet Sister Celia will be asking for equal time.' I smiled, for I know she drives around with a bumper sticker that says, 'PRAY TO GOD. SHE WILL HELP YOU!' The sisters here are nothing like those I remember in Winona. They don't wear habits; and in visiting in their dorm, I noticed they're reading many of the books we read.

"John gave me all the instructions of how we'd process behind the altar boys to the back and up the center aisle. Just as we started processing, he turned and said, 'Vi, I'd like to give you communion.' I drew a deep breath and wished we'd had time for a long Unitarian discussion. But there I was on my way, knowing I was to receive Holy Communion in front of the whole congregation.

"In the service I quoted Father Greeley from an article in *Time* magazine about what Jesus would think if he were to come back today, and also shared Cardinal Cushing's words at a Methodist church back when I was in Provincetown. He'd said, 'People try to be ecumenical and come in wanting a Catholic priest with a rabbi and a Protestant minister to come together to plant a tree on Boston Common. For the Lord's sake, why can't they get three children and go plant their tree!'

"As Communion started, I was first. John came toward me, the Host in his extended hand. Without thinking, I reached out, took it from him, and put it on my tongue. Then, as I watched, I was aghast as I realized the Pope had not as yet given them dispensation to put the Host wafer in their own mouth! I had to hurry off immediately to do our Unitarian Universalist service.

"I called John on Monday morning, 'I hope I didn't get you into any trouble. . . .' He replied, 'Not at all, Vi. They liked you. And I was going to call you. Father B. is to be in California this week. Ernie's cooking dinner Friday. Please join us at six.'

"There were five of us single souls—Ernie and John and I, and two young campus clergy, one from the University of Chicago and one from Princeton. We had drinks before the big roast beef dinner. During after-dinner drinks someone said, 'Let's go to a movie.' We walked in for free because there were Catholic ticket takers."

Sometime later I got a note from John, sending a picture he'd taken of "our great get together," and saying how good it was to be able to look back on such happy memories, as we look forward to new experiences. He closed with, "Peace and love."

Our whole congregation became part of the St. Pat family. They invited our choir to sing at one of their masses, and entertained us all one evening as a thank you. I thought of my warm close association with the two young priests. Since Kent had only a visiting rabbi from Cleveland, they more or less took the place of Rabbi Garfein in Tallahassee. I shared this good feeling in a letter to Stan Garfein, which brought forth the bonus of a long update on my former congregation.

In the same mail was a letter from a former Kent member who had moved to California. The writer asked me to share her letter with the congregation and I did in the March 27, 1977, issue of *The Gazette.* "I've been thinking a lot about the Unitarian Universalist church and its effect on my life, where I experienced more growth and more education than I think I ever had before. Each of us were teachers, I think, of each other. Those years were the seed of my life, the tiny spark of light that will burn within me throughout this life. Many of us have gone separate ways now, but to those who remain I want to say, 'Thank you again!' There are never days that pass when I do not recall those experiences and share them with someone new in my life."

In a sermon, "The Fall of Man," I shared thoughts of Florida Scott-Maxwell from her book *Women & Sometimes Men*. I began by mentioning that each of us has masculine and feminine qualities and that significant men and woman were those who found a good balance. She commented on our society's need to label women "the weaker sex," when actually they could be wise and strong, while using their creative powers of love, care, and concern. She felt it could greatly help in the healing of our ailing society if men could balance their manhood with feminine qualities.

I then went on to caution women that with the equality we would now demand, we must exercise the wisdom that we have and avoid demanding powers that betray that wisdom. Always wary of women who go around with a chip on their shoulder looking for something to be unhappy about, I do believe that women will need to use their valor and wisdom to set balanced examples of masculine/feminine relationships for our next generation. I now find it intriguing that some Unitarian Universalist churches are once again forming special groups for men.

At another level, I realized that in our scholarly discussions we often ended up bashing "big business." I felt the need to explore this concept further and spent an evening with our two Bills—Bill Eldredge and Bill Meade—the only businessmen in our congregation. Bill Eldredge had the responsibility of deciding where his firm would establish outlets worldwide. Bill Meade's firm was highly involved with a mix of government and business. After an open, mind-expanding discussion that evening, I thanked them for giving me a new and larger perspective to share with our congregation.

Not too much later, Bill Meade took a position with his company in Kuwait. In sharing letters from the Meades and their children, I decided it was important for us all to better understand Islam—the fastest growing religion in the world, and one Unitarian Universalists could relate to and even emulate. I prepared two sermons that I have since been asked many times to share as a visiting speaker—"Islam, the Misunderstood Religion" and "Understanding the Muslim Mind."

I pointed out that Muslim scholars gave us foundations for the modern world in chemistry, architecture, astronomy, and literature. Then I suggested the mind-blowing idea that without their having given us the concept of the zero, we would not have known our computer world, which is based on the concept of zero/one.

Their holy book, The Koran, shares our own basic principle: Let there be no compulsion in religion and unto you, your religion, and unto me, my religion. They have much the same commandments for daily living as our Christian Bible. Yet, in our failure to live up to them, we are often critical in their doing just that. I shared the five pillars of Islam, and said in my sermon, "I thought of our fraud, usury and slander, alcoholism, drug culture, and mental illness, and our resulting payment of millions for more drugs, therapy, and self-help groups, searching to find quiet, direction, and meaning in our lives.

"Then I smiled to myself as I contemplated what might happen if, indeed, we all were disciplined to stop in the tracks of our individual rat races—five times each day—all together—on streets and freeways—at home, in factories, offices, and schools—to ask ourselves, as individuals and as a nation, What are we doing and where are we going, and why? Today, tomorrow, in our lifetimes and those of our children?"

In the opening of the service I used a tape the Meades had sent from Kuwait, which included that haunting minaret call to prayer. In the church newsletter, I shared letters from them with our members, especially our children who knew their boys Brian and Chris. The idea of starting with our children to learn about the larger world gave me an idea. In my column "Vi's Children's Corner" in *The Gazette*, I suggested they start exchanging letters with Brian and Chris and that they ask their folks to get a world map to hang by the kitchen table. Then, when places like Kuwait and other countries were in the news, they could be looked up and talked about.

I also gave the children a summer assignment. They were to find a little notebook and at the top of each of four different pages, write one of these things: good things that happened to us, things we did to make this a better world to live in, things we'd like to do in our church school next year, and funny things that happened. They would then talk about these topics with their family, keeping notes to share with the church next fall.

So parents would have background to share with their children, I continued my practice of sharing world religions—this time with "A Look at the Bible," "The Heart of Judaism," "From Judaism to Christianity," "The New Testament in Perspective," and "Christianity and the Dead Sea Scrolls." Many Unitarian Universalists who had repudiated Christian upbringing seemed eager to learn more about what they had discarded, especially with new findings in the Dead Sea Scrolls. I thought of my New Testament professor at Starr King, who had said if you're going to throw something out, you should know what it is you're throwing!

I had often felt the same about being critical of other peoples and their countries, and felt rich in being given the privilege of discovering colorful Central America. One of my members was a professor of geography at Kent State. "Frank" and his department head had been there with the Peace Corps and loved it. Instead of teaching summer school at Kent State, they would dream up trips with students for credit work in art, city planning, and other such areas.

Frank talked me into joining them. Sharing weeks in Panama, Guatemala, and El Salvador with people who knew and loved the countries and their peoples in the days before all the uprisings was truly a rich religious experience. Looking back, it was an unforgettable part of the great privilege I felt in my years at Kent.

∾

Coming to Kent didn't cut off my ministry to members in Tallahassee, and I was always pleased when it was the young people who kept in touch. Jeanne Miller wrote often with an historic example of the idealistic journeys of some of our youth in America of the sixties.

In Tallahassee, when Jeanne found her husband Tom was not truly a conscientious objector, but was using this ruse to keep from being drafted, problems started. After a move to Denver, they were divorced. There Jeanne found a kindred soul in poet Jim Redford, and their story is a sixties documentary. In deference to their families, Jeanne and Jim married and accepted the invitation of a New Hampshire woman to use a cabin in the mountains to fulfill their wish to live off the land.

Jeanne wrote that December, "Snow's up to the windows, but it's warm and cozy inside. The camomile tea is steeping on the stove. If we don't get cabin fever this winter, we'll make it." She also included news of a child to be born in April. They had bought land in Kentucky where they would go after the birth of the baby, for "New England is no place to be poor in!"

In February, I received a letter written, as they always were, on the back of used paper, posted in a used envelope, with the return address Redford's Ark, Lenox, Kentucky. The letter said that since no doctors or midwives would come to the cabin in New Hampshire, Jeanne and Jim had decided to deliver the child themselves. When she learned this, their landlady said, "Either you have the child in a hospital, or you get out." So Jim dug their twenty-year-old truck out of four feet of snow, loaded their goat, chickens, and what furniture they could take and headed for the hills of Kentucky to live.

In April a postcard arrived, "Dear Vi, Three hours ago a daughter was born to us. We have christened her Rebecca. The night is deepening and Jeanne and Rebecca sleep peacefully at my side. Both are safe, warm and exhausted. Jeanne experienced no great pain, no tearing, no hemorrhaging. We did it all alone. Rejoice with us! Love, Jim."

Jeanne had wanted me to come, and when I wrote to ask when they would be there, she answered, "All summer—maybe the rest of our lives." Some weeks later I did drive south to Kentucky, and at the time of that first visit, the Ark was unbelievable in its rugged simplicity. I decided to share the experience with my congregation in Kent. One Sunday, I said in my preface to "The Story of Redford's Ark," "A. Powell Davies, a famed Unitarian minister, once said, 'And so the world falls apart, not through evil—deliberately chosen evil—but because people resist the temptation to be good.'

"I believe I'm speaking for many concerned persons when I say that inwardly we know that if we're to make it as a human race, we're all going to have to be willing to give up some of the comforts we now take for granted. Now and then our conscience nags us, . . . but we keep resisting the temptation of honestly facing the future . . . and honestly facing our own consciences. We struggle in a sea of semantic mishmash, where the vagaries of morality and immorality have replaced honest moral decisions, until it often seems that we live in an amoral world."

I told about receiving letters from the young couple, and how touched I was with Jim's letters of sheer poetry in sharing his deep appreciation of nature, and his family of Jeanne, Rebecca, and their animal friends. Then I said, "I've shared this experience not to shock you—not to recommend it as a way of life for anyone else—but perhaps as a touchstone, to remind us of the ecological and moral crisis now threatening human survival—perhaps to help each of us to assess, or maybe reassess how we wish to live the rest of our lives—or even, perhaps just appreciate the conveniences and comforts we so take for granted, and to wonder whether, indeed, we could give them up if necessary.

"Jeanne and Jim made their choice. They have a ten-year plan. Each day we make a choice. But have you wondered where you'll be and what you will be doing ten years from now? Let's think about this for the next two moments. Then, as anyone feels moved to speak, please share any feelings you had in listening to 'The Story of Redford's Ark.'"

Most of those joining in the sharing were appreciative and sympathetic, though two persons expressed hostility in sensing a judgment of their own way of life. A small group of Kent members, who identified with the young couple, became involved in selling some of Jeanne's weaving and were eager for any information I could bring them from The Ark. My next visit was possible on my way to Roanoke, Virginia, to minister to Mike McGee, another Tallahassee youth I'd joined in marriage—now a protégé of mine in the ministry.

Mike had called, "Since I'm supposed to decide about my ordination, what should I do?" I explained how many ministers take the opportunity to fly in important people for the occasion to do the sermon, Charge to the Minister, and Charge to the Congregation. Then I told him what we had done in Kent, which I felt not only saved the group money, but was far more meaningful. Mike decided to do just that, though he insisted that I come to do the ordination sermon.

It was a great day, and I loved especially the boy Mike had chosen to Charge the congregation. Jeff, a precocious seventh grader, stole the show! This is what he said, "Mike McGee is Mike McGee is Mike McGee. Mike is the same Mike whether he is talking to me or to my Dad, or Frosty [their president] or anyone else here. I like that! And it's real neat if you happen to be a kid like me. He doesn't make me feel like a little kid and him like a big man. He talks my language. He listens to me and never says, 'Run along kid, I'll get to you later.' Mike dresses neat. I like the way he smiles. Did he learn that at minister's school? I don't think so. He goes at everything he does with a smile.

"Mike is not a ho-hum person. I've never fallen asleep during one of his sermons, and I don't think anyone else has either. I'm supposed to say what the congregation will do for Mike. Well, Mike McGee is Mike McGee is Mike McGee! What we can best do, is to never ask him to be anything else!"

As I thought of Jeanne and Mike and the enthusiastically active and supportive youth groups in my Tallahassee and Calgary congregations, I was saddened in the realization that the healthy, open relationships between young men and women with adults were gone with the winds of war and societal change. The fact that we had no high school or college groups in the Kent church was reflected across the country. Our national LRY program seemed to fade as we faced rising problems with our youth. In contrast to past years, one could only wonder how and why we let all this happen.

I did wonder. In Kent sermons, I didn't have to talk about "trial marriage." It was now "open marriage," which I used as a sermon topic in speaking to the pros and cons as I wondered about the new sexual freedoms. To our UU credit, we in Kent helped pioneer discussion in this area, which is just now receiving national attention. We used the UUA program, *About Your Sexuality*, with our junior high students.

Because sex isn't easy to talk about even with Unitarian Universalists, we first had parents check out the program. I recall parents who expressed concerns about the "Same Sex" part. I also recall some of our ministers being threatened with legal actions when it was introduced in their community. This general public reaction reinforced what I felt deeply— that this is a bewildering world for our youth at a vulnerable age, with questionable adult examples. I felt that in indicting our youth, we indict ourselves.

I did support some of our youth's protesting lifestyles on Easter Sunday in a sermon entitled "Profile of a Dropout." I began, "Once upon a time, about two thousand years ago, there was a youth whose law-abiding parents took him to a religious celebration in Jerusalem. But on the way home at the early age of twelve, and without telling us why, this son of Mary and Joseph disappeared. We gather it was to do 'his thing,' but have no valid record until he was in his thirties. Then pictures we have of him show a young man with long hair and a beard, who wore sandals and wandered about sandy desert country where there was little water for daily showers. For his short ministry of love and caring among his people, he was martyred. Today we celebrate his life and his death."

In speaking of this dilemma for today's parents and youth in "Paradox of Parenting," I began, "We have been called a nation of child haters and abusers; at the very same time, we've become over-concerned about our children in what has been described as a child-centered society—where it seems we often try to be too good as parents, and in this process of over-concern may be 'using' our children in a way which isn't good either for them or for us."

Many Unitarian Universalist parents enrolled their kids in so many classes or activities that there must have been little time for the child's own leisure, or significant parental relationships. I spoke to parents, suggesting that if we no longer need the stimulus or support of the old reward-and-punishment religion—if we would brush aside anyone or anything to emulate—just what truths are there in what we verbalize, or the examples we set for our youth, in the loneliness of their growing-up quandaries? I later spoke to this in a presentation entitled "Antidote to Loneliness," suggesting that our church community can be a saving place for youth if they can feel safe to be known as significant, accepted persons among adults.

I followed these with a sermon entitled "Parents Are People Too," suggesting that parents sometimes tried too hard and listened too much to educators, ministers, and specialists—that they should read and listen and then decide what's right for them and their children, perhaps saying, "I'm honestly going to be me—the real person I am, not just a 'parent' to my son or daughter. In spending time with them, really getting to know them, I'll let them be real and honest too. Then, perhaps, good things may happen between us."

One Sunday I spoke to the issue "Why Students Revolt," with the subtitle, "A Cleansing of the Academic Temple," perhaps indicting some of our own members in sharing this experience.

I think it significant that most of my counseling those days was with our young people. One of our students said to me, "Miss Kochendoerfer, I don't care if I ever get a degree, if I could only find someone who would guide me, excite me, want to teach me, instead of assigning pages in a textbook which actually starts out with basic premises I cannot accept."

This suggested a premise I'd had for years (one that might even have taken parents off the judgmental hook) that each child or youth needed some adult—actually a non-parent—to turn to, one who could listen, be looked up to, and provide guidance, excitement, and teaching by example. Today this is vitally important given the state of our much-indicted television and sports arenas, with few old-fashioned, wholesome heroes.

I reminded them again of that vital creative energy within—that need to create as a human being—that given no creative outlet can explode in destruction, seeming to say, "I'm an important human being! I'm here! Notice me!" I felt we were finding this creative expression unleashed on every hand in the youth violence we seem to misunderstand.

Vital youth problems kept mounting, and each phase of our lives and the lives of our children seemed to be posing questions in vital need of answers. Such answers, it seemed to me, would require new patterns we seemed unable to face until they become a crisis. I challenged us as Unitarian Universalist religious communities with a quotation from artist Diana Sitar, "The world is not a prison house, but a kind of spiritual kindergarten where millions of bewildered infants are trying to spell God with the wrong blocks."

∽

Just as I felt much at home and appreciated in the Kent State community and Kent Ministerial Association, the Ohio Unitarian Universalist ministers were great, just as they had been in Florida. I was not only one of them, they made me feel special because I, as a woman and a colleague, represented a new experience for them. The Cleveland area Unitarian Universalist ministers got together monthly, and the notices that came from the president would be addressed, "Dear Brethern and Sistern!" When it was my turn to hostess the group, I'd cook a big pot of clam chowder, with a huge green salad and French bread, which they loved. One year we had a national ministers institute at Buck Hill in Pennsylvania, and the trip over and back with my compadres was special. One can learn a lot about others in a long car ride together.

Bucky McKeeman, a Universalist minister in Akron, had been quietly helpful and supportive during my candidating days. During the drive I learned things I feel Universalists have to offer all Unitarian Universalists in their simple acceptance of a God of love at a time when that three-letter word was scarcely heard in many intellectually oriented Unitarian churches.

The ministers of the Unitarian Universalist Ohio/Meadville District had their annual Institute at Salt Fork, one of Ohio's impressive state parks. There we'd have a cottage with a huge living room and screened veranda all to ourselves. I'd get one of the two bedrooms. As a newcomer I was elected president of our Ohio/Meadville group. The following year I was re-elected because they said I did such an admirable job at keeping everyone in touch. Leon Fay, president of the Unitarian Universalist Ministers Association, wrote, "How glad I am to hear that the ministers in your area know a good person when they find one! Your election as president of Ohio/Meadville UUMA is certainly pleasant news to me."

I was also pleased when I received a letter from John Clark of the national Unitarian Universalist Ministers Association. "Dear Vi, You were first choice of the Nominating Committee for trustee-at-large of the UUMA exec. If elected, as you're sure to be, you'll be hearing from Pete about exec meetings for next year. It meets for three days four times a year on the West Coast. So if you do accept, please confirm immediately. I'm pleased with your nomination and hope you enjoy the work. See you in New York. Fraternally."

It turned out that the bylaws were amended that year to do away with at-large members from different areas to save travel expenses, and I didn't get to serve; but I did have another outside invitation. I was taken by surprise when the phone rang one day and heard the voice of Ric Neff in Farmington, Michigan, Starr King class of 1969, whom I had met in Seattle. When I recalled who he was, he said, "There are five of us [Starr Kingers] here now!" He invited me to the Michigan-Ohio Ministers Institute in Indiana the following week. Rick had a whole afternoon to address different styles of ministry and he wanted me on his program.

I was deeply touched that one of the young Starr King students would think of including me. In Ric's Styles of Ministry workshop, I told them I liked to pose issues I felt involved in the religious dimension of our lives and suggest possible solutions as I saw them for my parishioners to accept, reject, or just wonder about.

On the way home I did a Sunday service at Fort Wayne in

their series on women. I had several other speaking engagements in Ohio and around the district in Indiana and Kentucky, as I was often asked to speak on the subject of women in the ministry.

Shortly after I returned home from the Indiana Institute, I got a call from Michael O'Kelly, the minister of the Toledo Unitarian Universalist church, asking whether I would deliver the Charge to the Congregation at his Installation service. I wondered whether or not I should, because I didn't know Michael all that well. I had heard he had a stiff challenge measuring up to the well-known minister he was replacing. Then I learned that Paul Carnes, president of the Unitarian Universalist Association, was to give the Installation sermon.

Since I'd always been on the receiving end at Installations, I began wondering about my presentation. As I was thinking of Michael O'Kelly, Michael McGee came to mind, and I was intrigued with the thought of using the format of young Jeff's challenge to the congregation in Roanoke.

I'd never been to the Toledo church and took a deep breath as I gazed up the front of a huge, red brick Georgian building with impressive white columns across the front. Then when I learned that the robed procession was to include the mayor of Toledo and the president of the University there, my heart sank. My homey little Charge wouldn't fit at all in that hierarchy! But what was I to do? This is part of what I said, "I've never been in this position as a minister before—of giving a Charge to the Congregation! In one sense it seems preposterous, since I don't know you and you don't know me. In another sense it makes me think, what an opportunity! . . . except that I've been in the Unitarian Universalist ministry long enough to know that we can't tell our people to do anything . . . or, at least, that's the way I feel it should be. So, I guess I'd rather not charge you with anything, but give you some things to think about on this happy occasion, and hopefully in the days ahead.

233

"This evening as you install Mike as your minister, at a time when many are questioning the direction of our denomination, I would remind us of what Jack Mendelsohn said some years ago, 'The future of the liberal church is almost totally dependent on two factors—great congregations (whether large or small) and skilled, effective, dedicated ministers.' And the last line I want you to especially remember, 'The strangest factor of their relationship is that they create one another!'"

I went on suggesting that ministers aren't special people, just have special training, and shared some of my experience in Roanoke with Jeff's Charge for Mike McGee, closing with, "Mike O'Kelly is Mike O'Kelly is Mike O'Kelly. He's a human being like the rest of us, with strengths in which I hope you will exult and take delight, and with shortcomings for which he may need your understanding and support. Mike O'Kelly is Mike O'Kelly is Mike O'Kelly. What you can best do for him—which will pay very rich dividends to each of you—is never ask him to be anyone else!"

∾

In all four of my churches I had received kudos for the newsletters, partly, as I said, because I used them to share more than just "churchly" things. I was deeply interested in issues that are still with us today—the economy and taxes, gays, youth and sex, ecology, and, of course, the role of women.

Reading my "Verily from Vi" column in *The Gougler Gazette,* gives one a feel for parts of my larger Kent ministry. In one I said, with all my college professors in mind, "Over the past several years I've found myself saying in many different ways that if we ever needed what the church has to offer at its best, we need it today as never before! I found this feeling corroborated in an article in *Macleans* (Canada's foremost magazine) entitled 'Universities Rediscover the Old Values' by Robert Harlow of the University of British Columbia, who feels that unrest in universities today is deep and quiet, but a kind of 'visceral understanding that a familiar way of doing things is dying and something else is being conceived, which is going to be born, whether we like it or not.' He ended in suggesting that we've long been reminded—and refused to listen—to the fact that the great questions are all, in the end, religious ones."

It was a joy to have John Seiberling as our Congressman. I felt privileged to be included in his constituent luncheons with the business community and professionals. When I enthusiastically told him how good I felt at his voting record, he replied, "I'm glad to hear that, Vi; but please know that you still must keep the letters coming so I can open the desk drawer and show the opposition all my support." I shared some of John's feelings with our members, hoping it would help in their defining some of the labels we often use for ourselves, or are given by others.

"John is a liberal's liberal, saying he feels the word is often misused. We forget that being a liberal means we can have our own beliefs, but also allow this freedom to others. He said something we need to keep reminding ourselves—that what one believes does not make one a liberal. A willingness to listen to others with an open mind and a willingness to change our beliefs in light of new developments are what make a liberal. In this sense, one could be conservative and still be a liberal. John said he had run for Congress to do something about the war in Vietnam and because he wanted to play a part in the reform of the Washington merry-go-round. Here, too, his liberalism seems genuine in his wish to build rather than tear down."

One month in my column I asked, "Is the US Going Broke?" This had been the cover story of *Time* magazine. I had been helping a man who gave up a job to start a one-man tax reform drive that was backed by Congressman Seiberling. I tried to get signatures to a petition, which began, "To the Congress of the United States: We the undersigned, believe the time has come when we must change our entire tax structure. The obvious place to start is with the Federal Income Tax. We believe it to be immoral for a large percentage of our population to be underfed, ill clothed and underhoused at the same time the ultra rich avoid paying taxes because of built-in loopholes in our tax laws. We want the laws changed now."

On March 7, 1973, I received a note, "Congressman John Seiberling has asked me to inform you that you are scheduled to testify at 2:00 P.M. at the public hearing on federal income tax reform, March 9, in the auditorium of the Akron Public Library."

In another newsletter, I championed a ministerial colleague in circumstances the Unitarian Universalist Ministers Association only began supporting twenty years later. In an article entitled "A New Kind of Ministry," I told of receiving requests for support from a "nearly ex-Presbyterian" minister who was trying to set up a ministry reaching out to the gay communities of Akron, Kent, Oberlin, and Cleveland. "In comparing notes on Bob's contacts, we found that many otherwise 'liberal' ministers and laymen truly shy away from involvement. A reason mentioned—contrary to other minorities, a gay can 'pass' in society; so there's a greater possibility of 'guilt by association.' When they spoke of the gay orientation as 'sinful,' I was proud to say that gays would be welcome in our group. We seem to be the one denomination thus far which offers such invitation.

"I rode home with Oggie, minister at United Presbyterian. In the conversation with him and other campus clergy, I find we have no corner on 'liberalism' any more—only that perhaps ours is more 'secular'—which might actually call for some examination."

With all the basic human problems, which seemed only to grow, I have often wondered what our country would be like today had we taken action in areas of some of these concerns quarter of a century ago. Part of my 1973 Christmas letter to family and friends reflected such concerns,

I never dreamed so much could happen all so
    quickly . . .
Where everything we valued on so many fronts would
    come to be suspect and questioned . . .
When safety, trust, security, and just plain gracious
    living are taken from us.

It was so good this summer to leave the Cleveland
    news, where almost every night the arson and the
    murder made one wonder 'bout the human race.
And most frightening of it all—that it becomes a way
    of life we all accept like sheep.

Much is exciting, I'll admit; but scary too . . .
What bothers most is when I see small children, and
    wonder what they'll have to face as they grow up
    because of us.
Of course they will adapt, but at what price?

One feeling's rather fun—a feeling vindicated on so
    many fronts.
It's OK now, and really "in," to be a single woman,
    conscious of nutrition and prevention, and wear
    "reprocessed" clothes.
I hope so much the trend from cure to wise preven-
    tion grows,
And we can somehow find adjustment for economy
    to handle things that way.
And that perhaps the "haves" will find it could give
    deeper meaning to their lives to "have" to live
    on less.

With shades of Calgary, I expressed personal concerns in the *Kent Record Courier*. We had positive newspaper coverage, and always with bold headlines and large pictures. The religious editor was a young woman who often stopped by my office to talk. She had their photographer come by to take several unusual photographs which they continued to use. One was in a big spread, "Out of the Kitchen and into the Pulpit," which began, "Mention 'church women,' and many will draw mental pictures of nice ladies in the kitchen preparing the church suppers, the good soprano in the church choir, the smiling Sunday school teacher. Not many will envision a woman behind the pulpit.

"But, slow as it may be, women are moving out of the Sunday school classes and the ladies' aid societies toward the pulpit. They are still few, but they are there, and their presence may eventually change the whole face of traditional religion."

In the long article, an Episcopalian minister explained that his group was divided, with some camps feeling ordination of women would endanger their church's close relationship with the Roman Catholic Church. He also noted the reactions of church women who did not want a woman standing up in front of them, and that it went back to the male-oriented traditions. Then I was quoted, "The Rev. Violet Kochendoerfer, pastor of the Unitarian Universalist Church in Kent, pointed out that traditional theology—the father-image in the pulpit—has made problems for women throughout history. Even today, although ordination of women is now being officially approved in many churches, the official decision is very different from actual practice. She hastened to add, however, that prejudice against women in the ministry is often dissolved once congregations actually meet a woman pastor and get used to the idea. Since she came to Kent two years ago she has been accepted with little question, she said. 'In fact, the subject seldom comes up.'"

The article mentioned the Kent State symposium that I had presented along with the Rev. Ogden White, associate pastor of the United Presbyterian Church, and the Rev. George Gaiser of the Lutheran Campus Ministries. I had conducted an unusual worship service there, in which all sexist references were removed. "For many at the service it was a first experience with a woman conducting a worship service. They had to look at biases that no one had ever really made them do before. Rev. White concurred that the symposium was one attempt to break through some of organized religion's patriarchal traditions and take a fresh look at religion's role in the modern world. 'We're taking strides,' he said, 'but we've got a long way to go.'"

On this same subject, I was featured in *Together* magazine in an article "Is God an Equal Opportunity Employer?" and in *Progressive Woman* with "Each Individual is Special."

My letters to the editor of the *Record Courier* were always printed with bold headlines. I spoke out on a health-screening program, on how to understand death and the Karen Quinlan issue, questioned the idea of a youth prison, and suggested that we establish a US Peace Department. Though I never spoke in the name of the church, most in Kent knew who I was.

It was a matter of satisfaction to me that in my sermons during the seventies, I often spoke to world problems that are still with us now. I repeated a Calgary sermon on Henry George economics called "Prophet of Progress and Poverty," which suggested that "poverty" is built into our concept of "progress," with the rich getting richer and the poor poorer, and that this progress is not real and cannot be permanant. I cautioned my parishioners with Thoreau's ideas in "Spending Money," in our moves away from simplicity to complexity—from country to city—away from the natural to man-made things, away from individual and inner responsibility toward external control.

Another group of sermons on the future of our little planet included "Of Cosmic Ecology," "Of Galaxies and Men," "In Search of a BioEthic," "Of Us and the Universe," and of course Loren Eiseley's *The Immense Journey*, and a second sermon, "Religion of Ecology," based on his visions, in which I opened, "There is an insidious logic that implies that men must adapt to machines, not machines to men . . . that production, speed, novelty, progress at any price must come first, and people second . . . that mechanization may be pushed as far as human endurance will allow. It ignores experience—which tells us we should not add new strains and pressures and discomforts to a high-pressure world. Our goal should be to accomplish both full production and the full life—a national prosperity that will include prosperity of the human spirit."

Most of my sermons fell under the "religious" column. Several congregations heard my "Big Rock Candy Mountain" and my "Paradox of Leisure" sermons expressing an important ingredient of my "theology." I opened with, "Joseph Pieper, the German philosopher, suggests that 'leisure is the basis of culture.' It's not time off the job, it's not idleness, free time, or even recreation. It's taking time to be—time for contemplation of the big questions of life, celebration of that life, with aspirations of what that life might be, which is closely related with what I feel we should be doing here together each Sunday morning."

I championed the positive Unitarian Universalist approach in our "I'm OK, You're OK Religion." In "A Liberal Case for Prayer," I suggested that it was not a question of "to pray or not to pray," for whether we admit it or not, we all do pray at those times we find a need to reach out to some power beyond ourself—to say "thank you" for the birth of a healthy child, "why?" at times of sudden death, or if it's only a "God damn it!" In "Unanswerable Questions—If This is All There Is," and "The Memory of a Future," I touched on some of the imponderables, including immortality. I also repeated "The Other Reality" from my Tallahassee days.

I often felt critical of our wariness to take a stand in the "religious" area. In my sermon "The Greatest Sin," I shared my feelings that "God is the experience of feeling a part of the on-going process in our universe, out of which we have evolved as the 'knowing' part, with capacity for further creation or destruction." In light of this I felt the greatest sin was involved in blocking or destroying this creation in our human relationships. Related to this premise was "On Violence and Pleasure," which presented the scientific findings that when babies and small children are not touched and loved there are consequences to pay.

In "Our Church Needs a Story," I suggested that, although we as Unitarian Universalists talk a lot and stress the "individual search for truth," we're not very good helpers or storytellers in our church for the new or searching self. I feel we have much to learn from primitive peoples and spoke of the Kalahari Bushman who was a wonderful storyteller. He knew what we need to remember—that without a story we have no nation, no culture, no civilization. Without a story of our own to live, we have no life of our own. I have often felt this is why Unitarian Universalism does not grow. We attract persons with our celebrated freedom "from"; but when they're with us, they do not find their basic needs fulfilled in merely a freedom "to."

The fall of 1976 brought decisions that influenced that last year of my ministry and corroborated my long feeling of "a charmed life." Franklin Delano Roosevelt had been elected for a second term on the day I was born, November 7, 1912. I was to be sixty-four! I mentioned this in a letter to Lyn, a friend in Vermont, and received a long letter back telling of happenings in her life. The last paragraph said, "I wonder what your plans are for the future. Have you thought of a warmer climate? Would you consider sharing a new solar house with me? You and I seem to have many interests in common—our love for people, our wonder at life all around us, our concerns for the world, and doing things with our hands. I'm eager to hear your ideas. If I don't build the solar house here next summer, would you like to drive out to Arizona and New Mexico and see how feasible a future there would be? Or go looking elsewhere?"

I answered immediately. So many times I stew and stew over small decisions. On bigger things I often "know." This was one of them. After two whole pages, including "solar reminds me of Santa Fe, where I've often thought I would like to live again," I said, "Well, as you can see, Lyn, the answer is 'yes.' It's something I can get really excited about. It could make planning this coming year and the rest of my life an adventure rather than a drag! So do let's plan to spend the summer—beginning the building in Vermont, or tripping around to look for another spot!"

Because I had started in Kent in January, I decided the January after my sixty-fifth birthday would round out my five years there. I told the board of this decision, but the congregation was not to be told until the next fall. That gave me time to tie things up not only for myself, but also to be helpful to my parishioners in bridging for the change and building for the future.

I prepared brochures for our literature table. *Adult Membership in the UU Church of Kent* had such sections as "Our Church is Not for Everyone," "We Feel We're Different," "Ours is a Ministry to Each Other," "Many Find Us Through Their Children." Another very popular brochure was *Unitarian Universalist Beliefs As They May Be Shared With Children of Different Ages, and Even Adults.*

That summer I went to General Assembly at Cornell, New

York, on the way to one of the Unitarian Universalist Star Island summer programs ten miles off the coast of New Hampshire. Returning through Vermont, I found "my new home" taking shape in the hills above Newfane. It was to be built into a hillside on two levels and heated by one wood stove, with tile floors and a greenhouse to capture the heat of the sun. The plans showed a special large room for me. On the trip home I was filled with plans for my last four months at Kent, for it was then that we were to announce my leaving to the congregation.

To begin a Sharing in Growth project, I repeated the Questionnaire Sunday we had done when I first came. We called it "Profile '77." Again I was delighted with answers written by members and friends in a fifteen-minute period, perhaps even more proud that my years with them had added depth to their religious lives. Some of the definitions follow:

Church is . . .

- ∾ a gathering of people trying to learn about and put into practice their religion
- ∾ a place where people sharing common beliefs join together to support each other and seek to live morally
- ∾ a place where one shares one's moral, spiritual, and social concerns and has them affirmed.

Religion is . . .

- ∾ a search for ultimate truths about life in an atmosphere of caring, and helping others
- ∾ a set of beliefs or attitudes about the great unanswerable questions of life
- ∾ that which begins where knowing leaves off— clearly recognizing the beauty and merits of all that is not explicitly known
- ∾ a search for the meaning of life.

A half page was full of wonderful things they expected from their church, such as intellectual and spiritual stimulation, fellowship, love, acceptance, leadership, and on and on, beautifully stated. The list of what they expected to give to their church would make any minister, board chairperson, or fundraiser proud—time, talent, skills, and financial support, plus understanding.

All but one felt worship should be part of our experiencing together, and a bit fewer than half said God was a meaningful concept for them. I felt as thought the whole experience was a great foundation with which to leave them, and followed it with the sermon entitled "Of God and Godlessness, or Our Godless Church."

I described the God we did not believe in as the God given lip service at the accepted proper time and place—that we were not "those godless people who don't have to believe anything." This description, which some lazy Unitarian Universalists rather enjoy, I felt warranted serious individual examination in light of our Judeo-Christian heritage. I felt the sermon would have great meaning to many emerging Unitarian Universalist congregations even today.

This was reflected in a letter from a member of great stature and commitment. She had been brought up Catholic, and we had often talked about this. She said, "This evening, totally exhausted, yet somewhat at peace, I'm allowing myself time to relax with leisure. I took out a folder labeled 'Censorship,' in which I found a copy of your sermon, 'Of God and Godlessness, or Our Godless Church.' I have read and reread it, and it has stirred my thoughts and feelings to purer mixture.

"If I had not found my church, I would have known it was here, having read this. Words must not lie mute, but must be spoken again and again, as a reminder of what it means to attempt community and high humanity.

"Not enough do we thank you for expressing all this to us so well on Sundays. This is my love letter of thanks at the end of a year in which I am especially grateful to be still alive and experiencing. May our warm and open climate continue, with you providing our direction."

I answered her letter. "Most of the time I know that I'm a good minister, especially when I compare myself to some of the men I've known. But I seem not to be able to rise above those times of doubt. So it takes letters like yours (and I have many in that file I mentioned that I've labeled Special Letters) where yours shall go. I'll treasure it all the more for having your marked-up copy and knowing how and why you wrote it."

Then I shared with her something I have often wondered about, especially these days when all too few women are "just housewives," and many must combine that with other commitments. "How much most of us need acceptance and approval, and need it over and over again. I've often thought this must be so true for many wives and mothers who cook a good meal, or do something for those they love, and are just taken for granted. I recall telling the men in a mixed gathering, 'You're missing the boat. You don't know what you could have for just a few words of appreciation now and then for all the little things women do for you over and over again.'"

In November of 1977, just after my sixty-fifth birthday, I wrote "To Far Flung Friends—I'm sending this early so you'll have my new address—where I expect to be after the first of the year. It's been sometime since I've announced a move; and this time it's East. Yes, East! So let me tell you how and why."

I explained that Lyn was an old friend who had been on my staff in the American Red Cross Olympic Club in Bavaria during World War II. She'd rediscovered me some years back when she accepted a secretarial job with the Unitarian Universalist church in Brattleboro, Vermont. In reading over material from the Boston headquarters, she ran across my name and thought, "There can be only one Vi Kochendoerfer!" Since then we'd been in touch, and I'd used Lyn's home as my eastern headquarters on summers in New England, one time joining her for a trip to Ireland. Then I told them about Lyn's invitation, and that even though friends had offered us a bit of land in my beloved New Mexico, Lyn purchased 8.6 acres of lovely land in Vermont. I closed with, "How heart-warming to have old friends like that!"

The Kent congregation rose to the occasion and hosted luncheons, dinners, and parties in my honor. *The Record Courier* sent a photographer with their religion editor. A huge picture of me packing boxes covered a third of the page, with an article entitled "New Year . . . A New Career—Kent woman minister retiring; will write war book." The article accounted all my ministries and gave another description of Unitarian Universalism as a liberal religion. "In addition to the importance of understanding of world religions, Rev. Kochendoerfer adds, 'Most of our problems stem from the lack of a religious dimension in our lives. The church is failing in its role to emphasize human values and morals. It should be a headlight out in front leading us, rather than a tail-light to the status quo.' She believes that often our increased education and affluence makes us doubt the existence of God. 'We've experienced what Dostoevski termed 'the death of God,' and taken on the role of God ourselves.'

"'As a unifying force within our lives,' she said, 'Religion brings together the intellectual, physical, spiritual, and emotional aspects and gives us hope for the future. It deals with the unanswerable questions. There is a boundary dividing what we know and what we do not know. Science keeps pushing that boundary line further and further out; but that area with the unanswerable questions is where religion must take over. Most often the greatest scientists are those with great humility. They are aware that we are not the measure of all things; and with all we do know, how little it is of all there is to know. . . .

"'A minister is one of the last generalists in this era of specialists, and helps bring sanity to our fragmented lives,' is how Rev. Kochendoerfer sees it."

My last service was during the holidays with a sermon on "Christmases We Remember." But my real farewell sermon was the week before, with a reminiscing and a kind of summing up of my fifteen years in the ministry, sharing thoughts of my spiritual teacher, Loren Eiseley and *The Immense Journey*.

Many of my sermons over the years had been filled with the humble wisdoms of this man in prose that was sheer poetry. In a childlike wonder of nature, he questioned our scientists who would play God and our direction away from the human being to the machine. Eiseley also felt there was a dimension denied to man—a dimension of time—that we are rooted in our particular century of the immense journey.

At the conclusion of my fifteen-year Unitarian Universalist journey, filled with memories of countless hours of searching for meanings to share with unforgettable Unitarian Universalists across my country and Canada, I closed that Sunday with adapted Eiseley words, "And perhaps there is no meaning in it at all save that of the journey itself. It has been filled with the chances of life; and the chances of my charmed life brought me here. But, it was a good journey—a good journey under a pleasant sun. So, I will not look for the purpose—only think now and then of the way I came, and be a little proud."

I arrived in Vermont after a winter's month in Minnesota to begin another chapter of my life. I had moved many times, but each had an exciting feeling of adventure and wondering who and what would be added to the long list of friends and experiences I'd had in far-flung places. To be a pioneer in the new solar experiment in progressive, colorful Vermont, and even find professional Unitarian connections on my own retirement terms, fulfilled my eager expectations once again.

After getting settled, I helped out at the Brattleboro church until they'd called a new minister. When they did, I became his friend, and we traveled together to ministerial meetings and institutes. After being in demand for speaking engagements in a large area, the nearby historic congregation at Northfield, Massachusetts, talked me into a half-time arrangement that I filled for nearly two years. But when even the part-time schedule conflicted with travel (including trips to Greece, Turkey, and the Orient), I chose to retire once again.

On a summer trip visiting Canadian Unitarian friends in Pincher Creek, Alberta (a small town in the fabulous foothills country just north of Watertown National Park), the possible purchase of the local travel agency was mentioned. When it seemed I could be part of that picture, the Canadian Rockies overshadowed staying on in New England. However, the situation changed during the several months of the immigration process, and I moved back to Duluth, Minnesota, where I still owned the home I'd purchased between Tallahassee and Kent.

My lovely small home is just blocks from the north shore of Lake Superior, and next to a huge park with two streams, waterfalls, swimming holes, and miles of trails. Here in the lovely Northland, where I still love the change of seasons, I enjoy to the full the freedom to do whatever I choose at any time, which often includes travel and visiting the many Unitarian Universalist friends I have all across the United States and Canada.

Because I had always enjoyed writing sermons, I went on writing. After doing articles for publication, I started the long manuscript of "A Single Life—A Story of My Life for Family and Friends." At a writer's conference, the feedback I received was that I had at least two books, if not more. One was the story of my three and a half years as the director of American Red Cross military on-base service clubs in the European Theater during World War II. That was before my move to Santa Fe, New Mexico, and my leaving there to become the first woman to graduate from Starr King School for the Ministry. It was also the beginning of my education in the publishing field. The University Press of Kentucky published *One Woman's World War II* in May of 1994 on the fiftieth anniversary of D-Day!

Over all these years, between the writing and travel, it was good now and then to be a visiting speaker at Unitarian Universalist groups. In 1993 I was elected to the board of the UURMA (the retired ministers association) which met at the UUA in Boston three times each year. This provided the opportunity to meet with the board of the Unitarian Universalist Women's Heritage Society, who felt a record of my years of modern pioneering should be preserved, and provided an editor for my manuscript.

I call this book *A Modern Pioneer*, because no one would have guessed back in 1962 that in a matter of decades women would outnumber men at theological schools, and a woman would head the UUA Department of Ministry in Boston.

I think also of an historical record I must hold as a woman pioneer. My ministries began the year following the beginnings of the UUA, with the merging of the Unitarians and Universalists in 1961. George Spencer, director of the Department of Ministry, did my ordination sermon in Provincetown. I then participated in some way with each of our UUA presidents since the merger. Dana McLean Greeley, the first president of UUA, was my Installation speaker in Calgary. I was a Starr King buddy of UUA President Bob West, participated in an Installation service with UUA President Paul Carnes, asked UUA President Eugene Pickett to deliver the Charge to the Congregation at my Tallahassee Installation, and followed UUA President Bill Schulz in my church in Kent. On the board of the UU Retired Ministers Association, I shared dinner and an evening with UUA President John Buehrens. In addition to the UUA pioneering, my ministries have covered historic decades that have changed the face of our nation and our world.

As a child of the Great Depression, one of my own short-comings was trying to save congregations money, such as not insisting on outside guests for my Installations. For years I had earned my living as a secretary and office manager; and it was easier to do things myself rather than demand a secretary. I now feel I might have received a more professional kind of respect had I made more demands.

My life has been filled with wonderful friends—male and female—through my years in the business world, the military, and my privileged years in the Unitarian Universalist ministry all across the country and Canada. Maybe this assurance allowed me to become a pioneer woman in our ministry without a feeling of discrimination, asking only to be accepted for the person I am. This stance was validated for me in reading Charles Johnston's *Necessary Wisdom*, when he suggested that to almost all of our familiar isms, we needed to consider effective bridging that says, "Yes, in part, but things are bigger than just that. . . ."

Johnston especially helped me in self understanding when he suggested that to find a wholeness for oneself one must be comfortable with sometimes feeling alone, and be ready to accept not always having the security of popular support or understanding. Although I had felt "alone" among some at times in taking unpopular stands, I did feel privileged in not having to feel "alone" as a pioneer woman in our male Unitarian Universalist ministry.

In light of the unbelievable changes of the past thirty years, it will be interesting to look ahead to changes that are sure to come about with more women in our ministries. And in our present practice of having to learn the hard way, our difficult dilemmas may just be the catalyst to promote our human values in a religious dimension. The religious dimension is back in the picture, and today as never before there is a challenge for us in our Unitarian Universalist churches and fellowships to reach out to all who would seek more meaningful human relationships—for self and for children at home and around the world.